MONETARISM

Praeger Studies in
International Monetary Economics and Finance

General Editors: J. Richard Zecher
D. Sykes Wilford

MONETARISM

Theory and Policy

George Macesich

PRAEGER SPECIAL STUDIES • PRAEGER SCIENTIFIC

Library of Congress Cataloging in Publication Data

Macesich, George, 1927-
    Monetarism, theory and policy.

    Bibliography: p.
    Includes index.
    1. Chicago school of economics. 2. Money. 3. Monetary policy.
I. Title.
HB98.3.M3   1983   332.4′6   82-19040
ISBN 0-03-062877-6

Published in 1983 by Praeger Publishers
CBS Educational and Professional Publishing
a Division of CBS Inc.
521 Fifth Avenue, New York, New York 10175 U.S.A.

Printed in the United States of America

FOREWORD

In this book, *MONETARISM: Theory and Policy*, Dr. George Macesich suggests that monetarism not only has become a force in economics over the past twenty years, but has become a new policy force. This has not occurred without controversy. Neo-Keynesians, Keynesians, Monetarists, and International Monetary Economists have been debating monetarism for years. With so-called monetarist policies being adopted around the world—in an attempt to undo the inflation that was created during the 1970s with expansive neo-Keynesian monetary and fiscal policy—the need for an international view of monetarism has never been greater.

Dr. Macesich has succeeded in taking many of the debates about monetarism out of the academic arena and into a real world context. He concludes that monetarism will survive the present crisis. He notes that in many instances the so-called monetarist policies being adopted in many countries are not monetarist at all. He demonstrates that monetarism of some form or another, especially in an international environment, is useful in analyzing the economic dilemma of low output and high inflation.

He compares basic philosophies of the monetarist, Keynesian, and Austrian school of economic thought and goes on to incorporate this synthesis into the development of a comprehensive understanding of the theory of monetarism. From that point, he focuses on the policy problems associated with implementing theory in the real world. His analysis covers the familiar models that we live with and read about in the daily newspapers and economic literature. For example, he discusses the Klein-Goldberger model, the Brookings-SSRC model, the Federal Reserve MIT model, and the St. Louis Federal Reserve Bank model.

In attempting to understand some of the international aspects of monetary policy, he presents information concerning the monetary approach to balance of payments, a theory that has much to say about the implications—as well as the proper conduct—of monetary policy in an open economy. This international aspect of policy is increasingly essential in the real world since capital markets are so well integrated.

Dr. Macesich's comprehensive analysis of monetary policy demonstrates the pitfalls of using simple monetarist tools in a complex world, and, by the same token, shows why some policies that are called monetarist certainly are not. One of his most interesting points is that monetarist policies of any form must be systematic and pre-announced. This is underscored by Friedman and others in the literature. Dr. Macesich notes that the credibility of the monetary authority is absolutely essential if any monetary policy is to be effective. One reason for monetary rules is that they enhance policy credibility. He emphasizes that credibility is the fundamental issue of monetary policy in the real world. Indeed, he notes that it is unfortunate that stricter monetary rules have not and may not be adopted in the future.

Dr. Macesich concludes that monetarism is paid lip service by almost everyone now, but this lip service itself is not sufficient for monetarist policies to be successful in today's environment.

D. Sykes Wilford
J. Richard Zecher

PREFACE

The role and importance of money in macroeconomic theory and policy has been the subject of considerable controversy. Keynesian and neo-Keynesian theories developed since the Great Depression tend to regard money as having only limited importance with respect to the determination of macroeconomic variables. In contrast to this belief an alternative view, with antecedents in the 1930s and earlier, was developed principally in Professor Milton Friedman's money and banking workshop at the University of Chicago. This view stresses the importance of money and the quantity theory of money. Economists who subscribe to this view are now called Monetarists; they place emphasis on the role of the quantity of money in the determination of economic activity.

This study focuses on the theoretical and empirical foundations upon which monetarism rests. Since monetarism is now a worldwide phenomenon, this volume draws upon the experiences of several countries. It also involves an examination of public policy prescriptions of monetarism. At the same time it provides an account of the issues involved in the lingering dispute between monetarists and Keynesians over the role of money in the economy.

The adoption and apparent triumph of monetarism in many countries is not the beginning of its downfall. It is not, as its critics assert, that the theory was safe until put fully into practice. Monetarism will survive that experience provided it receives more than mere lip service from policymakers.

Part I is devoted to examining the basic ideas and theoretical underpinnings of monetarism. Part II deals with policy issues. Wherever possible, a verbal and geometric presentation is used. The aim is to make the study accessible to people in fields other than monetary economics, while at the same time making it sufficiently useful to satisfy the expert and the needs of students taking monetary and macroeconomics courses.

I am grateful to Marshall R. Colberg and Anna J. Schwartz, Walter Macesich, Jr., Dimitrije Dimitrijević, Branimir M. Janković, Rikard Lang, Dragomir Vojnić, and John Karasinski, for useful comments and suggestions. A note of thanks is due to Mary Martha McWilliams for her assistance in typing the manuscript.

CONTENTS

Part II
Policy

In memory of my father,
Walter Macesich, Sr.

PART I
THEORY

1

MONETARISM

THE BASIC IDEAS

The principal tenet of monetarism is that inflation is at all times and everywhere a monetary phenomenon. Its principal policy corollary is that only a slow and steady rate of increase in the money supply—one in line with the real growth of the economy—can insure price stability.[1]

Milton Friedman summarizes the monetarist view on the relationship between the money supply and the price level as follows:

1. There is a consistent though not precise relation between the rate of growth of the quantity of money and the rate of growth of nominal income.
2. This relationship is not obvious to the naked eye largely because it takes time for changes in monetary growth to affect income, and how long it takes is itself variable.
3. On the average, a change in the rate of monetary growth produces a change in the rate of growth of nominal income about six to nine months later. This is an average and does not hold in every individual case.
4. The changed rate of growth in nominal income typically shows up first in output and hardly at all in prices.
5. On the average, the effect on prices comes about six to nine months after the effect on income and output, so the total delay between a change in monetary growth and a change in the rate of inflation averages something like 12 to 18 months.

6. Even after allowance for the delay in the effect of monetary growth, the relation is far from perfect. There's many a slip "twixt the monetary change and the income change."
7. In the short run, which may be as much as five or ten years, monetary changes affect primarily output; over decades, on the other hand, the rate of monetary growth affects primarily prices.

The monetarist view, as summarized by Friedman in *Counter-Revolution*, questions the doctrine advanced by John Maynard Keynes that variations in government spending, taxes, and the national debt could stabilize both the price level and the real economy. This doctrine has come to be called "the Keynesian Revolution."

The battle between neo-Keynesians and monetarists has been waged for almost a half century. It has long since moved into the policy area. The critics of monetarism declare that the proposed monetarist cure for inflation can work only by imposing excessive burdens of huge losses in real output and prolonged output losses on the economy. The monetarists respond that the burden must be borne because there is no other way to restore the economy to price or economic stability.

Critics are quick to point out that monetarism in isolation does not work, as the British and U.S. experiences show.[2] Its lack of "success" can be attributed to difficulties at three levels: first, there is the difficulty as to what is "money"; second, there is the problem that what a central bank elects to call "money" cannot either in quantity or velocity be controlled; third, there is the certainty that efforts at vigorous control will substitute for the problem of inflation the alternatives of high unemployment, recession, or depression, and disaster for those industries that depend on borrowed money. In effect, monetarism, which places its sole confidence in stabilizing the growth of some "esoteric monetary aggregate" to the exclusion of other concerns, is a prescription for calamity.[3]

These critics are distressed that monetarism, which began with the slogan "money matters" and manifested a healthy skepticism to Keynesian views, has over the years blossomed into all-out opposition to such discretionary Keynesian stabilization policies as compensatory use of fiscal and monetary measures. It is also upsetting to such critics to hear monetarist charges that an active-stabilization policy causes more problems than it cures.

Critics charge that monetarists have never really provided a convincing theoretical foundation for their policy prescriptions. There is not, so the critics argue, a clear conceptual basis for a sharp distinction of "money" from its substitutes and for ignoring systematic and random variation in velocity. Apparently, the empirical evidence presented by monetarists is insufficient.

Monetarists, moreover, are charged by their critics of converting long-run equilibrium conditions into short-run policy recommendations. Thus, natural rate theory argues that no permanent reduction of unemployment can be gained by accepting inflation. Anti-inflationary policies produce protracted social costs in lost output and unemployment. These costs are not fully addressed by monetarists. This is not surprising, so the critics argue, given their free market ideology; they will not entertain wage or price controls or income policies as alternatives or complements to anti-inflationary monetary restrictions.

Milton Friedman identifies monetarism with the quantity theory of money, suggesting thereby that monetarism is not a new development. It is also consistent with the quantity theory he freed of dependence on the assumption of automatic full employment, the focal point of Keynesian ridicule of traditional quantity theory. In Friedman's University of Chicago monetary workshop during the 1950s (in which this writer had the privilege of participating as a graduate student), studies on inflation and the role of money in inflation received considerable attention. Friedman's work changed professional thinking on matters pertaining to the role of money.

Harry Johnson has described changes in monetary theory as owing much to Friedman's efforts, which made

> monetary economics exciting and concerned with crucial issues. More fundamentally, the Friedman analysis gave a central place to expectations about future price movements and to Fisher's distinction between real and money rates of interest—in contrast to Keynesian analysis which always started with the assumption of stable prices—and in so doing steered theory and empirical research and monetary economics towards concepts and methods far more appropriate to the inflationary-cum-recessionary development of the past decade than Keynesian economics was capable of providing.[4]

It is, in fact, unfair to present Friedman as just another ideologue who lets his politics dominate his economics. To do so is to distort the actual situation. Karl Brunner writes:[11] The remarkable fact is that many of Friedman's political or policy views were guided by a strong commitment to a relevant empirical use of economic analysis. His "politics" emerge to a major extent as a consequence of his economic analysis. Analysis led him to a series of quite radical questions bearing on many of our social institutions, or more specifically, on the prevalent views of stabilization policies. The proposal for a monetary rule was not motivated by any 'laissez-faire preconception' but evolved from his appreciation of the unpredictable variability of monetary lags."[5]

Indeed, Keynesian emphasis on the basic instability of the private sector and the stabilizing function of a stable government sector is a central idea that Brunner correctly notes is turned on its head by Friedman on the basis of his work with Anna Schwartz on the Great Depression. Their argument is that it is essentially the stable private sector that operates as a shock absorber to the shock imposed by an erratic and unstable government sector. This inversion has generated a considerable amount of intellectual and political heat, but no resolution.

A case in point is an illustration reported by David Cobham[6] in attempting to sort out if monetarism is politically right-wing, left-wing, or neither. The beginnings of an answer, writes Cobham,

> are provided, curiously enough, by a recent criticism of Milton Friedman made by Samuel Brittan, himself a monetarist journalist who could hardly be described as left-wing. In an 'open letter' to Friedman in the *Financial Times* (December 2, 1976) Brittan criticized him for not distinguishing between 'Friedmanite economics and the personal opinions of Professor Milton Friedman,' on the grounds that 'Your eminence as an economist does not deprive you of your right to express your views as a citizen on those gray areas which are halfway between academic analysis and personal opinion. But there is danger that your strong expression of what is purely speculative or personal may discredit the more securely established parts of your analysis.'

In other words, writes Cobham, "Friedman's economics do not logically imply his politics; monetarists do not have to ' . . . denounce the whole welfare state . . . or . . . suggest that the developments of the last 70 years in Britain and Chile alike have been predominantly in the wrong direction."

There are four important issues in monetary theory that tend to dominate the current world scene: first, the impulse problem; second, the nature of the transmission mechanism; third, the stability of the private sector of the economy; and fourth, the relevance of allocative detail for the analysis of aggregative behavior. Monetarists, especially Friedman, have made important contributions to our understanding of each of these issues.

Concerning the impulse problem, Friedman focused attention on the need to distinguish between monetary growth and monetary accelerations. The latter influences employment and output, while the former dominates the average inflation rate.

On the issue of the transmission mechanism, Friedman's reservations on the nature and interpretation of the relation between unemployment and inflation as summarized in the Phillips curve have been borne out by the worldwide inflationary policies followed in the 1970s. The argument that a larger inflation could not permanently lower unemployment is now amply supported by worldwide evidence.

Friedman argues that the dynamic structure of the private sector is basically stable, absorbing shocks and transforming them into a stabilizing motion. This is at odds with the traditional Keynesian view, which rests on the assumption of an inherently unstable economy in which government activity is designed to offset swings in the level of economic activity.

Monetarists express little interest in allocative detail in explaining and predicting short-run changes in income. Since changes in the stock of money are dominant in explaining changes in nominal income, focus is placed on the behavior of the market for real cash balances. A sharp distinction is made between the general level of prices, which is affected by the quantity of money, and relative prices, which are affected by particular market conditions in various sectors. This is also the reason for monetarists' preference for small-scale econometric models. Again, this is in contrast to Keynesian preferences for large-scale econometric models which, presumably, provide detailed information on various sectors believed to influence significantly the aggregative behavior of the economy.

SUPPLY SIDE ECONOMICS

In marked contrast to previous U.S. administrations, President Reagan, within eight months into his first term in 1981, quickly deflated a Democratic-majority House of Representatives by reducing the budget and cutting taxes. This began what appears to be the dismantlement of social welfare programs adopted by the federal government during the previous 50 years. In addition, Reagan aims to abolish many governmental regulations that his supporters claim have handicapped U.S. industry. It appears that the liberal-reform philosophy that has dominated the U.S. political, social, and economic scene for the better part of the twentieth century will be replaced by neoliberalism.[7]

President Reagan's economic program calls for tax reduction that will stimulate business expansion, tax revenues, and employment, thereby resulting in lower outlays for unemployment compensation, welfare payments, and interest on the national debt. This program is based more on the neoliberal philosophy of individualism, limited government, free enterprise, and competition than any U.S. administration since Franklin Roosevelt put into place the reform-liberal philosophy of the New Deal. Should it fail, the economic and political consequences will be severe, and Reagan will be chastised as another Herbert Hoover. In either case Reagan will be remembered not as a president who continued more or less the reform-liberal philosophy of his predecessors, but as a Roosevelt who put into place a "different" philosophy and as one of the most radical and revolutionary U.S. presidents of the twentieth century. It is interesting that the young Ronald Reagan admired Franklin Roosevelt. If is optimistic scenario is realized, Reagan will go down in history as being as courageous a chief executive as his hero.

The dramatic shift in government policy engineered by the Reagan administration to stimulate the economy and contain inflation is under attack. Keynesian liberal-reform followers who advocate stimulating demand to make the economy grow argue that Reagan policies will not work. Wall Street's doubts were expressed in the beginning in stock prices that refused to go up and interest rates that refused to go down. Even more significant, a number of supply-side economists who supplied the intellectual force behind the Reagan program have turned skeptical.

Perhaps more important is the debate between the supply-siders pushing for a return to the gold standard and the monetarists arguing for control of the economy by regulating the money supply, mainly M-1B, the measure of cash, demand deposits, and NOW accounts. Supply-siders predict that Reagan's program will flounder in a collision between fiscal stimulation, caused by the tax cut, and Federal Reserve monetary policy, reflected in high interest rates that will choke off both the boom in private investment and the era of strong economic growth promised in Reagan's program. All these issues can be readily resolved, according to some supply-siders, by an immediate return of the U.S. dollar to a gold standard. This return will lower inflation and stimulate growth.

Monetarists disagree with these arguments that strong economic growth and lowering of inflation can be achieved simultaneously in the short run. Interest rates, monetarists argue, will decline as pressure on the economy is reduced by a consistently tight monetary policy. It is important to understand that the disagreement between monetarists and supply-siders is not simply between supporters and critics of the Federal Reserve System. It is, in fact, a significant doctrinal difference.

The supply-siders insist on a brand of monetarism that differs from conventional monetarist policy. Monetarists maintain that a central bank can control the stock of money. Supply-siders insist that quantitative control of the money supply by the central bank is not possible. Monetarists argue that control of the money supply is the key to everything else. Supply-siders believe such control is an inappropriate goal of policy. In the politically sensitive area of interest rates, only with a return to gold and further cuts in government spending, argue the supply-siders, will interest rates decline. They claim that individuals must have confidence in the long-term inflation outlook to be willing to hold a 30-year bond at lower rates.

Monetarists hold that there is good evidence of a relationship between growth in the money supply and inflation and interest rates. Moreover, there does not appear to be any systematic evidence that credit demand has any sustained effect on inflation, interest rates, or real growth. The real problem is to prevent the central bank from engineering policy lurches in money growth. Return to a gold standard advocated by supply-siders will not necessarily bring about stability and lower interest rates. In fact, the operation of the gold standard in the past was very different from that envisioned by the supply-siders. More important, the supply-siders and monetarists in their differences over the gold standard and money supply represent two separate wings in neoliberal philosophy on the importance and role that money and monetary institutions play in an economy.

PHILOSOPHIES OF MONEY: MONETARISTS, KEYNESIANS, AND AUSTRIANS

The monetary vision—for which philosophers as distant as Locke, Law, Cantillon, Hume, and Aristotle are called in evidence—is that inflation results from too much money chasing too few goods. Such members of the Austrian School as Carl Menger, Georg Simmel (actually a sociologist), Ludwig von Mises, and Friedrich von Hayek provide useful insights into the monetary system as an integral part of the social structure. They differ significantly from both Keynesians and monetarists, though Friedman and some monetarists come closer to the Austrians in their stress on "monetary rules" and a stable monetary order.

According to the Austrian view, money and the monetary system are the unintended products of social evolution in much the same fashion as the legal system.[8] Money is a social institution—a public good. It is not simply another durable good held in the form of "real balances" by utility-maximizing individuals or profit-maximizing firms as Keynesian and monetarist views hold. However useful the tools of demand and supply analysis applied to money as a private durable good, Keynesians and monetarists miss the full consequences of monetary instability.

In essence, the monetary system is an integral part of the social fabric whose threads include the faith and trust that make possible the exercise of rational choice and the development of human freedom. This is misunderstood by the very people who benefit from it. It is this misunderstanding of the social role of money as a critical element in the market mechanism and the need for confidence in the stability of its purchasing power that came to dominate much of Keynesian and monetarist thought in the postwar period. This misunderstanding is the ideological key to the use of discretionary monetary policies for monetary expansion as an unfailing means of increasing output and employment and reducing interest rates.

Frankel writes that Keynes, following Georg Friedrich Knapp, presents the monetary system as a creation of the state, and as such is available for manipulation by a government consisting mostly of wise and well-educated people disinterestedly promoting the best interests of society. The fact that such an arrangement curtails individual choice and decision did not disturb Keynes, who saw little reason to believe that those choices and decisions benefit society. In essence, it is at best an elitist view of government so familiar to Great Britain at the turn of the century; at worst, it is a totalitarian government on the model of the Soviet Union.[9]

Laidler takes exception to Frankel's argument that Keynes is the architect of a short-run monetary policy that seeks to exploit monetary illusion in order to trick people into taking actions which, did they correctly foresee their consequences, they would not take. Such "trickery" is not the policy product of the 1930s, when Keynes believed that undertaking an activist monetary policy to deal with unemployment would be what individual agents desired, but were prevented from accomplishing on their own owing to the failure of the price and market mechanism. Keynes, in effect, thought he was dealing with the issue of involuntary unemployment. It was in the 1950s and 1960s that the idea of a stable inflation-unemployment trade-off generated a money illusion available for exploitation by policymakers. I have argued elsewhere that such policy availability also assisted in the pursuit of the cold war as well as the Vietnam War with indifferent results, except to produce much of the recent worldwide inflation and speed the entrance of the third world as an outstanding world problem.[10]

Laidler is correct in that policies derived from a Keynesian philosophy of money may not be the fundamental reason that faith in the institutions of a free society is threatened. However, the policies of the 1950s, 1960s and 1970s do owe much to Keynes' followers if not to Keynes himself. These policies did indeed fool the population into providing more labor services and resources, which did permit the Western world to compete with the Soviet Union and its friends while presenting an aura of prosperity at home. Keynes did provide the theoretical apparatus to make possible the articulation of his post-World-War-I vision. It was in the late 1970s and the 1980s that the "chickens came home to roost," so to speak, with the era of rational expectations and growing distrust of government.

The interwar collapse of the international economy can be attributed more to unforeseen political factors than to often cited economic factors.[11] In essence, the British Empire collapsed, taking with it its role as a world stabilizer. The United States, the only other world power of sufficient strength to act as a stabilizer, refused to do so with predictable consequences.

The rise of socialism in the 1930s promoted central economic planning and redistribution of income policies. The Keynesian revolution for its part stressed the failure of the economic system, which was avoidable by the application of scientific knowledge. Harry Johnson is surely correct when he writes that these two movements reinforced one another.[12] This in turn led to the view that economic backwardness can be traced to the defects in the private enterprise system and not to the backwardness of people and their cultures in relation to the requirements of modern industrial society. The third world promoted this view to the top of world's development agenda since the 1960s in the form of demands for a New International Economic Order (NIEO).

In drawing on Georg Simmel's ideas for a free and stable monetary order, Frankel does not take into sufficient account the above largely political factors. As a result, he attributes too much responsibility to Keynes and his followers for the lack of faith and trust in the "old order." The free monetary order that underpinned Simmel's turn-of-the-century society can be defended on moral grounds as "an ideal—the pursuit of trust." The durability of the old order was questioned by Simmel, as Frankel points out, long before Keynes and his followers appeared.

Its durability is questioned by Simmel throughout his *Philosophy of Money*. This study is concerned not simply with money as a unit of account, a store of value, and medium of exchange, but with the free market economy in which the monetary system is an integral part, and the relationship between the institutions of such an economy and the matters of justice, liberty, and the nature of man as a social being. The focus is on exchange as one of the most fundamental functions that tie individuals into a cohesive social group. Since barter exchange is inconvenient, there naturally developed a group of individuals who are specialists in exchange and the institution of money, which solves the problem of the dual coincidence of barter. As soon as money enters the picture and the dual coincidence of barter is resolved, exchange ceases to be a simple relationship between two individuals. Simmel notes that the ensuing generalization of claims made possible by money transfers places these claims for realization upon the general economic community and government as its representatives.

Unlike other things that have a specific content from which they derive their value, money derives its content, according to Simmel, from its value. Its value, in turn, owes much to the implicit guarantee given by society and the community and little to the physical properties of money. It is, in effect, based on confidence in the sociopolitical organization and order. In this view, the British pound sterling formerly and the U.S. dollar currently owe their value more to the political and economic power and prestige of their institutions than to the physical properties of the pound and dollar. This confidence in the political and economic institutions of a country, and which Laidler and Rowe and Frankel attribute to Simmel in translation, is "trust."

Trust is the cement of society. The more trust individuals have in a society's institutions in general and in its money in particular, the more extension and deepening in the use of money will occur in an economy. By and large the consequences of such developments are beneficial to society in that an individual's achievements are enhanced not only in the economy but in all other endeavors. Indeed, freedom and justice are promoted by the development and growth of exchange and the monetary economy.

As a consequence, the individual can act independently of others, while at the same time becoming more dependent on society as a whole. That is, an individual becomes more dependent on the achievements of individuals and less so on the peculiarities of personalities. The loosening of bonds serves to promote economic freedom. It may or may not promote political freedom at the same time.

Simmel underscores two likely sources of trouble for a free monetary order. The problems are serious enough to threaten the survival of the order. First, the receipt of money wages instead of payment in kind, while promoting individual freedom, exposes the recipient to the uncertainties and fluctuations of the market, originating in turn in fluctuations in the purchasing power of money. Second, the very success of the free monetary order encourages the development of socialist ideas, which serve to undermine the individualistic order based on free markets and money. Laidler and Rowe and Frankel underscore

Simmel's concern regarding fluctuations in general and inflation in particular since the uncertainty so generated undermines trust in the monetary order.

Laidler's evaluation of the significance of the Austrian view of money is basically correct. If money is taken to be one among a complex of social institutions, one consequence of inflation is to move the social order away from the use of money and toward a greater reliance on one form or another of greater government control, or command organization. Such a development, Laidler notes, increases the dependence of individuals upon other specific personalities and decreases freedom. So much for anticipated inflation.

In the instance of unanticipated inflation, the Austrian view foresees an increase in uncertainty inherent in a money economy, which undermines the mutual trust essential for monetary exchange. The net effect would be a decline in the number of mutually beneficial exchanges taking place. Since monetary instability and market failure are closely linked in the Austrian view, both anticipated and unanticipated inflations serve to weaken the social fabric.

"In short," write Laidler and Rowe,

> if monetary theory is best approached along Austrian lines, then we must conclude that mainstream monetary theory, for all its considerable accomplishments, not only trivializes the social consequences of inflation in particular . . . but that it grossly underestimates the destructiveness of monetary instability in general. . . . Note that we here refer to modern monetary theory and not to its proponents. The principal authors of "shoe leather" approach to analyzing the cost of inflation such as Friedman have expressed far more concern about the importance of controlling or avoiding inflation than their theories could possibily justify, as their opponents (e.g. James Tobin ["Inflation Control as a Social Priority," 1977, cited by Laidler and Rowe]) have been quick to point out. In this their instincts have, in our view, run far ahead of their analysis."[13]

According to Laidler and Rowe, Keynes too was concerned with monetary stability, the fragile nature of a money-using market economy, and the social order that went with it. He was also well aware of the need for trust in the stability of purchasing power if the market mechanism was to function properly. Indeed, to Keynes money is not just another commodity. A money economy is very different from a barter economy. This idea was lost, write Laidler and Rowe,

> as the Hicksian IS-LM interpretation of the General Theory came to dominate monetary economics "monetarist" as well as so-called

"Keynesian." The dominance of this incomplete version of Keynes in subsequent debates has also surely been the main reason for participants in them having neglected "Austrian" ideas on these matters.

The story, however, is very different on the conduct of monetary policy, where Keynes and his followers depart significantly from the Austrian and monetarist paths. These differences are so profound as to overwhelm areas of agreement. As we have had occasion to note elsewhere, Keynes believed firmlly in discretionary monetary policy and viewed the gold standard as a relic. Modern Austrians hold to the gold standard and, as noted, to some supply-sider tenets. The monetarists argue for a given growth rate in the stock of money. The difference between the Austrians and the monetarists is essentially about means to achieve agreed-upon ends, though the latter do not stress the role of stability in promoting trust and so in facilitating the functioning of markets. The Austrians, while distrusting bureaucrats, are more skeptical than monetarists about the stability of the demand for money function. They opt for pegging the price of money in terms of gold, relying on the stability of the relative price of gold in terms of goods in general.

In *Two Philosophies of Money*, Frankel directs attention to the erroneous "nominalist" theories of money, which imply that money is something external to the fabric of society, a thing or commodity in its own right, which governments are entitled to manipulate in pursuit of their own limited economic or social ends. He draws and compares the views of Simmel and Keynes, arguing that both understood the economic uses and psychological power of money. Simmel and Keynes were also sensitive to its resultant influence on human character and behavior. More important, Frankel demonstrates how the views of Simmel and Keynes summarize the conflicting ideologies of the nineteenth and twentieth centuries and serve to place in perspective contemporary monetary problems. According to Frankel:

> It (conflicting ideologies) arises out of the conflict between money as a *tool* of state action and money as a symbol of social trust. The two concepts are incompatible. I go so far as to contend that for several decades we have been witnessing an intense reaction against traditional concepts of monetary order: it is not far removed from a revolt against it.[14]

The traditional view of money focused on a free monetary order that "implies the possibility for individuals of choosing between a multiplicity of conflicting goals or ends. It postulates the existence of principles, enforced by customs, convention and law, which ensure that its operation will not be arbitrarily, capriciously, or lightly altered in favor of particular groups, individuals, or interests."[15] The real nature of the monetary debate, argues Frankel, "is basically not about inflation or deflation, fixed or flexible exchange rates, gold or paper standards and so forth, it is about the kind of society in which money is to operate."[16]

The survival of the free monetary order is questioned by some for the reason that it might not prove possible to make it work in terms of specific goals that society should, in their opinion, pursue. This view, shared by Keynes, leads to utopian attempts to make the uncertain certain by control of society according to plan as well as by transformation of man.[17] This is reflected, writes Frankel,

> in the ongoing highly sophisticated debate about the scope, legitimacy and effectiveness of monetary policy. On the one hand, there are the optimists who believe that we now possess the technical tools and scientific knowledge to enable us to control monetary behavior, not only within a nation, but even internationally, and thereby not only the rate of economic change, but progress also. On the other hand, their opponents would support Milton Friedman's view that "We are in danger of assigning to monetary policy a larger role than it can perform in danger of asking it to accomplish tasks that it cannot achieve and, as a result, in danger of preventing it from making the contribution that it is capable of making"[18]

To use the monetary system to pursue changing goals and objectives is incompatible with monetary order, argues Frankel. It will make it "capricious and uncertain and prey to conflicting and varying political objectives."[19] Intended to reduce uncertainty, monetary manipulation actually increases it by casting in doubt the monetary system itself. A monetary policy, writes Frankel, "which is directed to shifting goals—as for example, full employment, economic growth, economic equality or the attempt to satisfy conflicting demands of capital and labour—cannot but vary with the goals adopted."[20]

According to Frankel, Keynes made the revolt against the predominant nineteenth-century view of money respectable. It was George Simmel, especially in The Philosophy of Money, who first suggested the sources of the revolt and foresaw its likely consequences. In essence, Simmel does not see the institution of money in mechanical terms but, as Frankel writes, "a conflict between our abstract conception of money and the social trust on which it rests. He was concerned to elucidate the moral basis of monetary order in contrast to the subversion of morals through money, in the abstract, which he feared." Simmel is pessimistic that the free monetary order will survive the revolt again it.

The nineteeth-century view of society's responsibility to maintain trust and faith in money was supported by the bitter eighteenth-century experiences with currency excess. Most classical economists, and certainly the Austrians, underscored society's monetary responsibilities for preserving trust and faith in money. Simmel's contributions to monetary thought are in keeping with the spirit of that tradition. It is against the use of discretionary monetary policy for the purpose of exploiting the presumed short-run nonneutrality of money in order to increase permanently employment and output by increasing the stock of money. Though an arbitary increase in money, according to Simmel, will not necessarily disrupt relative prices permanently, such manipulation sets into motion forces whose consequences for social stability are very serious indeed. Since no human power can guarantee against possible misuse of the money-issuing authority, to give such authority to government is to invite destruction of the social order. To avoid such temptation it is best to tie paper money to a metal value established by law or the economy.[21]

NOTES

1. "I must say that personally I do not like the term 'monetarism'," writes Friedman. "I would prefer to talk simply about the quantity theory of money, but we can't avoid usage that custom imposes on us." Milton Friedman, "Monetary Policy: Theory and Practice," *Journal of Money, Credit and Banking* (February 1982): 101.

See, for example, R.T. Selden, "Monetarism," in Sidney Weintraub, ed., *Modern Economic Thought* (Philadelphia: University of Pennsylvania Press, 1976), pp. 253–74; T. Mayer, "The Structure of Monetarism," *Kredit und Kapital* 8, Nos. 2 and 3 (1975): 190–218, 293–316; Thomas Mayer, *The Structure of Monetarism* (New York: Norton, 1978); George Macesich and H. Tsai, *Money in Economic Systems* (New York: Praeger, 1982), Chapter 12; L. Anderson, "The State of the Monetarist Debate," *Federal Reserve Bank of St. Louis Review* (December 1978); Anna J. Schwartz, "Why Money Matters," *Lloyds Bank Review* (October 1969), George Macesich, *The Political Economy of Money* (forthcoming).

W. Poole, *Money and the Economy: A Monetarist View* (Reading, Mass.: Addison-Wesley, 1978); R.E. Lucas, Jr., "Tobin and Monetarism: A Review Article," *Journal of Economic Literature* (June 1981): 558–67; Thomas Wilson, "Robertson, Money and Monetarism," *Journal of Economic Literature* (December 1980): 1522–38; S. Fischer, ed., *Rational Expectations and Economic Policy* (Chicago: University of Chicago Press, 1980) and B. Kantor, "Rational Expectations and Economic Thought," *Journal of Economic Literature* (December 1979): 1422–41, for a useful review of a number of outstanding monetary issues; F.H. Hahn, "Monetarism and Economic Theory," *Economica* (February 1980): 1–17; Franco Modigliani, "The Monetarist Controversy or Should We Forsake Stabilization Policies?" *American Economic Review* (March 1977): 1–19; O.D. Purvis,

"Monetarism: A Review," *Canadian Journal of Economics* (February 1980): 96–122; Milton Friedman and Anna J. Schwartz, *Monetary Trends in the United States and the United Kingdom: Their Relation to Income, Prices and Interest Rates, 1867–1975* (Chicago: University of Chicago Press, 1982); Friedman and Schwartz, *A Monetary History of the United States, 1867–1960* (Princeton: Princeton University Press, 1963); Friedman, *The Optimum Quantity of Money* (Chicago: Aldine, 1969); David Meiselman, ed., *Varieties of Monetary Experience* (Chicago: University of Chicago Press, 1970). Milton Friedman summarizes the Monetarist view in *The Counter-Revolution in Monetary Theory, First Wincott Memorial Lecture* (London: Institute of Economic Affairs, 1970).

2. John K. Galbraith, "Up from Monetarism and Other Wishful Thinking," *New York Review of Books*, August 13, 1981, pp. 27–32.

3. E.A. Birnbaum and P. Braverman, "Monetarism—Broken Rudder of Reaganomics," *Wall Street Journal*, July 23, 1981. See also Benjamin Friedman "The Theoretical Nondebate about Monetarism," Discussion Paper No. 472, April 1976, Harvard Institute of Economic Research, Harvard University, Cambridge, Mass.

4. Harry Johnson, "The Nobel Milton," *Economist*, October 23, 1976, p. 95.

5. Karl Brunner, "The 1976 Nobel Prize in Economics," *Science*, November 5, 1976, p. 648.

6. David Cobham in *Lloyds Bank Review*, April 1978 and reprinted in T.M. Havrilesky and J.T. Boorman, eds., *Current Issues in Monetary Theory and Policy* (Arlington Heights, Illinois: AHM, 2d ed., 1980), p. 566. See also George Macesich and H. Tsai, *Money in Economic Systems* (New York: Praeger 1982), for discussion of ideology and monetary theory and policy.

7. See Macesich, *Political Economy of Money*.

8. See for example David Laider and Nicholas Rowe, "Georg Simmel's *Philosophy of Money*: A Review Article for Economists," *Journal of Economic Literature* (March 1980): 97–105; S. Herbert Frankel, *Two Philosophies of Money: The Conflict of Trust and Authority* (New York: St. Martin's Press, 1977), and review of Frankel's study by David Laidler in *Journal of Economic Literature* (June 1979): 570–72; S. Herbert Frankel, *Money and Liberty* (Washington, D.C.: American Enterprise Institute for Public Policy Research, 1980).

9. See George Macesich, *The International Monetary Economy and the Third World* (New York: Praeger, 1981), Chapters 1–2.

10. Ibid.

11. Ibid., Chapters 2–3.

12. Harry Johnson, "The Ideology of Economic Policy in the New States," in D. Wall, ed., *Chicago Essays on Economic Development* (Chicago: University of Chicago Press, 1972), pp. 23–40.

13. Laidler and Rowe, "Georg Simmel's *Philosophy of Money*: A Review for Economists" *Journal of Economic Literature*, March 1980, p. 102.

14. S. Frankel, *Two Philosophies of Money*, p. 86.

15. Ibid., p. 4.

16. Ibid., p. 95.

17. Ibid., p. 6.

18. Ibid., p. 6, and Milton Friedman "The Role of Monetary Policy," in *The Optimum Quantity of Money and Other Essays* (Chicago: Aldine, 1969), p. 99.

19. Frankel, *Two Philosophies of Money*, p. 89.

20. Ibid., p. 92.

21. "The most serious repercussions upon exchange transactions will follow from this situation, particularly at the moment when the government's own resources are paid in devalued money. The numerator of the money fraction—the price of commodities—rises proportionately to the increased supply of money only after the large quantities of

new money have already been spent by the government, which then finds itself confronted again with a redeemed supply of money. The temptation then to make a new issue of money is generally irresistible, and the process begins all over again. I mention this only as an example of the numerous and frequently discussed failures of arbitrary issues of paper money, which present themselves as a temptation whenever money is not closely linked with a substance of limited supply. . . . Today we know that only precious metals, and indeed only gold, guarantee the requisite qualities, and in particular the limitation of quantity; and that paper money can escape the dangers of misuse by arbitrary inflation only if it is tied to metal value established by law or by the economy." Georg Simmel, *The Philosophy of Money*, trans. T. Bottomore and D. Frisby, Introduction by D. Frisby (Berlin: 1907; London and Boston: Routledge and Kegan Paul, 1977, 1978), p. 160.

2

THE QUANTITY THEORY AND INCOME-EXPENDITURE THEORY

MONEY IN ECONOMIC ACTIVITY

Monetary theory is primarily concerned with interpreting and explaining changes originating in monetary supply and demand to the behavior of the economy. This has been a matter of concern in the writing of economists for more than two hundred years. It is in this sense, as Friedman observes, that monetarism has a long lineage. Consider the views of the eighteenth- and nineteenth-century economists on the role of money in economic activity.[1] Conditions of economic instability at the beginning of the eighteenth century promoted examination of the connection between money and output. The most outstanding contributors were John Locke (1632–1704) and John Law (1671–1729). In essence, they focused on the obvious fact that total monetary receipts must equal total monetary payments. Locke and Law contended that increases in the quantity of money and in the velocity of circulation not only raised prices but also expanded output. Their policy prescription was to increase the quantity of money, which included policies designed to create a favorable balance of trade.

Richard Cantillon (1697–1734) focused on the processes by which variations in quantity of money lead to variations in prices and output— thereby providing useful insights into monetary dynamics. He also recognized what many would later point out: that nominal quantity of money is beneficial to trade only during the period in which money is *actually increasing.* Once a new equilibrium is reached, output would return to its original level only with a higher price level. This process of increasing the quantity of money, however, cannot last indefinitely for the reason that the process leads to an adverse balance of payments and so to an outflow of money. How to buy the benefits of the inflationary process without generating balance-of-payments problems is a dilemma all too familiar to contemporary society.

David Hume (1711–1776) and Henry Thornton (1760–1815) draw implications for monetary policy identical to those of Cantillon. Both had little confidence in a policy that would continuously increase the stock of money for any length of time. Ultimately, such a policy would lead to balance-of-payment problems. In effect, Cantillon dealt with money in transition periods, Hume with money in transition periods and comparative equilibria, and Thornton almost exclusively with comparative equilibria.

David Ricardo and John Stuart Mill focused attention on the role of money in comparative statics thanks largely to events in the nineteenth century. We have it from other studies that the "Industrial Revolution"—if one chooses to call the culmination of events and circumstances that occurred in the nineteenth century by this name—did indeed change the economic situation in the 1800s as compared to what went before. Cost reductions, innovations, movement of money including financial capital, when coupled with the inflation rate during the Napoleonic wars, underscored the importance of "real" forces. Unlike the eighteenth century when Cantillon's model appeared most applicable, Ricardo's model in which output is independent of money seemed most appropriate. Mill was straightforward in his argument that the quantity of money was unimportant provided that it was not allowed to get out of order. Economists, however, have been quick to add that money does indeed get out of order, especially during periods when its quantity undergoes rapid change. Indeed, it is the one area into which government intervention (however limited) is allowed by neoliberal doctrine.

To Keynes writing during the upheaval of the post-World-War-I period, the nineteenth-century model of Ricardo and Mill offered little in the way of guidance. Money, in fact, was out of order. The uncertainty generated by monetary disturbances effected expectations. People are reluctant to undertake investment in the face of uncertainty generated by such disturbances. If rapid monetary changes have occurred in the past and are expected to be repeated in the future—in which direction no one knows—people will refuse to bear the risk of investment.

Keynes concluded that rapidly fluctuating prices—such as characterized the post-World-War-I era—would create uncertainty on the part of businesses, which would then reduce the investment so necessary if economic stability was to be achieved. The only recourse, under the circumstances, was for government to undertake the necessary investment. In view of the Bank of England's preoccupation with restoring the pound to prewar gold parity and the willingness to accept and enforce any price fluctuations necessary, Keynes became convinced that Britain would have to place emphasis on means other than monetary policy to stabilize output and prices.

Friedman too deplores the uncertainty generated by monetary disturbances, arguing that marked instability of money is accompanied by instability of economic activity. Keynes and Friedman both desire a stable growth rate in the money supply as a way of minimizing fluctuations in prices, output, and employment. They differ, however, in how to achieve the benefits of monetary stability. Keynes thought that exclusive reliance on monetary policy was unrealistic on political grounds and opted for fiscal policy. Friedman has little confidence in the role political authorities may play in providing monetary stability, and opts from both monetary and fiscal authorities to a fixed rule.

The vexing problem of unemployment with simultaneous inflation received a most explicit and unique examination by Nobel Prize winner F.A. Hayek.[2] His ideas on the possibility of a simultaneous occurrence of unemployment and inflation were put forward in the 1930s, which was not a propitious time for such views. Unemployment so dominated the times that almost no attention was paid to theories purporting to explain the simultaneous occurrence of the two. The 1960s, 1970s, and 1980s, however, are another matter. Keynes's views advanced for the 1930s provide little guidance to contemporary policymakers. But Hayek's views require modifications if they are to be used as aids to understanding the economic scene since 1960.

Hayek's basic theory is that bank credit (or money supply) expansion, by lowering the market rate of interest below the natural rate, benefits private investment at the expense of consumers owing to a shift of resources for the production of more producer goods. This shift reduces the supply of consumer goods and so raises prices. Consumers are unwilling to pay the now higher prices and are "freed" to save.

Eventually, the banking system cuts back on its credit advances to producers. If additional savings are not forthcoming, the market rate of interest rises to the natural rate, making additional investment unattractive. Consumer prices, however, continue to advance thanks to supply reductions and incomplete investment projects that allow nothing to consumer supply. Since workers in the producer goods sector cannot readily shift to the consumer goods sector, the economy is faced with unemployment and rising prices.

Conditions have changed since the 1930s when Hayek presented his analysis. It is government, not private investment, that benefits by bank credit or money supply increases at the expense of consumers. For example, in the U.S. economy consumer expenditures as a percentage of GNP declined from 75 percent in 1929 to 63 percent in 1974, whereas government spending increased over the same period from 8 percent to 22 percent. On the other hand, investment, which was at 16 percent of GNP in 1929, fell to about 15 percent in 1974.

We should keep in mind that Hayek's views on money and the monetary system are those of the Austrian school and very close to the views of supply-siders who urge a return to the gold standard. Accordingly, money is a social institution—public good. In essence, the monetary system is an integral part of the social fabric whose threads include faith and trust, which make possible the exercise of rational choice and the development of human freedom.

When we turn to the analytical apparatus for examining money, we find that three approaches to monetary analysis have dominated the past few decades: the quantity-velocity approach, the cash-balance approach, and the income-expenditure approach. The Great Depression tended to overshadow the first two approaches, commonly grouped under the quantity theories of money, giving rise to the income-expenditure approach.

The quantity theories, however, have never been completely repudiated. On the contrary, they have experienced a remarkable revival, as this study demonstrates. An analytical review of these more traditional theories as well as of the income-expenditure theory against the background of past and contemporary experience will permit us to appraise monetary questions from several points of view. It will also establish the usefulness of the conceptual framework for understanding much of past and current monetary debate.

Closely associated with classical and neoliberal thought, monetarist quantity theories have tended to separate monetary from "real" influences. In interpreting swings in the price level or the value of money, they rest on the assumption, usually implicit, that the structure of relative prices, rates of interest, levels of employment and output, and the rate of economic growth are determined in the long run by "real" (nonmonetary) forces. In this view the theories of value and distribution explained how the forces of supply and demand determine the relative prices of goods and services. This is accomplished exclusive of money, which is viewed simply as a common unit or measure of account. "Real" forces are, in effect, the important factors underlying economic welfare; money, though useful, is only secondary.

Reform-liberalism and Keynesianism, on the other hand, tend to be associated with the development of the income-expenditure approach. As a result, the traditional separation between monetary and real forces has receded into the background. The scope of monetary theory has broadened so as to take into account the effects of monetary change on real income and employment and the processes of short-run economic adjustments.

QUANTITY THEORY EQUATIONS: VELOCITY AND CASH-BALANCES

Irving Fisher's (1867–1947) best known contribution to the field of money is the equation of exchange usually expressed as MV=PT.[3] This is a simple statement of identity, although it is often confused with the quantity theory of money. It states that the quantity of money (M), multiplied by the average number of times each unit of money is used during a given period (V), is equal to the sum total of goods and claims traded (T) during the period, multiplied by the average price (P). Since the equation is not a theory but an identity, it provides no basis for prediction. As a consequence, it is not open to disputes as to its "truth" or "falsity." The only problem presented by the equation of exchange is its usefulness as an analytic framework.

On the criterion of usefulness, a modification of the equation of exchange restricts transactions to those involving real income (y) and a price level (p_y) corresponding to this income. Thus, $P_y y$ represents total money income or receipts. By dividing total money income by M, income velocity (V_y), or the average number of times each unit of money enters into income in a given period of time, is obtained. The corresponding identity becomes:

$$MV_y = P_y y$$

This modification of the equation of exchange or, as it is usually called, the income-velocity approach, has the advantage of ready availability of statistical data on income and prices.

The identities so far discussed are converted into theory and thus capable of providing a basis for prediction by making various assertions about the terms in either the equation-of-exchange or income-velocity approach. Assertions about the various terms, however, result also in more than one version of the quantity theory of money. Thus, the answer to what determines price level changes in the "rigid" version of the quantity theory is simply changes in the stock of money. A looser version of the theory asserts that price level changes are the consequence of a combination of three factors: the quantity of money, its rate of turnover, and the balance of transactions or income. Both versions of the theory, however, accept the assertion that the price level is passive. We will now consider the quantity theory view of money's effect on output and interest rates.[4]

Money's Effect on Output

"Nominal money" refers to the money stock, or the actual dollar (dinar, pound, franc, and so on) amount of money (currency and deposits) in the economy. Real cash balances, on the other hand, can be thought of as the total dollar amount of money adjusted for changes in the price levels. If, for example, the nominal money stock stays constant but prices double, the amount of real cash balances in the system can be thought of as declining by 50 percent. The quantity theorist assumes that the nominal quantity of money can be controlled by the monetary authorities, but that the amount of real cash balances is determined by activities within the economic system.

The relationship between changes in nominal money and changes in real cash balances lies at the heart of the quantity theory. Increasing (decreasing) the rate of growth of the money supply is hypothesized to leave households and businesses with excess (deficient) cash balances. People have three options with which to dispose of these excess funds: they can purchase credit instruments; they can purchase goods and services; or they can do both. Increasing the demand for goods and services will affect prices, however; this, in turn, will affect the level of real cash balances.

The extent to which an increase in nominal money leads to an increase in real cash balances depends on the extent to which prices change. Generally speaking, in periods of high unemployment—such as during a recession—increasing the amount of nominal money would be expected to increase aggregate demand and output of goods and services relatively more than prices. On the other hand, when the economy is fully employed—such as during a boom period—increases in the amount of nominal money would be expected to lead to an increase in prices.

Money's Effect on Interest Rates

The second major aspect of the quantity theory is the relationship between changes in the nominal quantity of money, in prices, and in interest rates. To explain this relationship, quantity theorists like to talk about three effects of changes in the rate of growth in the money supply on interest rates: the liquidity effect, the income effect, and the price anticipation effect. The magnitude of each of these effects and the time lag before they are felt depend, in part, on how fully employed the economy's resources are.

The first effect to be felt is the liquidity effect. This effect results from the fact that increasing (decreasing) the rate of growth of the money supply will leave households and businesses with more (less) money than they wish to hold. Increases cause them to shift some portion of these excess balances into credit instruments, increasing the price of these instruments and, therefore, decreasing interest rates. According to the quantity theorists, increasing the stock of money will also lead to an increase in the demand for goods and services. This will stimulate, after a three- to six-month lag, the demand for credit on the part of businesses and households. This increased demand for credit, called the income effect, leads to a decline in the price of credit instruments and an increase in market interest rates.

In addition, the quantity theorists say, the increased aggregate demand for goods and services will increase prices. The amount of inflation, however, depends upon the extent to which resources are employed. More important, as households and businesses begin to feel the effect of inflation, they expect more of it. This, in turn, will add to the credit demand. If people expect prices to increase and if interest rates are low, it is logical that people will want to go into debt.

The increase in the demand for credit caused by inflationary price expectations leads to the price anticipation effect on interest rates. Lenders also come to expect inflation, and therefore require a higher return to compensate for the expected loss in purchasing power.

As a result of this price anticipation effect, quantity theorists like to speak of interest rates as being made up of two parts. One portion of the interest rate relates to the "real" return on capital assets (assuming no expected inflation), while a second portion relates to changes in expected prices.

Let us assume an individual anticipates no inflation and receives a 4 percent return on an investment. Now let events change and assume the individual anticipates 3 percent inflation to continue indefinitely. It is hard to be content with a 4 percent return. Instead, the individual will want the 4 percent return plus 3 percent additional to compensate for the expected inflation. Market interest rates thus reflect these price expectations.

This theory explains the often-heard contention by quantity theorists that increasing the money supply, while admittedly decreasing interest rates in the short run (the liquidity effect), will eventually lead to higher interest rates (the income and price effects). Because quantity theorists believe the economy is inherently stable, they contend that the real rate of interest, as opposed to the market rate of interest, does not change very much. Most of the changes, therefore, that are observed in the market rate of interest result from erratic historical changes in the money supply.

Much of the criticism of the quantity-velocity formulation of the quantity theory rests on challenging the basic assumptions underlying the theory, especially in its more rigid form. Neither velocity nor income nor transactions, it is argued, are stable. All are subject to rapid change even in very short periods of time. Indeed, velocity changes at times may be an even more important factor than the quantity of money in accounting for short-run changes in the level of prices.

Another criticism deals with the passive nature of the level of prices. It is asserted that P, far from being passive, may in fact contribute to changes in the other factors. Thus, for example, a rise in the level of prices may encourage people to dispose of their money for fear that its purchasing power will decline even further. Such disposals are registered in an increase in velocity.

Under a specie standard, moreover, a change in prices may affect the production of the monetary metal and so the stock of money (M). A rising level of prices may increase the costs of producing specie, which leads to a falling level of prices. The net effect is that P is not necessarily passive and may even influence M—albeit after a considerable period of time.

An alternative approach to the quantity-velocity view of money is the so-called Cambridge cash-balance view.[5] Essentially, this view considers the demand for money as the demand to hold a stock of liquid assets against the money stock made available by monetary authorities and banks. Attention is focused on the conditions necessary for the money stock to find willing holders and on the consequences when such conditions are not met. Economists have described the differences between the quantity-velocity view and the cash-balance view as that the former considers money "on the wing," while the latter considers money as "sitting" and examines the question of why it has not yet been spent.

In symbols, the cash-balance view is stated as $M=KyP_y$. M is the money stock, y is annual real income, and P_y is the appropriate price level, so that yP_y is aggregate money national income. Thus, K is simply the proportion of income held in monetary form. At times the cash balance equation is also stated in the form $K = M/yP_y$.

Clearly, an increase in M may be accompanied by an increase in K and so in the proportion of annual income held in the form of money balances; or by an increase in y and so increasing money and real balance but not their proportion to income; or by an increase in P_y and so in money balances but not real balances, thus keeping constant the ratio between money balances and real balances; or by a combination of all three.

The quantity theory of money can be expressed in cash-balance terms by imposing certain conditions on K and y. By imposing the conditions that K is relatively stable and that y tends to be maintained at relatively full levels of employment, the cash-balance identity is converted into the quantity theory of money. The demand for money balances is represented by KyP_y. If the desired demand for money balances (KyP_y) is equal to the supply of such balances (M), no attempt will be made to change the rate of monetary expenditures so as to increase or decrease the command over real income held in the form of money balances. As a consequence, prices (P) will remain stable and in equilibrium with the supply of money (M).

Suppose now that M is decreased. People's cash balances would be less than their desired holdings. Their attempts to increase cash balances would reduce the level of expenditures, thereby reducing general monetary demand for output. With the contraction of demand, prices would tend to decline, thereby increasing the real value of cash balances until the reduced money supply once again bears the desired (and, in the case of the rigid quantity theory, constant) relationship to the money value of output. Since the demand for money in the rigid quantity theory formulation is determined by custom, institutions, and the like, it changes slowly over time and thus may be asumed as given at any point in time. Accordingly, price changes are in proportion to changes in M.

The relationship between the quantity-velocity and cash-balance approaches to monetary analysis can be illustrated in terms of income velocity. The relationship is straightforward, following from the definitions of K and V_y. They are reciprocals. Thus, $V_y = 1/K$ and $K = 1/V_y$.

The important contribution of the cash-balance approach is that it introduced into monetary analysis considerations of demand and supply of money. It also introduced into the analysis of demand for money the powerful tool of marginal analysis. Typical criticism of the cash-balance view is that it continued to treat money primarily in terms of the so-called transactionsmotive. Accordingly, money is held in anticipation of expenditures for goods and services. Any increase in M resulting in an increase in undesired liquidity is promptly spent on goods and services. Another criticism is that this view does not provide a systematic analysis of the holdings of cash balances, uncertainty, and the rate of interest. According to some, an even more basic criticism is that the cash-balance view (and quantity-velocity view), when cast in the quantity theory, provides little insight into the level of income or output, or the interaction among income, the money supply, value of money, and the demand for cash balances.

INCOME-EXPENDITURE THEORY: INVESTMENT MONEY AND THE RATE OF INTEREST

The income-expenditure theory associated with Keynes sheds light simultaneously on income determination, the interaction between income, the money supply, the value of money, and the demand for cash balances.[6] Thus, it attempts to meet the criticism raised against simple versions of the quantity theory of money. This view relates monetary expenditures to income sources instead of to the stock of money, as in the quantity theory of money. The equation of exchange identity $P_y y = M V_y$ indicates that aggregate income is equal to the money supply multiplied by the number of times that it is spent in producing income. On the other hand, the Keynesian identity adopted by the income-expenditure view indicates that aggregate income is equal to the expenditures of four sectors of the economy: households, business, government, and foreign sector. These classifications are used to construct the income-expenditure theory. Although this view considers the stock of money as important, it does not play the dominant role it does in the quantity theory.

For purposes of illustrating the simple income-expenditure view of money, let us assume constant prices. This implies a perfectly elastic supply curve at the current price level so that aggregate income is determined by demand. Let us also assume that demand consists of consumer demand and investment demand. Consumer demand is assumed to be a function of several factors, including the level of income and its distribution, size of population, changes in living standards, interest rates, taxes or transfers, price level, and the wealth effect. For the sake of simplicity, attention is usually focused on the level of income. When income rises consumer demand also rises but not as much as income; as a consequence, savings also rise. Investment demand is assumed to depend on an array of objective and subjective factors. One of these factors appears to be the profit expectations of entrepreneurs, though other factors may be as important. Such a collection of assumptions serves as a basis for a simple version of the income-expenditure theory whereby the level of income is determined by the level of investment.

An illustration of the determination of equilibrium income is useful. In Figure 2.1 the curve $C + I$ indicates the planned level of expenditures measured vertically, associated with each level of income measured horizontally. The 45-degree line indicates all the points in the plane of the diagram at which expenditures equal earned income. The intersection of curve $C + I$ at E on the 45-degree line is the equilibrium income. When earnings are OY_1 expenditures are EY_1. The equilibrium level of consumption corresponding to this equilibrium level of income is DY_1.

The same results can be obtained in terms of the saving and investment curves presented in Figure 2.2. Saving (S) is plotted as a function of income (Y). In terms of Figure 2.1, saving is the difference between the C curve and the 45-degree line. Investment in Figure 2.2 is shown as a horizontal line an appropriate distance above the zero line. The equilibrium level of income is indicated by OY_1 at E' where $S = I$, which is equal to $C + I$ in Figure 2.1.

According to Figures 2.1 and 2.2, the equilibrium level of income depends on the characteristics of the consumption function and the

Figure 2.1
Determination of the Equilibrium Level of Income

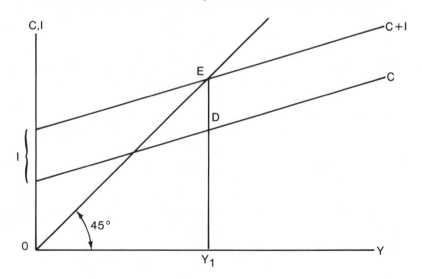

Figure 2.2

Saving and Investment
And the Equilibrium Level of Income

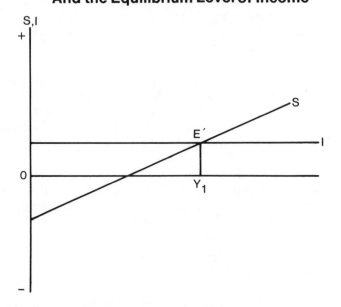

level of investment. This suggests that changes in the level of income can be traced either to shifts in the consumption function (C) or to changes in the rate of investment (I). How much income (Y) will change as a result of a change in C or I can be determined by simply substituting the changed values of C or I in the diagram in Figure 2.1.

Given the consumption curve C and the rate of investment I in Figure 2.1, equilibrium income is OY_1. If investment now rises by an amount ΔI to I_2, this is indicated in Figure 2.3 by an upward shift in the planned expenditures curve to $C_1 + I_2$. Planned expenditures on output AY_1, however, now exceed the former equilibrium level of income EY_1 by an amount AE, which is equal to the amount by which planned investment I_2 exceeds planned savings ED. Income ultimately expands to OY_2 thus bringing about a new equilibrium between planned expenditures and current income.

It is obvious from Figure 2.3 that the rise in income from OY_1 to OY_2 or ΔY will be greater than ΔI. This is because the rise in income resulting from a rise in I indicates an increase in consumption expenditures—a consequence of the implicit assumption that the marginal propensity to consume is positive. Thus, the difference between income levels OY_2

Figure 2.3
Investment Multiplier

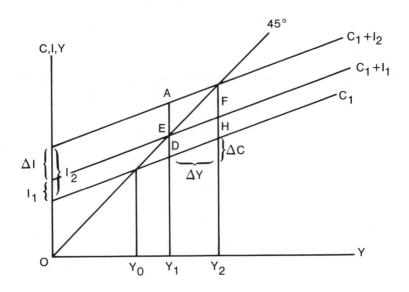

and OY_1 is equal to the change in investment BF, plus the changes in consumption HG induced by the change in investment.

It is also obvious that a similar analysis can be made for a change in the consumption curve. The income-expenditure theory, however, focuses attention on the investment multiplier and chiefly on the argument that investment tends to be more volatile than consumption expenditures. Accordingly, changes in the rate of investment tend to be the main source of instability in the rate of overall expenditures.

Symbolically, the investment multiplier can be stated as $K_1 = \Delta Y/\Delta I$ where K_1 is the amount by which a given change in investment must be multiplied to derive the induced changes in income. The change in income ΔY, however, is equal to $\Delta I + \Delta C$. Thus, $\Delta I = \Delta Y - \Delta C$. Substituting this expression for ΔI in the definition implies $K_1 = \Delta Y/(\Delta Y - \Delta C)$. Dividing through by ΔY, $K_1 = 1/[1 - (\Delta C/\Delta Y)]$. But $\Delta C/\Delta Y$ is the slope of the consumption curve in Figures 2.1 and 2.3 or in effect the marginal propensity to consume (MPC). Substituting MPC for $\Delta C/\Delta Y$ we obtain $K_1 = (1/1 - MPC)$, thus yielding the form in which the multiplier is usually expressed.

At times it is also argued that the multiplier is the reciprocal of the marginal propensity to save (MPS) since $1 - MPC$ is equal to MPS. This is correct for simplified versions of the expenditure theory. it does not, however, hold for more complicated versions of the theory where such leakages from the spending stream as imports or taxes are also taken into account. Thus, it is preferable to adhere to the more generally valid form of the multiplier that uses MPC.

The importance of the multiplier analysis is that it suggests a number of direct policy applications. If investment is as volatile as some would have us believe, other things being equal, we should expect fluctuations in national income that are some multiple of those in investment. Thus, if an economy is assumed to have a multiplier of five and if the current level of income is $50 billion less than that consistent with the desired level of employment, the size of the multiplier suggests that total expenditures need not be raised by $50 billion but by $10 billion.

Although useful in presenting the salient features of the income-expenditure theory, the simple version discussed above is not completely satisfactory for at least two reasons. In the first place, it fails to take into account the role of the stock of money. In the second place, it leaves both the rate of interest and the rate of investment undetermined.

In the more sophisticated versions of the theory, the rate of interest is determined by the stock of money and the "liquidity preference" demand for money. The rate of investment, on the other hand, is determined by balancing the rate of return on investment or "marginal efficiency of capital" against the rate of interest so that at the margin the marginal efficiency of capital should be equal to the rate of interest.

Investment

Let us examine the rate of investment and its relation to the rate of interest. An investor in a newly produced asset expects some rate of return on the invested funds. This rate is called the "efficiency" of the asset. It is estimated on the basis of the current cost of producing the asset and on the amounts and timing of the series of prospective money receipts that may be expected. This stream of money receipts may be called the "prospective return" of the asset, as distinct from its "efficiency." It is a stream of net money receipts rather than a net income stream for the reason that depreciation or interest costs of financing are not deducted. The net money receipts concept includes the sale value of the series of outputs that an additional unit of equipment makes possible over its useful life, minus the cost of such cooperating factors as labor and raw materials, including taxes.

The efficiency of an asset can be obtained from the equation

$$C = \frac{R_1}{1 + r} + \frac{R_2}{(1 + r)^2} + \ldots + \frac{R_n}{(1 + r)^n}$$

where C is the present cost of the capital goods, R is the series of returns from the asset, and r is the rate that makes both sides equal and whose value represents the efficiency of the asset under consideration. A numerical example may help to illustrate the point. Consider an asset with a series of ten net annual returns of $1,000, after which the asset does not possess even scrap value. The rate of return on this asset will depend on its cost. If the asset costs $10,000, only its initial cost will be retrieved at the end of ten years and its yield is zero. However, if the cost of the asset is less than $10,000, a positive rate of return can be anticipated; moreover, the lower the cost, the greater would be the expected rate of return. Indeed, anything that reduces C, assuming prospective Rs constant, or anything that increases prospective Rs, assuming C constant, raises the efficiency (r) of the asset under consideration.

Although there exist many possible efficiencies relating to the production of various additional units of assets, there is only one most efficient way of utilizing a small addition to the total stock of society's capital. The highest of potential rates of return from adding one more unit of capital is called the marginal efficiency of capital (MEC). The MEC concept can be illustrated with the aid of Figure 2.4(a).[7] The MEC is measured along the vertical axis and the stock of capital in value terms along the horizontal axis. For example, the marginal efficiency of the stock of capital at K_0 is r_0 and at K_1 it is r_1 and so on. The declining value of the r's is derived from the principle of diminishing returns, whereby each additional unit of capital adds less to the increase in output than preceding units. Assuming such factors as technology, population, and expectations are constant, the various rates of return appropriate to the alternative stocks of capital trace a marginal efficiency of capital curve (MEC_0). A change in any of these conditions such as for example technology causes a shift of the MEC curve.

The situation presented in Figure 2.4(a) indicating that the interest rate i_0 is below the marginal efficiency of capital r_0 for K_0 capital stock should encourage new investment in capital assets. An individual firm may increase its flow of profits and increase its present value by the capitalized value of the increase in prospective income by borrowing at interest rate i_0 and investing at the expected rate of return of r_0. Capital

Figure 2.4
Rate of Return on Capital and the Demand for Investment

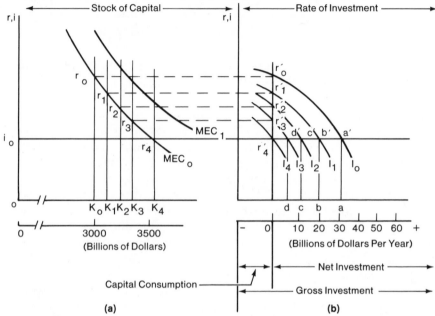

(a)   (b)

will continue to accumulate to K_4 where MEC_0 of r_4 is equal to the rate of interest i_0.

How rapidly the gap between K_0 and K_4 is closed is indicated by the rate of investment which is, in effect, the growth of the capital stock per period. With a given stock of capital we expect increasing amounts of investment per period to involve declining rates of return. This relationship is called the marginal efficiency of investment (MEI) curve. For each rate of interest an appropriate rate of investment exists on which the MEI curve would equal the rate of interest. As a consequence, investment is a function of the rate of interest. The MEI schedule describing the amount of investment that would occur at various rates of interest is called the investment demand schedule.

The relationship between the marginal efficiency of capital and investment demand is illustrated in Figure 2.4(b). The horizontal axis now shows the rates of change in the current capital stock. Net positive investment is measured to the right of the 0 axis, while the distance 0'0 indicates the rate of capital accumulation appropriate to the current stock of capital, so that distances to the right of 0' axis provide a measure of gross investment.

Thus, given the stock of capital K_0 in Figure 2.4(a), the MEC of r_0 corresponds to the marginal efficiency of investment of a rate of production of capital goods $0'0$ in Figure 2.4(b), or zero net investment. For greater quantities of investment per period, the marginal efficiencies will fall because of increasing risk and cost tracing out the MEI curve I_0. Moving along the I_0 curve, the marginal efficiency of investment becomes equal to the rate of interest at a', leading to the rate of net investment of 0a. It should be clear that with interest rates higher or lower than i_0 the corresponding amount of investment is indicated by appropriate points on the I_0 curve. The I_0 curve is thus the investment demand schedule.

According to Figure 2.4(b), investment takes place at 0a per period and the stock of capital shifts to the right so that the marginal efficiency moving along MEC_0 falls. As the stock of capital increases and reaches K_1, the marginal efficiency is r_1 and the gap between the yields on assets and interest rate is reduced, shifting the investment demand curve to I_1. As the process of capital accumulation continues and the marginal efficiency of capital falls, investment demand shifts to the left until K_4 capital stock is reached where the marginal efficiency r_4 is equal to the rate of interest i_0. This point corresponds to zero net investment.

Investment can be sustained if there is an upward shift of the MEC curve, say, from MEC_0 to MEC_1. A shift to the right of the investment demand schedule occurs as a consequence, thus permitting more investment despite a greater stock of capital. Factors underlying shifts in the MEC curve are those that reduce the cost of capital or raise expected returns without at the same time an offsetting change in the other. Investment that occurs as a result of shifts in the MEC curve is called autonomous investment, as distinct from induced investment, which refers to the growth of capital stock caused by the growth of output.

Money and the Rate of Interest

Supporters of the income-expenditure theory assert that people are motivated to hold money for reasons of transaction, precaution, and speculation. The transaction motive is straightforward. It exists because receipts and payments in society are not perfectly synchronized. Analytically, the money balances held to fulfill the transactions motive are considered in the aggregate as proportional to national income.

The precautionary motive for holding cash balances arises as a result of uncertainty about future payments and receipts. Cash balances serving the precautionary motive are above the level necessary for transactions requirements. These balances act as a cushion to absorb the shock of unexpected expenditures or a decline in receipts. Since interest rate movements are also uncertain, capital loss is ever present; consequently, assets other than money will not fulfill the precautionary motive. Thus, the demand for precautionary cash balances appears to depend on national income, degree of uncertainty, and interest rates.

Much of the transaction and precautionary demand for cash balances can be combined since both are largely a function of income. Let us call this component of the demand for money as the L_1 demand and indicate it as $L_1 = L_1(Y)$. As shown in Figure 2.5(a), it is assumed that holders of cash balances will hold some fixed proportion of their monies in the form of L_1 balances. At income OY_1, L_1 cash balances will be 01. When income rises to OY_2, L_1 balances will be 02.

The speculative motive for holding cash balances simply reflects the belief that, other things being equal, money is the best asset to hold. This demand plus some undetermined part of the precautionary demand constitute the L_2 demand for cash balances. The L_2 demand is taken as a function of the rate of interest $L_2 = L_2(i)$.

Figure 2.5(b) indicates the inverse relationship between the interest rate i and the L_2 demand for cash balances. This inverse relationship of the interest rates and demand for cash balances is based on three considerations. First, the higher the interest rate the greater is the return for assuming the uncertainty entailed in holding bonds and the greater is the cost of holding money. Second, some part of any increase in the total value of assets will be held in the form of cash balances. Third, the existence of some "normal" or average interest rate encourages expectations that any significant rise or fall in rates is temporary. The higher the rate the greater are the chances for a fall and the greater the chance for a capital gain. Conversely, the lower the rate the greater are the chances for a rise in the rate and the less are the chances for a capital gain.

The L_2 curve is drawn to suggest that at some high interest rate the L_2 demand for cash balances is zero—that is, the L_2 curve cuts the i axis. Furthermore, at some low interest rate the L_2 curve becomes perfectly elastic, suggesting that any additional money will go into cash balances rather than into securities.

The total demand for money is thus $L = L_1(Y) + L_2(i)$. Given the total quantity of bonds, the total money supply, and income, the interest rate must be whatever is necessary to make the supply of money equal to the demand. Figure 2.6 shows the determination of the rate of interest.

Given the supply of money M_0 and level of income, the L_1 demand would be 01 in Figure 2.6. By adding horizontally the L_2 demand, the total demand money L is formed.

Figure 2.5
Demand for Money

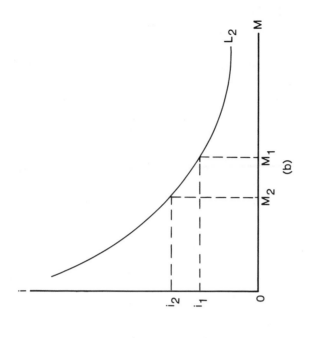

(b)

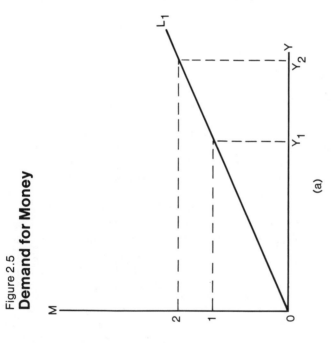

(a)

37

Figure 2.6
Determination of the Rate of Interest

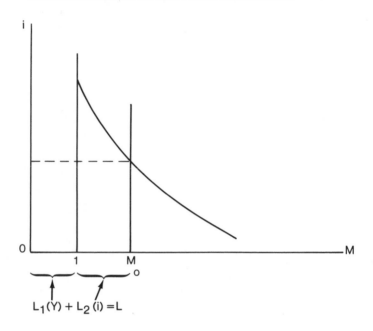

$$L_1(Y) + L_2(i) = L$$

Integration of Money, Interest, and Income

The several elements of the income-expenditure theory can be brought together as in Figure 2.7.[8] The quantities are measured mostly from the origin: saving and investment to the right, quantities of money to the left, interest from the origin up, and income from the origin down.

Consider first the money market presented in quadrant IV. Assume that the quantity of money is given and measured by the distance OO'. A secondary axis is erected at O'. The L_1 cash balances are measured from 0 to the left and the supply of L_2 balances from the O' axis to the right. Thus, if OO' is total money supply, and OS is absorbed in L_1 balances, the supply of L_2 balances is O'S. The rate of interest that provides equilibrium in the money market is i_0. Turn now to quadrant I and the axes measuring interest and investment. Given the demand for investment I, the rate of interest i_0 brings forth OI_0 rate of investment.

In quadrant II the level of income consistent with investment is OI_0. For this purpose a curve is constructed relating saving, measured to the right, to income, measured from the origin downward. When the rate of

Figure 2.7
Integration of Money, Interest, and Income

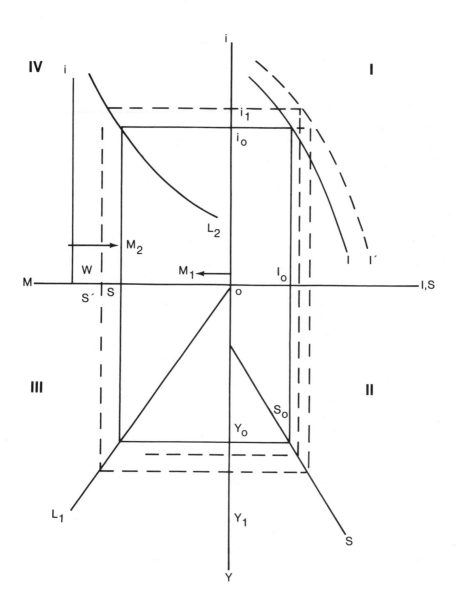

investment is OI_0 the level of income bringing about an equal flow of planned savings is Y_0.

Quadrant III represents the L_1 demand for money as a function of income. Given the L_1 demand schedule and the level of income Y_0, the required L_1 cash balances are OS, which in Figure 2.7 are equal to the level of balances we assumed originally in bringing about equilibrium in the money market in quadrant IV.

Figure 2.7 illustrates how the dependent variables of the economy are related to given quantities and behavioral relationships in the system. The given factors are: the quantity of money; L_1 curve; L_2 curve; I curve; and the saving function. The variables determined are: the interest rate; the rate of investment; the level of income; amount of L_1 cash balances; and amount of L_2 cash balances.

NOTES

1. In some of the early writers we see anticipations of theories advanced much later, e.g., Thomas Joplin (1790–1847), Thomas Attwood (1783–1856), Nicholas Barbor (1640–1698), William Lowndes (1652–1724), and Bishop George Berkeley (1658–1753). D. Vickers, Studies in the Theory of Money, 1690–1776 (Philadelphia: Chilton, 1959) makes the point that there was more Keynesian-type economics in the early period than has often been recognized.

2. F. A. Hayek, The Constitution of Liberty (Chicago: University of Chicago Press, 1960).

3. Irving Fisher, Purchasing Power of Money (New York: Macmillan, 1911); see also Milton Friedman, "Money: Quantity Theory, II," The International Encyclopedia of the Social Sciences (vol. 10, 1968); Don Patinkin, Money, Interest and Prices (Evanston: Row, Peterson, 1965); Robert L. Hetzel, "The Quantity Theory Tradition and the Role of Monetary Policy," Economic Review, Federal Reserve Bank of Richmond (May/June 1981): 19–26.

4. See Friedman, "Money: Quantity Theory, II," A. G. Hart, "Money: General I," and R. T. Selden, "Velocity of Circulation, III," all in Encyclopedia of Social Sciences (vol. 10); Milton Friedman, "The Optimum Quantity of Money," in The Optimum Quantity of Money and Other Essays (Chicago: Aldine, 1969), pp. 1–50; George Macesich and H. Tsai, Money in Economic Systems (New York: Praeger, 1982).

5. See for example D. H. Robertson, Money (London: Nisbet, 1948).

6. This section draws from the following: John M. Keynes, The General Theory of Employment, Interest and Money (London: Macmillan, 1936); Joan Robinson, Introduction to the Theory of Employment (London: Macmillan, 1937); Lawrence R. Klein, The Keynesian Revolution (New York: Macmillan, 1947); Alvin H. Hansen, A Guide to Keynes (New York: McGraw-Hill, 1953); Kenneth K. Kurihara, ed., Post-Keynesian Economics (New Brunswick: Rutgers University Press, 1954); Don Patinkin, Money, Interest and Prices (Evanston: Row, Peterson, 1956).

7. See for example Abba P. Lerner, "On the Marginal Product of Capital and the Marginal Efficiency of Investment," Journal of Political Economy (February 1953): 1–14. Figure 2.4 draws on results presented in Martin J. Bailey, National Income and the Price Level (New York: McGraw-Hill, 1962), Chapter II; R. W. Clower, "Productivity, Thrift,

and the Rate of Interest," *Economic Journal* (March 1954): 107–15; Milton Friedman, *Price Theory* (Chicago: Aldine, 1962), Chapter 13.

8. Figure 2.7 is adapted from J. R. Hicks, "Mr. Keynes and the 'Classics': A Suggested Interpretation," *Econometrica* (1937): 147–69; Franco Modigliani, "Liquidity Preference and the Theory of Interest and Money," *Econometrica* (January 1944): 45–88; Ira O. Scott, Jr., "An Exposition of the Keynesian System," *Review of Economic Studies* 19 (1951): 12–18.

3

THE THEORIES COMPARED

A GENERAL FRAMEWORK FOR MONETARY ANALYSIS

The theoretical framework set forth by Milton Friedman in "A Theoretical Framework for Monetary Analysis" is one that most economists would accept, even monetarists and Keynesians.[1] It is ideologically neutral and thus useful in analyzing fluctuations in income and prices in a wide variety of institutional and sociopolitical arrangements.

Assuming a closed economy and neglecting the fiscal role of government, Friedman's framework, cast into a basic IS-LM apparatus, can be described as follows:

$$\frac{C}{P} = f\left(\frac{Y}{P}, i\right) \qquad (1)$$

$$\frac{I}{P} = g(i) \qquad (2)$$

$$\frac{Y}{P} = \frac{C}{P} + \frac{I}{P} \qquad (3)$$

$$M_d = P\, 1\left(\frac{Y}{P}, i\right) \qquad (4)$$

$$M_s = h(i) \tag{5}$$

$$M_d = M_s \tag{6}$$

where: C = Consumption
P = Price level
Y = Income
i = Interest rate
M_d = Demand
M_s = Supply of money

Friedman does not consider in dispute the demand-for-money equation, which is here written in a general version acceptable to most economists. At issue is the method of completing the system that has seven variables, but only six equations in it. According to Friedman the choice is either

$$P = P_0 \tag{7}$$

as in the income-expenditure theory or

$$\frac{Y}{P} = y = y_0 \tag{8}$$

as in the quantity theory. Equation (7) represents the case of rigid prices. In this instance the price level is determined outside the system, which again reduces the system to one of six equations in six unknowns. It assumes that prices are set or administered by the bargaining power of respective parties such as unions, oligopolies, and/or other institutional arrangements that restrict price flexibility. Views attributing inflation to one or another variety of cost-push causes are a manifestation of equation (7).

A number of cost-push and administered price inflation theories are discussed in subsequent chapters. These theories of inflation will be called antitraditionalist or cost-pusher views. Phillips curve contributions represent attempts, for the most part, to link real magnitudes and the rate of change in prices to their initial historically determined level. This is discussed in a later chapter.

Equation (8) is a statement that the economy is operational at the full employment level of real income. That is, real income is determined outside the system by appending the Walrasian equations of general equilibrium to it and regarding them as independent of equations defining the aggregates. Again the system is reduced to one of six equations determining six unknowns. Friedman notes that this is the essence of the so-called classical dichtomy. In effect, the division between consumption and investment and the "real" interest rate is also determined in a Walrasian "real" system, one that admits of growth. It is for this reason that quantity theorists and monetarists tend to concentrate on equations (4), (5), and (6). In their view equations (1), (2), and (3) are a summarization or aggregation or subset of the Walrasian system.

This suggests one reason why quantity theorists and monetarists focus on increases in aggregate demand and specifically on increases in the money stock as primary causes of inflation. These theories of inflation will be here called traditionalist or demand-pull theories. Since changes in aggregate demand can be engineered also by fiscal policy manipulation, some advocates of demand-pull inflation may not share the monetarist conviction on the important role of the money stock.

Following Friedman, for the simple quantity theory given that $Y/P = y_0$, equations (1), (2), and (3) become a self-sustained set of three equations in three unknowns: C/P, I/P, and r. Substituting (1) and (2) into (3) we have

$$y_0 - f(y_0, r) = g(r), \tag{9}$$

or a single equation that determines r. If we let r_0 be this value of r, from equation (5), this determines the value of M, say M_0, which, using equation (6) converts (4) into

$$M_0 = P.1(y_0, r_0), \tag{10}$$

which now determines P.

Equation (10), however, is simply the classical quantity equation that was discussed in the preceding chapter. This may be seen by multiplying and dividing the right-hand side by y_0 and replacing $1(y_0, r_0)/y_0$ by V, which is its equivalent. Thus,

$$Mo = \frac{Py}{V}, \tag{11}$$

or

$$P = \frac{MoV}{y}. \tag{12}$$

For the income-expenditure theory, setting $P = P_0$ does not in general permit a sequential solution. The manner in which it is established is discussed above. By substituting equations (1) and (2) into (3) we have

$$\frac{Y}{P_0} - f\left(\frac{Y}{P_0}, r\right) = g(r), \qquad (13)$$

an equation in two variables, Y and r. This is in fact Hicks's IS curve of his IS-LM analysis. By substituting (4) and (5) into (6) we have

$$h(r) = P_0 . 1\left(\frac{Y}{P_0}, r\right), \qquad (14)$$

a second equation in the same two variables, Y and r. It is Hicks's LM curve. The simultaneous solution of the two determines Y and r.

In keeping with the discussion in the preceding chapter, our simplified model (which Friedman points to as being faithful to Keynes's) can be obtained by supposing that Y/P is not an argument in the right-hand side of equation (4) or that absolute liquidity preference holds so that equation (4) takes the special form:

$$M_d = O \text{ if } r > r_0$$

$$M_d = OO \text{ if } r < r_0. \qquad (4a)$$

In these cases equations (4), (5), and (6) determine the interest rate, $r = r_0$, as in the simple quantity theory equations (1), (2), and (3) do. Substituting the interest rate in equation (2) gives us investment say of $I = I_0$, and in equation (1) makes consumption simply a function of income; so that real income must be determined by the requirement that it equate saving with investment.

Moving along with Friedman, if we approximate the function f(y/p, r_0) by a linear form, say,

$$\frac{C}{P} = C_0 + C_1 \frac{Y}{P} \qquad (15)$$

and substitute in equation (3) and solve for Y/P, we have

$$\frac{Y}{P} = \frac{C_0 + I_0}{1 - C_1} \tag{16}$$

which is the simple Keynesian multiplier equation with $C_0 + I_0$ equalling autonomous expenditure and $1/1 - C$ equalling the multiplier.

The key differences between the Keynesian view and monetarist view are that: Keynesians argue that change in the quantity of money affects spending via the interest rate effect on spending; and the monetarist view underscores wealth in portfolios and then on final spending.

Neither the quantity theory nor the income-expenditure theory model is satisfactory as a framework for short-run analysis. According to Friedman, this is so mainly because neither theory can explain

> (a) the short-run division of a change in nominal income between prices and output, (b) the short-run adjustment of nominal income to change in autonomous variables, and (c) the transition between the short-run situation and a long-run equilibrium described essentially by the quantity-theory model.[2]

A third way to determine the above system of equations is provided by Friedman in the monetary theory of nominal income.[3] This method draws on Irving Fisher's ideas on the nominal and real interest rates and Keynes's view that the current long-term market rate of interest is expected to prevail over a long period. The Keynes and Fisher synthesis is then integrated into a quantity theory model, together with the empirical assumptions that the real income elasticity of the demand for money is unity, and that a difference between the anticipated real interest rate and the anticipated growth of real income is determined outside the system. In effect, this is the counterpart assumption to equations (7) and (8) of income expenditure and quantity theory, respectively. The result is a monetary model in which current income is related to current and prior quantities of money.[4] This monetary model of nominal income, according to Friedman, corresponds to the broader framework implicit in much of the theoretical and empirical work that he and others have done in analyzing monetary experience in the short run, and is consistent with many of the empirical findings produced in these studies.

The quantity theory of money is basically a theory of the demand for money. It is at its best when the demand for money is a stable function of a few key variables. For instance, its stability is important because it ensures that, mutatis mutandis, inflationary pressures from a change in the supply of money are transmitted to the general level of prices.

MONEY DEMAND FUNCTION

In the neoclassical analysis, the demand for money is functionally related to income, interest rates, and some types of wealth. The question of the nature of the income in the money demand function is still under debate: the current nominal income, real income, or Friedman's permanent income. The nature of the interest rate also commands attention: the short-term or long-term government bond rate, or the money market rate on private debt. In effect, the arguments or variables that enter the demand function for money, and the definition of the quantity of money appropriate for the demand function, have received substantial attention in both the recent and distant past. A number of studies seem to suggest that in the long run the demand for money function may not be stable. To judge from some of these studies, the function shifts over different phases of the cycle; no unique and stable function would therefore be obtained.[5]

Money is one of the forms in which individuals can hold their assets. In some economies a small interest income is to be had from assets that are also used as money. But the desire to hold cash cannot be explained by this fact; there are many instances of money yielding no interest and being held nevertheless. Two peculiar and interrelated characteristics of money have usually been emphasized in theories that set it apart from other assets. The first is that money is acceptable as a means of exchange for goods and services, and the second is that its market value is generally highly predictable. These two characteristics are not the exclusive property of money. Other assets also possess them in varying degrees. However, unlike other assets, money is universally accepted as a means of exchange, and its value is usually more predictable than that of other assets. The three motives introduced by Keynes are the transactions, the precautionary, and the speculative motives. Keynes said, in developing in detail the motives of liquidity preference, that the subject was "substantially the same as that which has been sometimes discussed under the heading of the Demand for Money":

> It [the analysis of the motives to liquidity preference] is also closely connected with what is called the income-velocity of money—for the income-velocity of money merely measures what proportion of their

incomes the public chooses to hold in cash, so that an increased income-velocity of money may be a symptom of a decreased liquidity preference. It is not the same thing [as the analysis of the motives to liquidity preference], however, since it is in respect to his stock of accumulated savings rather than his income, that the individual can exercise the choice between liquidity and illiquidity.[6]

Keynes postulated that the level of transactions undertaken by an individual and also by the aggregate of individuals would be in a stable relationship to the level of income. Hence, the so-called transactions demand for money would be proportional to the level of income. The use of the term "transactions motive," however, was confined to describing the necessity of holding cash to bridge the gap between the receipt of payments and the disbursement of such proceeds, or to bridge the interval between purchase and realization.

According to Keynes, the precautionary motive concerns the two aspects of the demand for balances: first, the demand for cash as a proportion of assets "to provide for contingencies requiring sudden expenditure and for unforseen opportunities of advantageous purchases"; and second, the demand for an asset whose "value is fixed in terms of money to meet a subsequent liability (e.g., bank indebtedness) fixed in terms of money."[7] Keynes suggested that the demand for money arising from the precautionary motive would also depend largely on the level of income.

Marshall and Pigou suggested that uncertainty about the future was one of the factors that might be expected to influence the demand for money. Keynes's analysis of the speculative motive represents an attempt to formalize one aspect of this suggestion and to draw conclusions from it:

> The aggregate demand for money to satisfy the speculative motive usually shows a continuous response to gradual changes in the rate of interest, i.e., there is a continuous curve relating changes in the demand for money to satisfy the speculative motive and changes in the rate of interest as given by changes in the price of bonds and debts of various maturities.[8]

Furthermore, he said, it is "important to distinguish between changes in the rate of interest . . . due to changes in the supply of money . . . and those which are primarily due to changes in expectations affecting the liquidity function itself."[9]

Accordingly, the Keynesian theory of liquidity preference separates the demand for money into two parts:

$$M^D = L_1(Y) + L_2(r).\tag{17}$$

The first part, $L_1(Y)$, based on transactions and precautionary motives, is treated as a function of income; the second part, $L_2(r)$, is based on speculative motives as a function of the interest rate. This analytical breakthrough by Keynes was significant in that it placed the demand for money in a behavioral framework consistent with the concept of utility maximization in an uncertain world, and away from the restrictive notion of institutionally determined payment schedules. Later economists, however, have found that the demand for transactions balances was also interest elastic.[10] Since the alternative to holding cash for transactions purposes is short-run assets or time deposits, their rate of return should influence the money demand and the short-term rate of interest should be treated as an argument in the demand function for money.

Moreover, people's behavior in holding cash balances is affected not only by the transactions, precautionary, and speculative motives as dictated by the Keynesian theory, but also by their expectation of changes in the price level.[11] The alternative cost of carrying over one's wealth from one period to the next in the form of cash balances is the profit one could obtain by carrying over this wealth in the form of other assets, such as commodities and bonds.

> The profit that can be obtained by carrying over a bond is measured by the rate of interest. Similarly, the profit that can be obtained by carrying over commodities is measured by the anticipated rate of increase in prices. Hence just as we assume a negatively sloping demand curve for money as a function of the rate of interest, so can we assume one as a function of the rate of price increase. In both cases the negative slope expresses the fact that the higher the alternative cost of holding cash balances, the smaller the amount demanded.[12]

This symmetry between the rate of interest and the rate of price increase brings out the fact that even the existence of certain anticipations of a price increase will not cause an absolute flight from cash. Instead, just as in the case of the interest rate, it will simply cause the individuals to adjust their holdings of real cash balances so that the marginal utility of the liquidity cash balances provide compensates individuals for the opportunity costs of holding these balances.[13]

Therefore, the expected rate of change of the price level must be interpreted as an expected rate of return on money holding. Other things being equal, the higher is the expected rate of return to money holding, the more of it will be held; the lower it is, the less will be held. The expected rate of change of the price level becomes a potentially important variable in the demand-for-money function. Since the actual rate of change in prices of the immediate past is probably the basic determinant of present expected change in prices, for simplicity, the former may be substituted as an argument explaining the demand for money. The demand for money may assume the basic form

$$\frac{M}{P} = f\left(r^s, \frac{Y}{P}, Z\right) \tag{18}$$

where M^D is nominal money stock, P is the price level, r^s is the short-term market rate of interest, Y/P is the real income, and $Z = (P - P_{-1})/P_{-1}$ is the rate of changes in the price level. In equation (1) partial derivatives of M^D/P with respect to r^s and Z are expected to be negative, and that with respect to Y/P to be positive.

MONEY SUPPLY FUNCTION

The pure theory of the demand for money assumes that the nominal supply of money is given and is varied at the discretion of the monetary authorities and government. Demand theory sets out to analyze the effects on general equilibrium of a change in the nominal quantity of money or of a change in demand for money arising from an exogenous change in tastes. Demand theory also explicitly assumes that the monetary authorities and government can control the nominal quantity of money. In contrast to this view there is a school that sees the money supply responding to demand; it therefore concludes that there is no point in attempting to control the economy by monetary policy. Hence, a theory of money, if it is to be consistent, requires that supply be determined independently of the money demand, and if the theory is to be of use, it must allow that the central bank can control the quantity of money in the hands of the public.[14]

Early theories of money supply developed a mechanistic approach that did not allow for the possibility of ratios being behavioral functions of economic variables. This stage of the theory's development is evocative of early quantity theory and Keynesian multiplier analysis. There is now considerable evidence showing that the supply of money can be expressed as a function of a few variables.[15] Basically, these functions are two types. First, Brunner (1961) and Brunner and Meltzer (1962, 1972) consider money supply as a function of the monetary base, currency-deposit ratio, and reserve-deposit ratio. They contend that, with the monetary base given, the current rate of interest can have very little effect on the supply of money. Second, in contrast, Teigen (1964), Goldfeld (1966), Smith (1967), Modigliani, Rasche, and Cooper (1970), and Bhattacharya (1974) attach importance to the interest rates. A bank's ability to vary the level of excess and borrowed reserves it wishes to hold provides an important reason for treating the money supply as an endogenous variable. The interest responsiveness of excess and borrowed reserves implies a supply function of money that is similarly responsive. To allow this dependence, Teigen has estimated a relationship in which the money supply is made a function of certain Federal Reserve parameters and of interest rates. While the study by Goldfeld is "a slightly high-order approach" in that he derives the money supply from bank behavior, a function of the Teigen-type is implicit in his model. In particular:

> when studies of money-supply determination are reviewed, two main theories emerge. One is that in general there is a stable relationship between the money supply and the reserve base, so that when the stock of reserves increases or decreases the money supply will change in a predictable way. According to this theory, therefore, a central bank can control the money supply by controlling total reserves or the banking and monetary system. The other main theory is that in the United States the volume of member-bank borrowing from the Federal Reserve System and the volume of excess reserves of the member banks (or the net of these two in "free" reserves) influence bank behavior in such a way that the rate of change of bank deposits and money supply can be predicted from these variables. An implication of the second main theory for the operation of a central bank is that attention should be focused on excess reserves and borrowings, or on free reserves, rather than on total reserves in attempting to control the money supply.[16]

The two main theories are not so clearly alternative to one another as they might at first seem to be. Each contains useful insights regarding the behavior of the monetary system. If they are combined, each may contribute an essential element of a more satisfactory explanation of changes in money supply than can be obtained from either of them separately.

In this section, we will develop a way to incorporate variation in excess reserves and borrowings, or in the two as combined in free reserves, in a theory of money supply determination. By so doing, we synthesize the two basic approaches described above.

The derivation of the money supply model proceeds as follows: monetary base (H), or high-powered money as it is frequently referred to, is defined to include all monetary assets capable of being used as banking reserves. It is represented by

$$H = C + R \qquad (19)$$

where R = high-powered money inside the banks (banking reserves), and C = high-powered money outside the banks (currency supplied by the government). C is defined as

$$C = C_p + C_b \qquad (20)$$

where C_p = currency held by the nonbank public, and C_b = currency held by commercial banks.

In the United States, currency held by commercial banks (vault cash) can also be counted as required reserves. It can also be used for excess reserves. In this case, high-powered money is defined as

$$H = C_p + R \qquad (21)$$

where total bank reserves (R) are then defined as

$$R = R_r + R_e + C_b. \qquad (22)$$

In either case, the definition of high-powered money is not changed.

Similarly, total bank reserves (R) are defined as

$$R = R_r + R_e \qquad (23)$$

where R_r = required reserves of member banks, and R_e = excess reserves of member banks. Money supply is defined as

$$M_1^S = C_p + DD \qquad (24)$$

or

$$M_2^S = C_p + D \qquad (24')$$

where DD refers to demand deposits and D the sum of demand and time deposits.

Regardless of whether definition (24) or (24') of money supply is used, the arguments will remain the same. But the data on R_r will be different for demand deposits and aggregate deposits. Without loss of generality, if we further assume that the public desires to hold a fixed proportion $g(0 < g 1)$ of money supply in currency, and that the banking system maintains a fixed cash-deposit ratio n $(0 < n < 1)$, then we get

$$C_p = g_1 M_1^S \qquad (25)$$

or

$$C_p = g_2 M_2^S \qquad (25')$$

and

$$C_b = n_1 DD = n_1(M_1^S - C_p) = n_1(1 - g)M_1^S \qquad (26)$$

or

$$C_b = n_2 D = n_2(M_2^S - C_p) = n_2(1 - g)M_2^S. \qquad (27)$$

If k is the required reserve ratio $(0 < k < 1)$, then we can write

$$R_r = k_1 DD = k_1(M_1^S - C_p) \qquad (28)$$

or

$$R_r = k_2 D = k_2(M_2^S - C_p)$$

$$(28')$$

Here we note that if k, g, and n are constant, the authorities can control the money supply by fixing monetary base (H). But if H is held constant and k or g or n changes, then the money supply does not remain constant. The reserve-deposit ratio rises as commercial banks keep larger reserves to ensure solvency in the fact of increased uncertainty.

Thus, the money supply at any moment is the result of portfolio decisions by the central bank, the commercial banks, and the public. Whether the central banks, by controlling the monetary base, can actually achieve fairly precise control over the money supply, depends on whether the link between the monetary base and bank reserves, and between bank reserves and the money supply (the monetary base-bank reserves-money supply linkage) is fairly tight and therefore predictable. If there is a tight linkage, the monetary authorities can formulate their policies and achieve any particular target for the money supply; on the other hand, if there is significant unpredictable slippage, and the central bank control over the money supply is not sufficiently precise to achieve a given target, it will necessarily have to formulate its policies in terms of other variables it can control. The variable used to confine the central bank's objective, or to implement its policy decisions, must therefore be one it can control within reasonable limits.[17]

Let U be the unborrowed monetary base, defined as

$$U = H - R_b \tag{29}$$

where R_b refers to the borrowings by commercial banks from the central bank. Then, from (2) through (9), we obtain

$$U_1 = C_p + C_b + R_b + (R_e - R_b) = (g + n - ng + k - kg)M_1^S + R_f \tag{30}$$

$$U_2 = (g + n - ng + k - kg)M_2^S + R_f \tag{30'}$$

where $R_f = R_e - R_b$ is free reserves.

"Free reserves" are used in this discussion rather than the component "excess reserves" and "borrowings" in part for convenience in exposition and in part because there are plausible theoretical grounds for this procedure. The question of whether excess reserves and borrowings should be treated separately or as combined in free reserves will be kept open.

Member banks hold excess reserves because they want to be able to meet the cash demands of their depositors without drawing down their legal reserves and hence incurring a penalty cost on reserve deficiencies. Excess reserves, however, are nonearning assets. The opportunity cost to the banks is the yield they must give up by not acquiring an earning asset such as government securities.

Banks are supposedly discouraged from borrowing from the central bank except to meet unexpected short-term contingencies. Nevertheless, there is some interest elasticity with respect to the discount rate.[18] If the discount rate is substantially below the yield that can be earned on short-term government securities, commercial banks will prefer to borrow from the central bank instead of selling these securities. Thus, the lower the discount rate relative to short-term market interest rates, the lower will be the level of free reserves if the central bank does not take offsetting measures. That is, the level of the discount rate determines to some extent whether banks sell short-term securities or draw down their excess reserves.

Banks will prefer to decrease their reserves by a greater amount the larger the (positive) spread between short-term interest rates and the discount rate, and they will sell more bills the smaller this spread. Because there is often considerable hesitancy about continued borrowing from the Fed, one would not expect the effects of changes in each interest rate to be symmetrical. A change of 1 percent in the short-term rate should have a greater effect on banks' reserve position than a change of 1 percent in the discount rate. . . . . But changes in both rates exert an influence on bank behavior.[19]

Without specifying the direction of causality between the discount rate and the short-term interest rate, the free reserves function can be treated as a function of the discount rate (r^d) and the short-term market rate of interest (r^s).[20] Free reserves will also vary with the lagged reserve ratio of commercial banks, v_{-1}, defined as the ratio of the holdings of reserves by banks to their deposit at the beginning of each year. v_{-1} is a lagged endogenous variable, as its components are all determined within the system.[21] These considerations suggest that the free reserves function may assume the basic form

$$R_f = h^*(r^d, r^s, v_{-1}). \tag{31}$$

In equation (31) partial derivatives of R_f with respect to r^d and v_{-1} are expected to be positive, and those with respect to r^s to be negative. Combining equations (21) and (22) and solving for M_q^S, $q = 1,2$, we obtain the basic form of money supply function

$$M_q^S = h(U, r^d, r^s, v_{-1}). \tag{32}$$

In equation (32) partial derivatives of M_q^S with respect to U and r^s are expected to be positive, and those with respect to r^d and v_{-1} to be negative.

If free reserves are assumed to be linear of the basic form

$$R_f = a_0 + a_2 r^d - a_3 r^s + a_4 v_{-1} \tag{33}$$

then we get the money supply function as

$$M_q^S = 1/m(-a_0 + a_1 U = a_2 r^d + a_3 r^s - a_4 v_{-1}) \tag{34}$$

where $q = 1,2$, and $m = (g + n - ng + k - kg)$.

The money supply function postulated in equation (34) differs from the money supply functions derived by Teigen and others. Teigen has distinguished the actual from the potential money supply. But this is not the case of equation (34). It also differs from that of Bhattacharya, who has introduced the differential between the discount rate and a short-term market interest rate as an explicit variable.

MONETARISM AND THE MONETARY APPROACH TO THE BALANCE OF PAYMENTS

The reemergence of the long dormant view, with roots going back more than two hundred years, that money and monetary policy are indeed important is underscored by the work on the monetary approach to the balance of payments undertaken by James Meade, Harry Johnson, Robert Mundell, Jacob Frenkel, J. Richard Zecher, Bluford H. Putman, D. Sykes Wilford, and others.[22] This approach can be summarized in the proposition that the balance of payments is essentially a monetary phenomenon:

> In general the approach emphasises the budget constraint imposed on a country's international spending and views the various accounts of the balance of payments as the "windows" to the outside world, through which excesses of domestic flow demands over domestic flow supplies are cleared.

> Accordingly surpluses in the trade account and the capital account respectively represent excess flow supplies of goods and of securities, and a surplus in the money account reflects an excess domestic flow demand for money. Consequently, in analysing the money account, or more familiarly the rate of increase or decrease in the country's international reserves, the monetary approach focuses on the determinants of the excess domestic flow demand for a supply of money.[23]

Though the approach is described as "monetary," it should not be confused with the term "monetarist" used in policy debates, especially over the use of monetary policy as contrasted with fiscal policy in economic stabilization. As Johnson and Frenkel put it:

> The monetary approach to the balance of payments asserts neither that monetary mismanagement is the only cause, nor that monetary policy change is the only possible cure, to balance of payments problems; it does suggest, however, that monetary processes will bring about a cure of some kind—not necessarily very attractive—unless frustrated by deliberate monetary policy action, and that policies that

neglect or aggravate the monetary implications of deficits and surpluses will not be successful in their declared objectives.[24]

As in the quantity theory statement of Milton Friedman, the
essential assumption in the monetary approach is that there does exist
an aggregate demand function for money that is a stable function of a
relatively small number of aggregate economic variables. In this sense it
makes the same assumptions as in the moderate Keynesian view. Like
the classical quantity theory of money, the monetary approach assumes
the longer run view for the most part of a fully employed economy as
the norm rather than the exception.

A country's size is irrelevant to the monetary approach. A small
country viewed as facing a parametric set of world prices and interest
rates presents no theoretical difficulty in taking demand and supply
functions as dependent on prices rather than prices themselves as
parameters. Johnson and Frenkel note that country size is important on
the monetary side of analysis. For instance, a large country such as the
United States whose national currency is internationally acceptable
may, as a result of following an inflationary domestic credit policy,
force an accumulation of its money in foreign hands and so lead to
world inflation rather than a loss in its international reserves. The
postwar era is a good illustration of such a case.

Of the several studies reported on by Harry Johnson up to about
1975, one is by M. Parkin, I. Richards, and G. Zis (1975):

> [An] empirical study of the determination and control of the world
> money supply under fixed exchange rates (1961–1971) reaches the
> important general conclusions that the growth of the world money
> supply in the study period was influenced in an important and
> predictable way by the growth of the world reserve money, but that
> even if there had been firm control of the growth of world high-
> powered money, this would not have prevented national control banks
> from pursuing domestic credit expansion policies unconducive to
> world price stability.[25]

Zecher properly puts the issues in perspective when he writes
that

> the emergence of the monetary approach in the late 1960's and 1970's
> marks a major swing in economic thought back to the concepts of
> Hume and Smith, and away from the balance of payments theories that
> emerged from the Keynesian revolution. . . . At the same time domestic
> monetarism was a rising force, emphasizing the importance of money
> and the general equilibrium nature of domestic economies. Given that

world goods and capital markets were becoming more and more integrated, international theorists were forced to rework their models; simultaneously, the importance of monetary demand and supply relationships on a world level was becoming integrated with this new general equilibrium approach to balance of payments questions.[26]

NOTES

1. Journal of Political Economy 78 (April/May 1970): 193–238; Friedman, "A Monetary Theory of National Income," Journal of Political Economy 79(April/May 1971): 323–37; See also George Macesich and H. Tsai, Money in Economic Systems (New York: Praeger, 1982).

2. Friedman, "A Theoretical Framework for Monetary Analysis."

3. Friedman, "A Monetary Theory of National Income."

4. Ibid.

5. H. P. Minsky argues in "Central Banking and Money Market Changes," Quarterly Journal of Economics, 71 (May 1957) that innovation in the money market may be responsible for such shifts. On the other hand, see Scott E. Hein, "Dynamic Forecasting and the Demand for Money," Review, Federal Reserve Bank of St. Louis (June-July 1980): 13–23. Hein rejects the notion of a constantly shifting money demand relationship and concludes the money is a useful policy instrument. Innovation has had little effect on the demand for money over the past decade.

6. John Maynard Keynes, The General Theory of Employment, Interest and Money (New York: Harcourt, Brace, 1936), p. 194.

7. Ibid., pp. 170–71, 195–97.

8. Ibid., p. 197.

9. Ibid.

10. In his later writings Keynes did permit the rates of interest to affect L_1 ( ) as well as L_2 ( ); see his "Theory of the Rate of Interest" (1937), reprinted in Readings in the Theory of Income Distribution, ed. W. Feller and B. F. Healey (Philadelphia: The Blakiston Co., 1949), p. 422.

11. Milton Friedman, "The Demand for Money—Some Theoretical and Empirical Results," Journal of Political Economy 67 (June 1959): 327–51; R. Selden, "Monetary Velocity in the United States," in Milton Friedman, ed., Studies in the Quantity Theory of Money (Chicago: University of Chicago Press, 1956); D. Laidler, The Demand for Money: Theories and Evidence (Scranton, Pa.: International Textbook, 1969), 106–97; Lawrence B. Smith and John W. L. Winder, "Price and Interest Rate Expectations and the Demand for Money in Canada," Journal of Finance (June 1971): 671–82.

12. Don Patinkin, Money, Interest, and Prices, 2d ed. (New York: Harper & Row, 1965), pp. 144–45.

13. Ibid., p. 145. The interested reader may profitably look into Patinkin's other studies dealing with one or another aspect of Keynesian economics. See for example Patinkin, Keynes' Monetary Thought (Durham: Duke University Press, 1976); Patinkin and J. Clark Leita, eds., Keynes, Cambridge and the General Theory (Toronto: University of Toronto Press, 1978).

14. Harry G. Johnson, Macroeconomics and Monetary Theory (London: Gray-Mills, 1971), p. 135.

15. For a survey of this evidence refer to A. J. Meigs, Free Reserves and the Money Supply (Chicago: University of Chicago Press, 1962); P. H. Hendershoot and F. De Leeuw,

"Free Reserves, Interest Rates and Deposits: A Synthesis," *Journal of Finance* 25 (June 1970): 599–614; Macesich and Tsai, *Money in Economic Systems.*

16. Meigs, *Free Reserves*, p. 1.

17. David I. Fand, "Some Issues in Monetary Economics," *Review*, Federal Reserve Bank of St. Louis (January 1970). It is for this reason that we have treated the unborrowed monetary base as the policy variable.

18. Goldfeld, loc. cit., pp. 43–50.

19. Michael K. Evans, *Macroeconomic Activity* (New York: Harper & Row, 1969), pp. 314–15.

20. The relationship between free reserves and the interest rates and the discount rates developed here is analogous to that by Meigs (1962), Goldfeld (1966), Teigen (1964), and Bhattacharya (1974). Based on his empirical evidence, Meigs concludes that the free reserves ratio is functionally related to market rate of interest and the discount rate. Bhattacharya assumes free reserves to be an increasing function of the differential between the discount rate and a short-term market rate of interest. If anything, borrowing is sometimes held to be a function of that differential. If that differential widens, banks may borrow additional funds, but they do not necessarily retain those funds as resources.

21. The studies that have related quantities of reserves supplied to the banking system to changes in volume of earning assets or deposits of the banks are: George Horwich, "Elements of Timing and Response in the Balance Sheet of Banking, 1953–55," *Journal of Finance* 12 (May 1957): 238–55; Allan H. Meltzer, "The Behavior of the French Money Supply: 1938–54," *Journal of Political Economy* 67 (June 1959): 275–96; Stephen L. McDonald, "The Internal Drain and Bank Credit Expansion," *Journal of Finance* 7 (December 1953): 407–21. An extensive discussion bearing on the reserve ratio and free reserves is given by Albert E. Burger, *The Money Supply Process* (Belmont, Calif.: Wadsworth, 1971), pp. 24–72. Reference should also be made to A. James Meigs's (1962) discussion on free reserves and the money supply.

22. See, for example, papers in Jacob A. Frankel and Harry G. Johnson, eds., *The Monetary Approach to the Balance of Payments* (London: George Allen and Unwin, 1978); Bluford H. Putman and D. Sykes Wilford, eds., *The Monetary Approach to International Adjustment* (New York: Praeger, 1978), contains useful theoretical and empirical studies on the monetary approach to international adjustment, as well as a statement by J. Richard Zecher and a bibliography of relevant studies. See also George Macesich, *The International Monetary Economy and the Third World* (New York: Praeger, 1981), Chapters 2 and 3; Macesich and Tsai, *Money in Economic Systems*, Chapter 11.

23. Frenkel and Johnson, "The Monetary Approach to the Balance of Payments: Essential Concepts and Historical Origins," in *The Monetary Approach to the Balance of Payments*, p. 21.

24. Ibid., p. 24.

25. Harry G. Johnson, "Monetary Approach to the Balance of Payments: A Nontechnical Guide," in John Adams, ed., *The Contemporary International Economy: A Reader* (New York: St. Martin's Press, 1979), p. 205. The empirical study is N. Parkin, I. Richards, and G. Zis, "The Determination and Control of the World Money Supply under Fixed Exchange Rates, 1961–71," *Manchester School* 43 (September 1975): 293–316.

26. J. Richard Zecher, Preface to *Monetary Approach to Internatonal Adjustment*, pp. ix–x.

4

ISSUES AND EVIDENCE

INTRODUCTION

The results of recent empirical studies have added significantly to our knowledge of money and monetary processes. A number of these studies have been undertaken with the specific objective of shedding light on the issues dividing the quantity and Keynesian theories.

These empirical studies focus on three issues. First, theoretical developments in modern Keynesian economics have scored the demand for money as a potentially unstable economic relationship. This is denied by modern quantity theorists and monetarists. In fact, they argue that the demand for money is perhaps one of the most stable of economic relationships. This is an issue of singular importance to the monetarist argument and to monetary policy, for if the demand function for money is stable and if other conditions are right, then monetary policy becomes a very potent policy instrument for economic stabilization. But if the demand for money is unstable, then monetary policy is a tool whose effects are erratic and additional stabilization devices are needed. Keynesians argue that fiscal policy provides a much more effective stabilization device than monetary policy.

The second issue deals with questions of whether the demand for money is a function of the rate of interest. It is also an issue that is perhaps settled at last. Most studies have shown that the rate of interest is an important determinant of the demand for money. This suggests that on the basis of reported empirical studies, traditional Keynesian criticism of the traditional quantity theory of money is valid.

The third issue is more important. It deals with the magnitude of the functional relationship between the interest rate and the demand for money. Modern quantity theorists and most monetarists accept the proposition that the demand for money is a function of the rate of interest. They do not believe, however, that it is a powerful relationship. In effect, a low-interest elasticity of the demand for money supports the quantity theory, while a high-interest elasticity supports the Keynesian theory.

The significance attached to the numerical size of the interest elasticity can be illustrated by considering the extreme values. For instance, if the interest elasticity of the demand for money is zero, this means that a 1 percent change in the rate of interest will cause a zero percent change in the quantity of money demanded. This in turn means that there is no relationship between the two. The traditional quantity theory is thus vindicated. The change in money supply is absorbed by a change in nominal income. On the other hand, suppose that a 1 percent change in the rate of interest will result in an unlimited change in the quantity of money demanded. This is, in effect, the extreme Keynesian view of the liquidity trap where the liquidity preference schedule turns horizontal. Monetary policy, as a result, cannot influence the real sector of the economy since it cannot influence the interest rate.

In principle, one can argue that a low interest elasticity supports the quantity theory while a high interest elasticity supports the Keynesian theory. This can be misleading. For instance, suppose we are told that given elasticity estimates range from about −0.1 to −1.0. These estimates appear to support the quantity theory. They are also within the range accepted by moderate Keynesians.

STABILITY OF MONETARY VELOCITY AND INVESTMENT MULTIPLIER

Some of the first studies of the stability of the demand-for-money function were carried out by Milton Friedman and David Meiselman for the United States, by George Macesich for Canada, and by Macesich and F. A. Close for several other countries. These studies attempt to compare the stability of the Keynesian concept of the multiplier with the quantity theory concept of velocity.

In order to compare the relative stability of the multiplier and velocity, these studies derive a series of equations and subject them to empirical tests.[1] The quantity theory and Keynesian income-expenditure theory is set out in the several studies by the following equations.

$$Y = Z + V'M \tag{1}$$

$$Y = \alpha + K'A \tag{2}$$

$$Y = V'M \tag{3}$$

$$Y = K'A \tag{4}$$

$$C = \alpha + KA, \text{ where } K = K' - 1 \tag{5}$$

$$C = \alpha + VM \text{ (V does not have the simple relation with V' that K has with K'.)} \tag{6}$$

$$C = \alpha + VM + KA \tag{7}$$

$$C = \alpha + VM + BP \tag{8}$$

$$C = \alpha + KA + BP \tag{9}$$

$$C = \alpha + BM + KA + BP, \tag{10}$$

where: Y = Income, C + A
 M = Stock of money
 V' = Marginal income velocity
 A = Autonomous expenditures
 K' = Marginal multiplier
 P = Index of prices
 C = Induced expenditures

In analyzing the Keynesian income-expenditure theory, it is important to understand that the term "investment" may be misleading. Accordingly, a change in investment will change people's incomes, and then, according to the marginal propensity to consume, they will change their consumption expenditures. But "investment" also includes expenditures by government, foreign trade, and similar items. As a result, a better insight into the Keynesian process is had in thinking about the multiplier by distinguishing between *induced* (C) and *autonomous* (A) expenditures. According to this view, induced expenditures are caused by changes in income (e.g., consumption). Autonomous expenditures are those that occur without respect to the level of income, such as government expenditures and investment. In effect, Keynesian multi-plier analysis argues that autonomous expenditures cause a change in national income, and that this changed income induces or causes other changes in income and so on. Autonomous expenditures thus trigger a chain reaction among the induced expenditures.

Having framed the issues in the above terms, these studies attempt to answer the following question: Which is more stable, K (the multiplier) or V (the velocity)? In this context, stable means which will give the higher coefficient of determination r^2 in a regression analysis. In short, do autonomous expenditures and the multiplier "explain" national income better than money and velocity, or otherwise?

The tests indicate that income velocity (for instance, in Canada) is consistently more stable than the multiplier. This is so for each of the tests and during every period studied, covering a wide range of experiences from 1926 through 1958. For the period 1926–58, $r^2 = .97$ for the quantity theory and an $r^2 = .43$ for the income expenditure. The Keynesian multiplier analysis achieves its best performance during the period of the 1930s when the Great Depression gripped Canada. Although it performed during these hectic years better than in other years ($r^2 = .72$, 1933–38), its performance in absolute terms is poorer than that of velocity ($r^2 = .97$, 1933–38). The same is true for the United States for the years 1929–34. It is thus a tribute to Keynes's insight into the contemporary events of the Great Depression that his multiplier theory did so well during these years.

These results are consistent with those obtained for the United States. For the period 1897–1958, $r^2 = .756$ for the income and $r^2 = .985$ for the quantity theory are reported by Friedman and Meiselman. Those estimates suggest that differences in institutions and dependence on external trade in the two countries were of minor importance in determining the outcome of the tests. Quarterly data reinforce results derived from annual data. The period of the business cycle selected does not subtract from velocity's overall performance. It performs better than the multiplier whether we conduct our analysis from peak to peak or from trough to trough of the cycle.

Albert Ando and Franco Modigliani take issue with the U.S. results reported by Friedman and Meiselman. In particular, they disagree over the way Friedman and Meiselman define "autonomous expenditures," which, as noted, are expenditures that do not change because national income changes. Friedman and Meiselman include such items as personal income taxes and imports in their definition of autonomous expenditures. But these items change as income change. They are induced expenditures rather than autonomous expenditures. By re-defining autonomous expenditures to account for such items and excluding World War II years (1942–45) when shortages and rationing had an effect on consumption expenditures, Ando and Modigliani for the period 1929–58 report an $r^2 = .992$ for the Keynesian income-expenditure theory. In effect, the results appear inconclusive. Accordingly, there is little to prefer in terms of performance and stability between the demand for money and the Keynesian multiplier.

The Ando-Modigliani criticism, however, is refuted by the fact that any definition of autonomous expenditure implies some definition of income. Suppose we have

$$Y = C + U + A$$

(11)

where U is a term representing elements of the national accounts that cannot be identified as either autonomous or consumption (that is, induced) expenditure. Then we should use $Y - U = C + A$, as Friedman and Meiselman do, as the expression for income. The fact that U moves with Y means that its addition will not affect the coefficients relating Y (no matter how defined) with C and A. Hence, consumption can be legitimately treated as a function of $(Y - U)$ in the Keynesian world.[2]

Several criticisms are directed at the Friedman-Meiselman analytical approach.[3] First, the money supply itself may be induced. This may be the case when the government deficit itself is financed through an increase of autonomous expenditures on income may be picked up as the influence of the money supply.

Second, issue is raised regarding the confidence in the predictive capacity of a single equation relying on high correlation coefficients. Critics argue for a full specification of the economy's interdependence. Friedman, Meiselman, and other monetarists argue that the methodology is satisfactory as an operative methodology.

To be sure, the issue of the stability of the demand for money cannot be regarded as being definitely settled. Nevertheless, the preponderance of evidence supports the hypothesis that this function is stable under almost any reasonable definition of the term "stability." Assuming that this conclusion is correct or at least approximates reality, what are the implications for Keynesian and quantity theorist or monetarist debate?

The various empirical studies substantially support the quantity theory and the monetarist position. They demonstrate that the demand for money is stable. If they had demonstrated the contrary, the quantity theory would be seriously challenged. On the other hand, a stable demand function for money does not present a serious challenge to the Keynesian theory. It does mean that early Keynesians are off the track in arguing that monetary policy is important. These empirical studies have pushed Keynesians into admitting that while other things matter, so does money. Indeed, this is a position readily accepted by contemporary Keynesians.

MONEY DEMAND FUNCTION AND DETERMINANTS: A REVIEW OF THE EVIDENCE

Liquidity-Preference Models

In the early studies by Kisselgoff (1945)[4] and Tobin (1947),[5] and in later work by Bronfenbrenner and Mayer (1960),[6] attempts were made to test a very faithful version of the Keynesian theory by estimating a relationship between idle balances and interest rates. It was assumed that only the demand for the idle balances was responsive to the rate of interest; the problem tackled was to measure the degree of responsiveness involved here. By constructing data on idle balances, these writers were successful in finding an empirical liquidity-preference relationship much like that postulated by Keynes.

More significant and more in line with modern liquidity-preference theory[7] are those studies by C. F. Christ (1963)[8] and H. A. Latane (1954, 1960),[9] which are concerned with the hypotheses that total money balances rather than idle balances are interest-elastic. These studies estimate functions relating velocity of circulation to interest rates, and have obtained results that give strong support to the liquidity-preference hypothesis. In his two articles appearing in the *Review of Economics and Statistics* in 1954 and 1960, Latane attempted to isolate a stable relationship between M/Y, proportionate cash balances, and r, the long-term rate of interest. The period covered in the 1954 study was 1919–52. Latane began with the following demand-for-money function:

$$M^D/P = aY + bY \cdot r^{-1} \qquad (12)$$

from which the function

$$M^D/PY = a + b(1/r) \qquad (13)$$

was derived. Using regression analysis, Latane found that the parameter, b, was significantly positive, indicating that the demand for money is negatively related to the interest rate. The equation fitted seemed to have some predictive power over data generated outside the time period in which it was initially fitted.

The two demand-for-money functions Latane actually tested statistically were:

$$M/Y = c/r + d \qquad (14)$$

and

$$1/r = g(M/Y) + h \qquad (15)$$

where M is demand deposits adjusted plus currency in circulation, Y is gross national product, r is the interest rate on high-grade, long-term corporate obligations, and c, d, g, and h are parameters. Equation (14) states that the proportion of income held in the form of currency and demand deposits is a linear inverse function of the interest rate. The demand for money is considered to be constrained by money income, and it is implied that the equation is homogenous of first degree in income. Latane bases the latter assumption on statistical data. He does not, however, test the homogeneity assumption explicitly.

Equation (15) reverses the direction of causality and makes the rate of interest depend upon proportionate cash balances. By the least-squares method, Latane derives the following regression equations:

$$M/Y = .0074328/r + .108874 \qquad (14')$$

and

$$1/r = 111.775(M/Y) - 7.233 \qquad (15')$$

These equations exclude the years 1932, 1933, 1942, 1946, and 1947, because they were not considered representative. The coefficient of correlation is .87173.

In his 1960 article, Latane extended his analysis forward by more than six years (through 1958) and back to 1909. He estimated a log-linear demand-for-money function of proportionate cash balances and the long-term rate of interest. The variables were defined as in the earlier study. He found some consistency of his regression equations with the hypothesis that there existed a relatively constant interest elasticity of the demand-for-cash balances of about .85, with the correlation coefficient of .88. Latane was thus able to find a stable long-run demand relationship defining money as currency plus demand deposits.

The drawback to all the tests is that "they each assume that the demand for money is proportional to the level of income, a postulate that would be challenged by those who regard wealth as a more appropriate variable to include in the demand-for-money function as well as by those who suspect that there may be economies of scale in money holding."[10] Apart from these generally applicable criticisms, these studies have the special weakness of constraining the income elasticity of demand for money to be unity.[11] This assumption of unitary income elasticity would lead one to expect equal percentage changes in the demand for money and income and it should have been tested explicitly. Even so, the consistency with which they point to the significance of the interest rate as a determinant of the demand for money is impressive. Two particularly advanced studies by A. M. Khusro (1952)[12] and R. J. Ball (1965)[13] have estimated equations that are more sophisticated developments of Keynes's hypothesis.

A major theoretical development of liquidity preference in the post-Keynesian era was the recognition that wealth should be an argument of the demand functions.[14] Bronfenbrenner and Mayer (1960) extended a Keynesian liquidity-preference equation to include a wealth variable.[15] Their results, however, fail to support any strong conclusions. In their study of the demand function for money in the U.S. economy during the period 1919–56, Bronfenbrenner and Mayer, by modifying Tobin's method,[16] analyze aggregate liquidity functions first by using total money balances and idle balances as alternative dependent variables, then by using interest rate and wealth as independent variables, and then by using last year's idle balances as a third independent variable. They further disaggregate the demand function for money by major holders, with major emphasis on year-to-year changes. By so doing, they attempt to provide answers to five fundamental questions concerning the demand-for-money function:

(1) Is there a definite observable liquidity function, i.e., a relation between money holdings and interest rates? (2) Assuming this function to exist, what is its interest-elasticity? (3) Assuming this interest to exist, what is its stability over time? (4) If shifts over time are observed, what are their causes, i.e., what other variables are important? (5) Does the liquidity function appear to impose an observable floor to interest rates?[17]

In their empirical testings, Bronfenbrenner and Mayer use the four- to six-month commercial paper rate to represent the yield on alternative assets, because "beside being available readily, this rate is nearly free of risk and appreciation factors, and it is also more sensitive to economic changes than are longer term rates."[18] The second independent variable used is the logarithm of national wealth. For this variable, the authors use Goldsmith's series on total national wealth in 1929 prices. Government-owned assets wealth was not excluded, but rather used as a proxy for the government securities omitted from the wealth of the private sector. The third independent variable used is the logarithm of prior year idle balances.

Bronfenbrenner and Mayer made three separate statistical estimates of the demand-for-money functions. The first two were estimates of the demand for idle balances and employed the modified Tobin technique. Income was not one of the independent variables. The third was an estimate of the demand for all private cash balances, and income was one of the independent variables. The first two estimates differ in that the first includes the years 1926 and 1927, while the second excludes them.

Using the ordinary least-squares method, Bronfenbrenner and Mayer obtained the following results:

$$\ln M_t^i = -4.2066 - 0.5304 \ln r_t + 1.6849 \ln W_t + 0.5416 \ln M_{t-1}^i \tag{16}$$

$$\ln M_t^i = -1.9552 - 0.2772 \ln r_t + 0.8269 \ln W_t + 0.7158 \ln M_{t-1}^i \tag{17}$$

$$\ln M_t^T = 0.1065 - 0.0928 \ln r_t - 0.1158 \ln W_t + 0.7217 \ln M_{t-1}^T$$
$$+ 0.3440 \ln Y_t \tag{18}$$

where M_t^i and M_{t-1}^i are current and lagged idle balances, M_t^T and M_{t-1}^T are current and lagged total money balances, respectively, r_t is the current short-term interest rate, W_t is current national wealth, and Y_t is current GNP. Equation (17) omits the years 1926 and 1927. The multiple coefficients of correlation are .901, .978, and .997, respectively.

The statistical fits are obviously close. All variables except the wealth variable, W, are statistically significant at the 1 percent level. All elasticity coefficients except that of wealth in equation (17) have the signs suggested by theoretical considerations. The negative wealth elasticity in equation (18) represents the extreme opposite of Friedman's conclusion that money is a luxury. While not statistically significant, according to Bronfenbrenner and Mayer, it suggests that "money may be an 'inferior asset', of which people hold less as their wealth (and credit worthiness) increases."[19]

A more plausible explanation of the unexpected result of the negative elasticity for wealth is that the use of wealth and income simultaneously in the money demand function results in a high degree of multicollinearity, such that little significance should be attached to these particular income and wealth coefficients. It is curious that Bronfenbrenner and Mayer did not mention this possibility.

The interest rate plays a relatively small role in the demand functions for money in Bronfenbrenner-Mayer's study, particularly in the total-balances function. They report that

> the interest elasticity . . . the nub of liquidity theory, is estimated at between 0.3 and 0.5 for idle balances. . . . There is no evidence for the proposition that any of these elasticities goes to zero for high rates of interest or for the proposition that some "floor" or "bottom stop" exists for interest rates at which the elasticity goes to infinity.[20]

That the interest elasticity is lower for total balances than for idle balances is to be expected from traditional economic theory, as transactions or working balances have usually been considered to be quite interest inelastic. The relatively low interest elasticity of the Bronfenbrenner-Mayer functions, however, is at variance with the results obtained by Latane. This divergence may be due, in part, to the fact that Latane used a long-term rate of interest in his analysis, whereas Bronfenbrenner and Mayer employed a short-term rate.

Bronfenbrenner and Mayer are criticized by Robert Eisner on this issue. Eisner argues that a long-term rate is more appropriate because "the Keynesian theory about the demand for money tending to become 'absolute' at low rates of interest, applies to long-term rates," and the efficacy of monetary policy in influencing economic activity can better be ascertained with reference to long-term rates.[21] Eisner provides empirical evidence to show that Bronfenbrenner-Mayer idle balances are considerably more interest elastic with respect to the long-term interest rate than they are with respect to the short-term rate,[22] which is not surprising since the long-term rate is less volatile than the short-term rate.

Utilizing additional data for the same 1916–56 period along with the original series that Bronfenbrenner and Mayer used in their study, Eisner refutes Bronfenbrenner-Mayer's conclusion that their data do not provide evidence for the existence of a liquidity trap. Eisner points out that "Measurement of appropriate elasticities and slopes does in fact give strong support to the Keynesian proposition 'that some "floor" or "bottom stop" exists for interest rates.' "[23] Eisner's particular criticism serves to bring out the fact that the definition of "liquidity trap" is not unequivocal. He points out that constant elasticity of demand, such as is given by the relation

$$\ln M^D = a + b \ln r \qquad (19)$$

where b is assumed to be less than zero, is consistent with the liquidity trap, for in arithmetic form this would appear as

$$M^D = A/\alpha^{-b} \tag{20}$$

and clearly as r goes to zero, M^D goes to infinity.

Eisner further argues that

> evidence that the elasticity goes to infinity or even gets larger at lower interest rates is quite unnecessary for the proposition that the money demanded goes to infinity as the interest rate is lowered. Findings that the elasticity does not get smaller in absolute amount as the interest rate gets smaller would be sufficient—but not necessary— evidence for the liquidity traps.[24]

In view of the implication of a "floor" or "bottom stop" from any constant interest elasticity, Eisner believes that in an actual trap situation (both the elasticity of demand and the demand itself are infinite, that is, the slope of the function is zero), to measure the responsiveness of the demand for money to changes in interest rates, it is more useful to measure the money-interest relationship in terms of arithmetic slope rather than elasticity. This is so because the demand for money can approach infinity as the rate of interest falls, even though the elasticity of demand is constant. "For the Keynesian theory would require the slope of the demand curve to be closer to horizontal for low interest rates or high amounts of idle balances."[25] Eisner provides empirical evidence to show that the demand curve for idle balances became flatter as the rate of interest fell during the period 1919–56.[26]

Bronfenbrenner and Mayer rejoin that in the *General Theory* and in the standard expositions of Keynesian economics, the concept of the liquidity trap is referred to in terms of elasticity rather than of slope of the liquidity-preference function; hence, they are not breaking with tradition. They maintain that their difference with Keynesian theory lies only "in considering the elasticity of the liquidity-preference function as a constant rather than as shifting inversely with interest rates and eventually approaching infinity at some interest rate significantly greater than zero." Furthermore, they believe that elasticity is a more convenient measure than the slope because of its greater independence of units of measurement.

Allan Meltzer participated in the above discussion. He asserts that "evidence for or against the liquidity trap must rest on a demand function for money which explains more than the period surrounding the supposed trap. The post-1920 data alone are inadequate to support or reject the trap hypothesis."[27] After estimating a money demand function using a long-term interest rate and total assets as independent variables, he concluded that the long-term interest elasticity of the demand for total money balances was constant over the period 1900–58, and there appeared to be no kink in the function. Meltzer uses these results to assert that a liquidity trap did not exist during the 1930s.[28]

There are good arguments for using slope and for using elasticity as measures of the responsiveness of the demand for money to changes in interest rates. But no decisive argument has been advanced.

In Bronfenbrenner-Mayer's study, since single-equation models rather than complete systems of equations were used, they were forced, at least implicitly, to make some assumptions about the supply function of money. In effect, they assume that the demand-for-money function is independent of the supply function; that is, the supply of money is unaffected by any of the independent variables in the demand function. This assumption is questionable, particularly with regard to interest rates and lagged money balances. Bronfenbrenner and Mayer partially tested their assumption by supposing that lagged money balances reflect "supply relationships rather than demand inertia." The supply relationship is in this view the unwillingness of the monetary authority to permit sharp year-to-year changes in the money supply.[29] Bronfenbrenner and Mayer reestimated their aggregate functions excluding the lagged-balance variable, and found that the multiple correlation coefficients are lower and significant autocorrelation in the residuals existed. They further showed that negative slopes predominated in their scatter diagrams, hence shifts in supply appeared to predominate over shifts in demand.[30] They thus concluded that they apparently had estimated demand functions.

Finally, Eisner makes a criticism of Bronfenbrenner and Mayer that is applicable to most empirical studies of the demand for money employing single-equation models. For instance, implicit in the estimation of the demand for money by Bronfenbrenner and Mayer is the assumption that the rate of interest can be taken as an exogenous variable to which it responds, according to the structural relation hypothesized, the quantity of money demanded. But this hardly accords with the economic theory to which it relates. More complete macroeconomic models generally assume that the quantity of money varies exogenously and that the rate of interest respond to it in accordance with the structural relation defined by the demand curve. Keynesian liquidity-preference theory, for example, was developed in the first instance as a theory of the rate of interest. Therefore, if the interest rate is influenced by the quantity of money, then specifying a one-directional causal relation in a single-equation model causes bias in the estimates of the parameters. Eisner maintains that "the effect of this kind of misspecification of the error is to cause underestimates of the elasticity of money with respect to the rate of interest or, perhaps more appropriately, to lead one to infer greater than true elasticities of the rate of interest with respect to the quantity of money."[31]

Eisner inverts the money-interest relation and makes interest rates a function of idle balances. Regression of short- and long-term interest rates on idle balances was performed and elasticity estimates of −0.69 and −0.2, respectively, were obtained over the entire 1919–56 period. Since other variables are included in these functions, it is impossible to specify the direction in which the coefficients are biased in the single-equation fits. The multiple coefficients of determination of the functions using idle balances as the dependent variable are significantly higher than those of the functions using interest rates as the dependent variable, suggesting that the former specification of the relation fits the data more closely.

However, since economic theory tells us that the rate of interest influences the demand for money, and that interaction between the supply of and demand for money influences the rate of interest, the only satisfactory way to analyze the money relations is within the context of a structural model of the monetary sector. This appears to be the only way to avoid specification error and simultaneous equations bias in single-equation estimates of parameters.

A somewhat similar test to that of Bronfenbrenner and Mayer was carried out by Laidler (1966) for the period 1892–1960. Laidler divided the whole time period between those years when the interest rate was above its average value for the period and those when it was below it.[32] Such a division was made both for the long-term and the short-term rate of interest, and regressions of the money stock on the level of permanent income and the interest rate were performed for these two sets of data separately. He employed both definitions of money, including and excluding time deposits. He failed to discover any tendency for the interest elasticity of demand for money to be higher for low-interest observations than for high; nor did he find any evidence that "the function was any less stable at low rates of interest." However, permanent income and the interest rate were found to be the best explanatory variables for both definitions of money, with the broader definition providing the more satisfactory results. Time deposits alone were better explained by nonhuman wealth and the interest rate.

On the basis of these results, Laidler argues that: any empirical definition of money must be an approximation, rather than a direct counterpart, of the theoretical concept; the definition that includes time deposits is the more appropriate; the demand for money is dominated by motives different from those that dominate the demand for other financial assets; and money is most approximately viewed as a consumer durable, rather than as an inventory of transactions balances or a risk-offsetting asset in the nonhuman wealth portfolio.

Wealth Models

More significant contributions to our knowledge of the role or wealth in the demand for money have been made by K. Brunner and A. Meltzer. Meltzer starts with a general demand function for money similar to that in Friedman's restatement[33] article. With some simplifying assumptions, Meltzer derives an equation showing that money demanded is a product of wealth and a certain function of the interest rate. That is, Meltzer formulates a money demand function containing variables that reflect wealth and substitution effects on the amount of money demanded. The general demand function for money as formulated by Meltzer is

$$M = f(r^*, z, d^*, W_n) \qquad (21)$$

where M represents the nominal value of the quantity of money demanded; r^*, the yield on financial assets; z, the yield on physical assets; d^*, the yield on human wealth; W_n, nonhuman wealth; and the f_i specifies the signs of the derivatives for each argument of the function. Meltzer hypothesizes that the demand function is homogenous of first degree in the money value of W_n; thus the function becomes

$$M = f^*(r^*, z, d^*, 1)W_n. \qquad (22)$$

Meltzer assumes that d^* can be divided into two components—$Y_h Y_h^*$, where Y_h is actual human income, Y_h^* is expected human income, and W_h is human wealth. That is, the yield on human wealth is now viewed as the product of two components. The first term, Y_h/Y_h^*, measures short-run deviations of actual from expected human income; it is an index of the transitory component of human income. In the short run, wealth holders may adjust the composition of their portfolios in response to changes in this index, but in the long run, actual income is assumed to be equal to expected income. Since Meltzer is primarily concerned with the long-run demand function for money, Y_h/Y_h^* is assumed to be constant. The second term, Y_h^*/W_h, the ratio of expected human income to its decapitalized value, is assumed to be stable in the long run and therefore is taken as a constant. The assumption that

$d^* = Y_h/Y_h^* \cdot Y_h^*/W_h$ is a constant eliminates the direct effects of human income from the long-run money demand function.

Another assumption Meltzer makes is that r^* and z have sufficiently high covariance and can be combined in a single long-term interest rate, r. Thus, with this assumption and those mentioned above, the demand function is shortened to

$$M = g(r)W_n. \tag{23}$$

In this form, the equation reflects the wealth constraint and substitution effect on the demand for money. Meltzer further hypothesizes that $g(r) = r^b$. A linear logarithmic demand function

$$\ln M = a + b \ln r + c \ln W_n \tag{24}$$

was estimated for the period 1900–58.

To test his hypothesis, Meltzer uses three definitions of money in his empirical study: the sum of currency plus demand deposits, M_1; M_1 plus time deposits at commercial banks, M_2; and M_2 plus savings deposits at mutual savings banks and the postal savings system, M_3. For the interest rate, Meltzer has used Durand's basic yield on 20-year corporate bonds. In the first estimates, wealth is defined as total wealth from Goldsmith's Table W-1[34] plus monetary and nonmonetary government debt minus government assets.[35] The regression estimates obtained are as follows:[36]

$$\ln M_1 = -1.65 - \underset{(13.5)}{0.781 \ln r} + \underset{(66.8)}{1.01 \ln W_n} + u_1 \quad \bar{R} = .994 \tag{25}$$

$$\ln \frac{M_1}{p} = -1.48 = \underset{(21.8)}{0.949 \ln 4} + \underset{(42.0)}{1.11 \ln} \frac{W_n}{p} + u_2 \quad \bar{R} = .992 \tag{26}$$

$$\ln \frac{M_2}{p} = -1.98 - \underset{(10.8)}{0.500 \ln r} + \underset{(53.2)}{1.32 \ln} \frac{W_n}{p} + u_3 \quad \bar{R} = .994 \tag{27}$$

In equations (26) and (27), p is the implicit price deflator for net national product.

Meltzer's findings suggest that a stable demand function of money is consistent with more than a single definition of money balances, and that nonhuman wealth and interest rates explain almost all of the variances in money balances whether money is defined inclusive or exclusive of time deposits at commercial banks. But they also suggest that the definition of money is relatively important for a proper appraisal of issues in monetary theory. A further result is that the interest rate and wealth elasticities differ substantially with different definitions of money—the more inclusive the definition of money, the lower the interest elasticity and the higher the wealth elasticity.

Meltzer's explanation of the lower interest elasticity is that when interest-bearing assets are included in the definition of money, part of the substitution effect of interest rate changes occurs within the money variable itself. The estimates of the wealth elasticity shed some light on two issues raised by Gurley and Shaw. First, Gurley and Shaw maintain that the liabilities of financial intermediaries are very close substitutes for currency plus demand deposits, and that a stable demand function for money requires a broader definition of money. Second, the Gurley-Shaw analysis presupposes that the demand for M_1 has declined relative to other assets.[37]

Meltzer's estimates suggest that the growth of financial intermediaries is a wealth effect and not primarily a substitution effect, and that, for a given percentage increase in real wealth, the community has chosen to increase its time deposits by a greater percentage than its demand deposits and currency: "In short, the public has chosen to hold a larger proportion of its wealth in the form of income-yielding assets."[38]

Finally, Meltzer's results strongly indicate that the demand to hold currency plus demand deposits is at least as stable as other alternative demand functions. Thus, there appears to be no compelling reason for broadening the definition of money to include time deposits at commercial banks (Friedman), or liabilities of financial intermediaries (Gurley-Shaw). The results further suggest that the measurement of yields on a variety of alternative assets by a single financial rate provides a reasonable approximation for the long-run function.

To distinguish between the income and wealth models, Meltzer experimented with a money demand function by incorporating real net national product as an argument. In some of the functions the interest rate and real income are the only independent variables; in others, real wealth is added. The functions are tested over three periods: 1900–58, 1900–29, and 1930–58. For the demand equation using only the interest rate and real income as explanatory variables, the interest elasticity for the long period (1900–58) was −0.79. For the period 1900–29 it was −0.05, and for 1930–58, −0.69. Meltzer concludes that "those who argue that the demand for money depends on real income must deny the importance of the interest rate during much of the time period we have considered."[39]

Meltzer, however, fails to point out that one of his earlier results for the period 1900–29, using nominal wealth and the interest rate as arguments, yielded an interest elasticity of only −0.15. The long-run interest elasticity for the same function was −0.78. When real wealth was used with the interest rate, the interest elasticity for the period 1900–29 was only −0.32, whereas the long-run interest elasticity for the same function was −0.95.

Indeed, most of the functions tested over the two periods yielded very low interest elasticities for the earlier period. This would lead to the conclusion that the demand for money was relatively unresponsive to changes in interest rates during the period 1900–29.

The estimates of the functions using both real wealth and real income along with the interest rate suggest that "real income has no significant effect on the demand for real money balances when real non-human wealth appears in the equation." Substantial multicolinearity due to the high correlation income and real wealth impedes interpretation of this finding. However, the interest rate and wealth coefficients are generally quite similar to those estimated in other regressions, while those for the real income coefficients are quite different. Thus, Meltzer concludes that "the addition of real income to the money demand equation does little to improve the explanatory ability of the demand function for money."[40]

Meltzer's wealth model of the demand for money was tested on the assumption that the effects of human wealth could be excluded from the empirical wealth measure without biasing the results. The yield on human wealth, $Y = Y_h/Y_h^* \cdot Y_h^*/W_h$, was assumed to be constant in the long run. Although he was unable to measure human wealth, Meltzer was convinced that the evidence suggested that the omission of human wealth (or the income received as wages and salaries) did not introduce a substantial bias to his wealth elasticities, and the elasticity of the demand for money with respect to human wealth is approximately the same as the elasticity with respect to nonhuman wealth.

In summary, Meltzer's findings suggest that a relatively stable long-run demand function for money can be isolated, and its principal arguments are interest rates and nonhuman wealth. They are of almost equal importance in explaining the demand for real cash balances. Interest rates have played the predominant role in determining the level of velocity. The demand-for-money functions defined inclusive of time deposits or time plus savings deposits are no more stable in the long run than the demand-for-money function defined exclusive of these financial assets. The use of broader definitions of money avoids the problem of mixing the effects of general and relative changes in interest rates on desired money holdings. Meltzer further suggests that "the observed growth of financial intermediaries relative to commercial banks reflects the effect of increased wealth on the desired allocation of wealth rather than a substitution effect as Gurley and Shaw have suggested." Thus, Meltzer maintains that money need not be defined more broadly than currency plus demand deposits. He also concludes that the demand function is more stable when a wealth rather than an income constraint is used.

The salient feature of the work of Meltzer is to place emphasis on wealth rather than income as an explanatory variable. The obtained result is supported by a different test published by Brunner and Meltzer (1963).[41] In their paper, Brunner and Meltzer tested theoretical explanations of velocity rather than money balances. They attempted to determine the short-run stability of the demand function for money based on the wealth-adjustment process. It differs, however, because it is concerned with the problem of predicting velocity in the short run. The criterion by which the theories were evaluated was not how well the regression equation fitted past data, but how well the regression equation with parameters estimated from past data predicted future velocity. The predictive performance of the wealth model is compared with the performance of a number of alternative theories of the demand for money to obtain both relative and absolute measures of the power of the various demand-for-money or velocity relations in the short run.

The various demand functions were used to predict velocity for each of the years in the 1910–40 and 1951–58 periods. (Data for 1941–50 were excluded from both the computations and the predictions since bond prices were pegged by the Federal Reserve during these ten years.) Predictions were obtained by regressing each money demand function or velocity equation for a moving 10-year period. The parameters thus obtained were used with the value of the independent variable in the "eleventh" year to predict the dependent variable for that year.[42] The mean absolute percent error and the root-mean square of standard deviation were then calculated and used as criteria to determine the predictive ability of the alternative equations.

Brunner and Meltzer tested six equations based upon the money demand hypothesis of Keynes' general theory. The first three were used to predict the demand for idle balances, the latter being computed by the same procedure used by Tobin and Bronfenbrenner and Mayer. The only independent variable in these equations was the long-term rate of interest. Two of the equations were tested in linear form, and the other was in the log-linear form. The statistical results for these equations led Brunner and Meltzer to conclude that

The predictions from the . . . hypotheses are extremely poor for the period as a whole and for each of the subperiods. . . . The model is virtually useless as a guide to predicting "speculative" balances, a result which casts doubts on the usefulness of the 1947 Tobin form of the Keynesian hypothesis.[43]

The other three Keynesian money demand functions tested were based on Latane's studies. Two of these equations, with money defined as currency plus demand deposits, were used to predict velocity, and the third was used to predict the demand for real balances. In the first velocity equation

$$\ln V_1 = a + b \ln r \tag{28}$$

the demand for money was assumed to be homogenous of first degree in money income (NNP), the independent variable was the long-term rate of interest, and the function was assumed to be in the log-linear form. In the second velocity equation

$$\ln V_2 = a + b \ln r + c \ln y \tag{29}$$

Brunner and Meltzer tested the homogeneity assumption explicitly by including income as an independent variable. This function also was assumed to be linear in the logarithms. Using the demand for real balances, they further tested the linear Keynesian equation

$$M/p = a - br + cy \tag{30}$$

which includes both the interest rate and real income as independent variables. The results suggest that this equation predicts with smaller percent absolute error and RMS than any of the other Keynesian-type hypotheses.

Brunner and Meltzer also tested three velocity equations based upon Friedman's permanent-income hypothesis. The first velocity equation hypothesized that permanent velocity (the money measure that includes time deposits at commercial banks) depends upon real per capita permanent income. The velocity equation is used to test the predictive power of the demand-for-money model that Friedman has prepared. The result shows that it has a smaller mean and root mean square absolute percent error than any of the previously tested money demand functions. The question arises as to whether this improvement results from the definition of money balances, from a more appropriate specification of the demand function for money, or from both. The other two velocity equations, which include variables representing transitory income and prices to account for short-run influence on income velocity, are used to predict measured velocity. Two definitions of money, M_1 and M_2, are used in the testings.

From the empirical results obtained, Brunner and Meltzer conclude that the Friedman-type equations are better predictors of velocity than both the naive and the Keynesian models, but that "the error in predicting velocity . . . is sufficiently large that it would fail to distinguish between predictions of prosperity or recession in a given year."[44]

Brunner and Meltzer further develop the wealth model of the demand for money. They tested the long-run wealth model of the demand for money in ratio form

$$\ln M_1/W_n = a - b \ln r \tag{31}$$

where money is defined as the sum of demand deposits and currency, and the long-run velocity function

$$\ln rW_n/M_1 = - a + (1+b) \ln r \tag{32}$$

where the income from nonhuman wealth is used as the numerator of the velocity relation in the long run.

Most emphasis, however, was placed on two short-run functions. In the short run, actual and expected human income need not be equal; thus, an index of transitory income is required in the short-run function to measure this ratio of actual and expected human income. Since there were no adequate measures of human income available back to 1900, Brunner and Meltzer used the ratio of measured to permanent income, (NNP), Y/Y_p, as a measure of transitory income. The short-run demand function

$$M_1/W_n = h^*(r, Y/Y_p) \tag{33}$$

was assumed to be log-linear and was tested in ratio form. This function predicted with smaller average error for the period as a whole and for two of the subperiods than any other demand or velocity function tested.

To predict measured velocity or measured income rather than the short- or long-run demand for money, the above equation was modified. The short-run velocity function was presented in the following form:

$$Y/M_1 = Y/W_n \cdot W_n/M_1 = U(r, Y_p/Y)(Y/W_n) = U(r, y_p/y, P_p/P_y)(Y/W_n) \tag{34}$$

The wealth model views measured velocity as composed of two principal elements. The first is "permanent velocity," expressed in equation (32). It reflects the long-run desire to hold part of wealth in the form of money. The second is the response to essentially short-run events that affect the short-run demand for money through Y_h/Y_h^* (or Y/Y_p) in equation (33) and affect measured velocity through Y_h^*/Y_h (or Y_p/Y) and Y/W_n in equation (34). Thus, short-run influences enter the velocity function via inverted indexes of real transitory income and transitory prices. It is assumed that an increase in the index of transitory income will lower the demand for money and increase velocity in the short run. This reflects the idea that money is not a shock absorber in the portfolios of economic units. Another short-run influence on the velocity function is shown by Y/W_n, the ratio of net national product to net nonhuman wealth of households and business. This ratio is a crude measure of the rate at which the stock results of the test show that "the predictions obtained from this equation are substantially closer to the actual values of measured velocity and are much less variable" than any of the Keynesian, Friedman, or naive equations.[45]

Both definitions of money, M_1 and M_2, are used in the wealth model to predict velocity. But the wealth model predicts velocity less accurately when M_2 is used.

In summary, the major conclusions of the Brunner-Meltzer study are the following:

The wealth model is a better predictor of short-run velocity than the Keynesian, Friedman, or naive models;

Interest rates play an important, independent role in the prediction of short-run measured velocity and income. The short-run wealth model includes as variables the rate of interest, transitory income and prices, and nonhuman wealth;

A comparatively stable demand function for money is observed when wealth rather than measured or permanent income is used as the constraint; and

The more appropriate definition of money is currency plus demand deposits, M_1.

The measure of wealth used successfully by Brunner and Meltzer is a measure of private sector nonhuman wealth. Theory suggests, however, that several alternative measures of wealth may be important influences in the demand for money. Of major importance in recent monetary controversies have been Milton Friedman's arguments in favor of including human wealth as an influence on the demand for money, in opposition to the Keynesian liquidity-preference theory. In its general form, wealth, both human and nonhuman, is regarded as a constraint on money demand, and the fundamentals of capital theory are applied to the problem of assets equilibrium. Friedman's empirical work is aimed at offering a theoretical explanation of the discrepancy between the secular and cyclical behavior of income velocity.[46] He finds that the stock of money generally rises secularly at a considerably higher rate than does money income. Thus, income velocity tends to fall over long periods as real income rises. During cycles, on the other hand, the money stock usually increases during expansions at a lower rate than money income, and either continues to rise during contractions or falls at a lower rate than money income. Over the cycle, therefore, income velocity rises and falls with income, that is, it moves procyclically. The issue, then, is that in the long run the income elasticity of the demand for money is considerably above unity, whereas in the short run it is less than unity (occasionally even negative).

Permanent Income Models

In an attempt to explain the economic behavior of this phenomenon and to examine the relationship between the stock of money and money income, Friedman has hypothesized that the demand for money, defined as currency plus demand and time deposits at commercial banks, is a function of permanent income rather than measured income. Permanent income is measured as an exponentially weighted average of prior measured income, and is considered to fluctuate less over the cycle than the corresponding measured magnitudes. If permanent income rather than measured income is used to compute cyclical velocity, then the latter would fluctuate countercyclically, and the conflict between secular and cyclical velocity would be resolved. As Friedman states:

> If money holdings were adapted to permanent income, they might rise and fall more than in proportion to permanent income, as is required by our secular results, yet less than in proportion to measured income, as is required by our cyclical results.[47]

The particular money demand function formulated by Friedman is

$$M/NP_p = a(Y_p/NP_p)^b \qquad (35)$$

where M is currency plus demand and time deposits at commercial banks, P_p is the permanent price level, Y_p is permanent nominal aggregate income, N is population, and a and b are parameters. This equation states that permanent real balances per capita are a function of permanent real income per capita. Friedman concludes that money is a luxury with a per capita income elasticity of 1.8. However, the rate of interest is shown to have negligible effects. In fact, of the many experiments that have been performed, only one, which was carried out by Friedman for the period 1869–1957, failed to find a relationship between the demand for money and the interest rate. Friedman reasoned that since the greater part of variations in the rate of interest take place within the business cycle, a demand-for-money function fitted to data that abstract from the cycle, if it is used to predict cyclical fluctuations in the demand for money, should yield errors in prediction related to the rate of interest. He therefore took data on the average values of the variables concerned over each business cycle. The variable used was money defined to include time deposits and permanent income, and to these was fitted a log-linear regression whose parameters were then used to predict annual variations in the velocity of circulation. He found no close relationship between the errors of prediction and the rate of interest.

However, if interest rates on time deposits are positively correlated with other interest rates, then demand for time deposits being directly related to their interest rates is also often positively related to other interest rates. This is why the inclusion of time deposits in the definition of money often leads to the rejection of the Keynesian liquidity-preference hypothesis in empirical analysis. No wonder that Friedman (1959) and many others have found no significant inverse relationship between money demand and the interest rate.

The finding of a relationship between money balances and permanent income data has been corroborated by other studies. Meltzer (1963) says that Friedman's equation fits 1900–58 data well, but he finds that the wealth hypothesis fits the data even better. Discovering that the explanatory power of Friedman's equation is improved by including interest rate as an independent variable, Meltzer rejects Friedman's findings on the unimportance of interest rates. He obtained a significant negative relationship between the demand for money, however defined, and the rate of interest, regardless of the other variables included in the equation. Meltzer's result also indicates that the wealth elasticity of the demand for real money balances does not support the view that money is a luxury. However, Meltzer points out that most of the empirical differences between his wealth model and Friedman's permanent income hypothesis can be accounted for by "differences in specification of the variables rather than by inherently conflicting implications."[48]

Using successively a short-term and a long-term rate of interest and using permanent income as the "other" variables, Laidler (1966)[49] finds, for the period 1892–1960, regardless of whether the definition of money used included or excluded time deposits, that permanent income is a better explanatory variable for the demand for money than is either measured income (NNP) or nonhuman wealth. Interest elasticities of the demand for money of about −0.7 for the long-term rate of interest and of about −0.15 for the short-term rate were found.

Meltzer's result was criticized by T.J. Courchene and H.T. Shapiro (1964) for its deficiency in the statistical treatment of neglecting autocorrelation in the random disturbances.[50] Using income rather than wealth as a determinant, they gave the estimates showing that the relevant parameters were stable for different time periods.

In his 1965 study, H.R. Heller used the interest rate as well as GNP and wealth for different definitions of money. The evidence led him to conclude that: wealth is more important as a determinant for time deposits, while income is the appropriate determinant for cash and demand deposits, which reflects the respective motives for holding these balances; the short-term interest rate is more significant than the long-term interest rate, supporting the argument that the closest available substitute for money should be used as an indicator of the opportunity cost of holding money; and the relevant elasticities are slightly higher in the downswing than in the upswing.[51]

Furthermore, for the years 1951–64, Lee (1967)[52] used data on the interest differentials between demand deposits and various other assets (including time deposits at commercial banks and savings and loan association shares) to explain the demand for money. The model employed for the analysis is a variety of Friedman's permanent income formulation of the demand for money. The demand function is specified as

$$M = f(Y_p, r) \qquad (36)$$

where Y_p is per capita real permanent income, M denotes per capita money stock in real terms for the traditional concept of money, and r represents a vector of interest rate differentials between yields on other assets and the yield on money. The yield on traditionally defined money is derived as the weighted average of rates of return on demand deposits and currency. The price deflator employed for real variables is current price rather than permanent price. This static model was then cast into a dynamic stock adjustment model of Chow (1966)[53] and Teigen (1964) varieties by introducing a lagged dependent variable, M_{-1}, as

$$M = g(Y_p, r, M_{-1}). \qquad (37)$$

Log-linear forms of the above two equations for both the traditional and Friedman's concept of money were fitted to the data by least-squares method, using: single interest rate differentials of alternative rates; two interest rate differentials, using both the yield on savings and loan shares and the yield on other assets; and three interest rate differentials utilizing the yield on savings and loan shares, the yield on time deposits, and the yield on the rest of other assets. The empirical evidence shows that the yield on nonbank intermediary liabilities is the most significant interest rate variable in affecting the demand for money. It also shows that distributed lags of the demand for money in response to interest rate changes are negligible when the yields on close cash substitutes are incorporated into the demand function. Thus, Lee concludes that his empirical results do not support the rationale used by Friedman et al. for the broad definition of money. Unlike M.J. Hamburger, however, he did not find the yield on corporate equities a potentially important determinant of the demand for money.[54]

Another important contribution to the study of demand-for-money function is Chow's article on the long-run and short-run demand for money.[55] Based on his statistically confirmed hypotheses on the demand for automobiles,[56] Chow formulated an equilibrium demand function for money with the long-term interest rate and the variable of the relevant constraint, such as permanent income, private wealth, and current income. His short-run demand for money is composed of two components—the long-run or equilibrium component, which reflects the effect of permanent income, and the short-run component, which shows the effect of the allocation of savings and hence the effect of current income. It also serves as a mechanism for the adjustment of the actual money stock to the desired stock. The rather long time series of annual data covering 1897–1957 are used for statistical tests of these two sets of equations, both in logarithmic and linear forms. Chow concludes that in an equation to explain the equilibrium money stock, permanent income is a better explanatory variable than either non-human wealth or net national product. The long-run interest and income elasticities of the demand for money are estimated to be −0.75 and 1, respectively. Current income, through its influence on savings, is a better variable than permanent income when the money stock of the previous year is introduced according to his short-run formulations of the demand-for-money equation.

As to other variables that might be important in the function, it is again difficult to be too decisive in one's conclusions. It is worth pointing out that Lerner's study (1956)[57] of inflation in the Confederacy, Cagan's study (1956)[58] of European hyperinflations, and Harberger's study (1963)[59] of Chilean inflationary experience all provide strong evidence of the importance of the expected rate of change of prices as a determinant of the demand for money. Both Friedman (1959)[60] and Selden (1956)[61] have looked, without success, for the influence of this variable on the demand for money in the United States.

Experience in Several Countries

Macesich and Tsai (1982) test the several money demand functions against the experience of ten countries over the period 1950–80.[62] Their results indicate that for the countries under review (Belgium, France, Germany, Italy, Netherlands, United Kingdom, Sweden, Yugoslavia, United States, and Canada), all income elasticities at sample mean levels are highly significant at 1 percent level for broad definitions (M_2) of money, and in most cases they are elastic (greater than unity) except for the United Kingdom (.7354) and Sweden (.9675). Moreover, a narrower definition of money (M_1) reduces the size of the income elasticities to less than unity, except in Germany (1.0537), Canada (1.1362), Italy (1.3431), and Yugoslavia (1.2863).

Their results show that while regression coefficients for the interest rate variable are for the most part with expected negative signs and are significant, there are exceptions. For instance, Macesich and Tsai report that the insignificance of the interest rate in most of the M_2 functions may be due partly to the fact that the positive relationship between the demand for time deposits and the short-term market interest rate has neutralized the intense relationship between money demand and the short-term market interest rate in the M_2^D functions.

Another important result reported by Macesich and Tsai, and which is also consistent with both theoretical considerations and other econometric studies, is that the interest elasticity of M_1^D/p, which excludes time and savings deposits, is in general greater than the interest elasticity of M_2^D/p, which excludes these deposits. When money is defined inclusive of time and savings deposits, part of the substitution effect caused by interest rate changes takes place among monetary assets; that is, part of the substitution effect is hidden by changes within the composition of money itself. This suggests that the definition of money and the method of estimation are therefore important factors in the test of the Keynesian liquidity-preference function.

The interest elasticities at the sample mean level are extremely low and statistically insignificant in four of the countries studied by Macesich and Tsai. In the cases of Canada (for $M_1^D/p = -.2643$), the Netherlands (for $M_1^D/p = -.1491$), and United States (for $M_1^D/p = -.1937$), Germany $(M_1^D/p = -.1368)$, the United Kingdom $(M_1^D/p = -.1432)$, and

Belgium $(M_1^D/p = -.1393)$, comparatively "high" interest elasticities are observed. They are, moreover, significant at the 5 percent level. This suggests that over the period 1951–80 cash balance holders in these countries were sensitive to variations in interest rates in their adjustment of desired real cash balances. The prompt and rational portfolio adjustments during the period are further confirmed by a comparison of the interest elasticities in the demand-for-money equations with the traditional (narrower) definition of money and those with the broader definition. In the latter set of equations, Macesich and Tsai report smaller interest elasticities. This is again consistent with earlier results discussed above.

In summary, the Macesich and Tsai study indicates that real income is the most important determinant influencing the demand for real cash balance in the ten countries studied. The interest rate apparently plays a supplementary role in augmenting the demand for real money balances. The rate of price changes is the least important influence in most of the countries. The exceptions are the United States, the United Kingdom, and Yugoslavia, where the rate of change in the price level appears to play an important role in influencing the demand for real cash balances. To judge from the high value of R^2 in most of the Macesich and Tsai estimates, the demand-for-money functions include most of the important factors that are responsible for the variations in the stock of real cash balances.

The Macesich and Tsai results are consistent with studies rejecting a constantly shifting money demand function, and thus reaffirm the usefulness of money as a policy instrument. Moreover, several other studies demonstrate that the magnitude of the downward shift in money demand relationship in the 1970s has been exaggerated.[63]

NOTES

1. What these results indicate is that a simple version of the quantity-theory approach to income changes is more useful than a simple version of the income-expenditure theory. The results, however, are not as strikingly one-sided in favor of the quantity theory as earlier studies indicated. Since the Canadian tests are based on comparatively simple versions of the two theories, the results are, like all scientific judgments, subject to later modifications as additional data and other ways of organizing these data become available.

George Macesich, "The Quantity Theory and the Income Expenditure Theory in an Open Economy: Canada 1926–1958," *Canadian Journal of Economics and Political Science* (August 1964): 268–90; C.L. Barber, "The Quantity Theory and the Income Expenditure Theory in an Open Economy, 1926–1958: A Comment," and Macesich, "Empirical Testing and the Income Expenditure Theory." *Canadian Journal of Economics* and *Political Science* (1966); Macesich, "The Quantity Theory and the Income Expenditure Theory in an Open Economy Revisited." *Canadian Journal of Economy* (1969); Macesich, *Economic Stability: A Comparative Analysis* (Belgrade: BGZ, 1973); Macesich, *Money and the Canadian Economy* (Belgrade: National Bank of Yugoslavia, 1967); Macesich and Frank Falero, Jr., "Permanent Income Hypothesis, Interest Rates, and Demand for Money." *Weltwirtshaftliches Archiv* (1969). See also F.A. Close, "A Study of the Comparative Stability of the Investment Multiplier and Monetary Velocity for Twenty-Two Countries" (Ph.D. diss., Florida State Univ., 1968); Milton Friedman and David Meiselman, "The Relative Stability of Monetary Velocity and the Investment Multiplier in the United States, 1897–1958," in *Stabilization Policies* (Englewood Cliffs, N.J.: Prentice-Hall for the Commission on Money and Credit, 1963), pp. 185–268; D.H. Meiselman CMC Paper, "Reply to Donald Hester," and Hester's "Rejoinder," *Review of Economics and Statistics* (November 1964); Albert Ando and Franco Modigliani, "The Relative Stability of Monetary Velocity and the Investment Multiplier"; Michael DePrano and Thomas Mayer, "Tests of the Relative Importance of Autonomous Expenditures and Money"; Friedman and Meiselman, "Reply to Ando and Modigliani and to DePrano and Mayer"; and rejoinders by Ando and Modigliani and DePrano and Mayer, *American Economic Review* (September 1965); Macesich and Close, "Monetary Velocity and Investment Multiplier Stability Relativity for Norway and Sweden," *Statsokonomisk Tidskrift* (1969); Macesich and Close, "Comparative Stability of Monetary Velocity and Investment Multiplier for Austria and Yugoslavia," *Florida State University Slavic Papers* (1969); David Meiselman, ed., *Varieties of Monetary Experience* (Chicago; University of Chicago Press, 1970); Macesich, *The International Monetary Economy and The Third World* (New York: Praeger, 1981); Macesich and H. Tsai, *Money in Economic Systems* (New York: Praeger, 1982); Macesich, *The Political Economy of Money* (forthcoming).

2. See, for example, Harry G. Johnson, *Macroeconomics and Monetary Theory* (Chicago: Aldine, 1967)

3. Ibid.

4. A. Kisselgoff, "Liquidity Preference of Large Manufacturing Corporations," *Econometrica* (October 1945).

5. James Tobin, "Liquidity Preference and Monetary Policy," *Review of Economics and Statistics* (February 1947).

6. M. Bronfenbrenner, and T. Mayer, "Liquidity Functions in the American Economy," *Econometrica* (October 1960).

7. H.G. Johnson, "Monetary Theory and Policy," *American Economic Review* (June 1962): 345.

8. C.F. Christ, "Interest Rates and 'Portfolio Selection' among Liquid Assets in the United States," in C. F. Christ and others, *Measurement in Economics: Studies . . . In Memory of Yehuda Grunfeld* (Palo Alto, 1963).

9. H.A. Latane, "Cash Balances and the Interest Rate—A Pragmatic Approach," *Review of Economics and Statistics* (November 1954).

10. David E. Laidler, *The Demand for Money: Theories and Evidence* (Scranton: International Textbook, 1969), p. 93.

11. R.L. Teigen, "The Demand for and Supply of Money," in W.L. Smith and R.L. Teigen, *Readings in Money, National Income, and Stabilization Policy* (Homewood, Ill.: Irwin, 1965), p. 54.

This renders the models different from Keynes's hypothesis and W. Baumol's and J. Tobin's hypotheses of transaction which are the theoretical basis of a relationship between total balances and interest rates. See W.J. Baumol, "The Transactions Demand for Cash: An Inventory Theoretical Approach," *Quarterly Journal of Economics* (November 1952).

12. A.M. Khusro, "Investigation of Liquidity Preference," *Yorkshire Bulletin of Economic and Social Research* (January 1952).

13. R.J. Ball, "Some Econometric Analyses of the Long-Term Rate of Interest in the United Kingdom, 1921–1961," the *Manchester School of Economic and Social Studies*, January 1965.

14. Johnson, "Monetary Theory and Policy," p. 346. See also J. Tobin, "Liquidity-Preference as Behavior Toward Risk," *Review of Economic Studies* (February 1958); R. Turvey, *Interest Rates and Assets Prices* (London, 1960).

15. Bronfenbrenner and Mayer, "Liquidity Functions," pp. 813–21.

16. Building on a formulation ascribed by Tobin, Bronfenbrenner and Mayer in effect define idle balances as

$$L_t = M_t - Y_t^{(M/Y)}\text{min}$$

where L represents idle balances, M represents the quantity of money (demand deposits plus currency), and Y represents private GNP, all in billions of dollars, and $(M/Y)_{min}$ represents the minimum ratio of the quantity of money to private GNP in the period under consideration, which was achieved in 1926.

17. Bronfenbrenner and Mayer, "Liquidity Functions," p. 811.

18. Ibid., p. 815.

19. Ibid., p. 818.

20. Ibid.

21. Robert Eisner, "Another Look at Liquidity Preference," *Econometrica* 31 (July 1963): 532–33.

22. Ibid., pp. 534–36.

23. Ibid., p. 531.

24. Ibid., p. 532.

25. Ibid.

26. Ibid., pp. 535–37.

27. Allan Meltzer, "Yet Another Look at the Low Level Liquidity Trap," *Econometrica* 31 (July 1963): 545.

28. Ibid., pp. 545–49.

29. Bronfenbrenner and Mayer, "Liquidity Preferences," p. 820.

30. Ibid., p. 823.

31. Eisner, "Another Look," p. 534.

32. David E. Laidler, "Some Evidence on the Demand for Money," *Journal of Political Economy* 74 (February 1966): 55–68, and "The Rate of Interest and the Demand for Money—Some Empirical Evidence," *Journal of Political Economy* 74 (December 1966): 545–55.

33. Milton Friedman, "The Quantity Theory of Money—A Restatement," in *Studies in the Quantity Theory of Money* (Chicago: University of Chicago Press, 1956).

34. R.W. Goldsmith, *A Study of Savings in the United States* (Princeton, N.J.: Princeton University Press, 1956).

35. A. Meltzer, "The Demand for Money: The Evidence from the Time Series," *Journal of Political Economy* 71 (June 1963): 224.

36. Ibid., p. 225.

37. J. Gurley, *Liquidity and Financial Institutions in the Post-War Economy*, Study Paper 14, Joint Economic Committee, 86th Congress, 2d Session, Washington, D.C., 1960.

38. Meltzer, "Demand for Money: The Evidence from the Time Series," pp. 219–46.

39. Ibid., p. 233.

40. Ibid.

41. K. Brunner and A.H. Meltzer, "Predicting Velocity: Implications for Theory and Policy," *Journal of Finance* (May 1963): 319–54.

42. Ibid., p. 324.

43. Ibid., p. 328.

44. Brunner and Meltzer, "Predicting Velocity," p. 333.

45. Ibid., p. 337.

46. Friedman, M., "Demand for Money: Some Theoretical and Empirical Results," *Journal of Political Economy* (June, 1959) n.p.

47. Ibid., p. 8.

48. Meltzer, "The Demand for Money: Evidence from the Time Series," p. 234.

49. Laidler, "Some Evidence on the Demand for Money," pp. 55–68.

50. T. Courchene and H. Shapiro, "The Demand for Money: A Note from the Time Series," *Journal of Political Economy* 72 (October 1964): 498–503.

51. H.R. Heller, "The Demand for Money: The Evidence from the Short Run Data," *Quarterly Journal of Economics* (May 1965): 291–303.

52. T.H. Lee, "Alternative Interest Rates and the Demand for Money: The Empirical Evidence," *American Economic Review* 57 (December 1967): 1168–81.

53. G.C. Chow, "On the Long-Run and Short-Run Demand for Money," *Journal of Political Economy* (April 1966): 111–131.

54. M.J. Hamburger, "The Demand for Money by Households, Money Substitutes, and Monetary Policy," *Journal of Political Economy* 74 (December 1966): 600–23.

55. Chow, "Long-Run and Short-Run," pp. 112–31.

56. G.C. Chow, *Demand for Automobiles in the United States: A Study in Consumer Behavior* (Amsterdam: North-Holland, 1964).

57. Eugene Lerner, "Inflation in the Confederacy 1861–65," in Milton Friedman, ed., *Studies in the Quantity Theory of Money* (Chicago: University of Chicago Press, 1956).

58. Phillip Cagan, "The Monetary Dynamics of Hyperinflation," in Milton Friedman, ed., *Studies in the Quantity Theory of Money* (Chicago: University of Chicago Press, 1956).

59. Arnold G. Harberger, "The Dynamics of Inflation in Chile," in Christ et al., *Measurement in Economics, Studies in Mathematical Economics and Econometrics* (Stanford, 1963).

60. Milton Friedman, "The Demand for Money—Some Theoretical and Empirical Results," *Journal of Political Economy*, (June 1959): 327–51.

61. Richard Selden, "Monetary Velocity in the United States," in Milton Friedman, ed., *Studies in the Quantity Theory of Money* (Chicago: University of Chicago Press, 1956).

62. Macesich and Tsai, *Money in Economic Systems.*

63. For instance, on the magnitude of the downward shift in the money demand function, Scott E. Hein, "Dynamic Forecasting and the Demand for Money," *Federal Reserve Bank of St. Louis Review* (June/July 1980): 30, writes "[has been] exaggerated and the pattern of the precise shifts has been obscured by reliance on the dynamic forecasting procedure to evaluate the temporal stability of the money demand relationship."

PART II
POLICY

5

STRATEGIES
OF MONETARY POLICY

GOALS OF MONETARY POLICY

The term "monetary policy," as it is usually understood by monetarists and other economists, focuses on the objectives, tools, and processes involved in the regulation of the supply of money. It is argued that monetary policy influences primarily the value and composition of assets. As a consequence, it is more circuitous than, for example, fiscal policy, which directly influences income and therefore economic activity. A contrary position is the argument that decisions regarding the demand to hold money really involve a decision as to whether it is best to hold wealth in this form or in securities or physical assets. Against such a background, asset holdings may be as significant as income in directly influencing economic activity. Monetary policy, through its effect upon assets, may theoretically have as direct an impact on economic activity as fiscal policy operating through income. The empirical evidence cited elsewhere also tends to support this view.[1]

Monetarists argue that the monetary authority can control nominal quantities and directly the quantity of its own liabilities.[2] By manipulating the quantity of its own liabilities, it can fix the exchange rate, the nominal level of income, and the nominal quantity of money. It can also influence directly the rate of inflation or deflation, the rate of growth of the nominal stock of money, and the rate of growth or decline in nominal national income. The monetary authority cannot through control of the nominal quantities fix real quantities such as the real interest rate, the rate of unemployment, the level of real national income, the real quantity of money, or the rate of growth of either real national income or the real quantity of money.

Economists are quick to point out, however, that this does not mean that monetary policy does not have important effects on these real magnitudes. Indeed, when money gets out of order, important repercussions are felt throughout the economy. Monetary history provides ample evidence on this point. In fact, the debate among the monetarists, Milton Friedman, and the Keynesians over the effectiveness of governmental monetary and fiscal policies as a means of influencing economic activity provides us with a valuable example. The latter argue that money and monetary policy have little or no impact on income and employment, particularly during severe economic depressions. Moreover, government taxation and spending, in effect fiscal policy, are most effective when dealing with problems of inflation and unemployment. Monetarists and Friedman, as we have noted elsewhere, stress the importance of money. They argue that a rule that requires the monetary authority to cause the nominal stock of money to increase by a fixed percentage annually would effectively reduce fluctuations in prices, real output, and employment.

It is thus generally agreed that by goals of monetary policy we mean ultimate aims or objectives. These agreed upon goals are price stability, economic growth, "full" or maximum employment, and balance-of-payments equilibrium. These are objectives shared by most countries.

When viewed individually, each of these goals appears straightforward. It is, however, another matter to achieve all these goals at the same time. Conflicts among goals do arise. Reaching one goal may make it impossible to reach another. Thus, the closer an economy is to full (or maximum) employment, the faster will prices rise. Under a system of fixed exchange rates, balance-of-payments equilibrium requires that the domestic economy be systematically inflated and deflated. Moreover, the goal of economic growth may conflict with any or all of these other goals. It is thus useful to distinguish between a necessary conflict and a policy conflict. A necessary conflict means an achievement of one goal necessarily means the nonachievement of another. An example of such a conflict is suggested in the Phillips's curve analysis, whereby a presumed trade-off occurs between full employment and price stability. A policy conflict example is furnished in the case where monetary policy cannot pursue both price stability and economic growth at the same time. The evidence suggests that any rate of economic growth is consistent with any rate of price increase. Other examples of potential conflict come to mind from the experiences of other countries. Except for price stability, argue monetarists, the achievement of other goals by monetary policy manipulation is an illusion.

In a recent study incorporating several countries, attempts are made to formulate and test statistically the objectives of monetary policy. Essentially, the monetary authority is envisaged as having as objectives of policy price stability, high employment, economic growth, and a satisfactory balance of payments.[3] Each objective is given a weight in determining monetary policy. The degree to which each objective is achieved is assumed to be reflected in an appropriately defined statistical indicator of the performance of the economy. The monetary authority is assumed to govern its policy—as reflected in a statistical indicator—by reference to the statistical indicators of achievement of the objective. The response of monetary policy itself to changes in the performance of the economy is subject to a distributed lag. The conduct of monetary policy is formulated in terms of a reaction function. This is done by relating a statistical indicator of monetary policy to statistical indicators monitoring the various objectives and the lag in the reaction of monetary policy to changes in the performance of the economy.

The application of the Dewald Johnson model described is applied by Macesich and Tsai to ten countries for the period 1956–80.[4] For simplicity, they select: the money supply as the control variable actually used by the monetary authorities; the consumer price index, the unemployment rate, and the balance-of-payments deficit as the variables relevant respectively to the objectives of price stability, high employment, and a satisfactory balance of payments; and real gross national product as an objective of economic growth. Annual data for the period 1956 to 1980 are used in the ordinary least-squares regression analysis.

Their results indicate a reasonably good statistical explanation of changes in the money supply in terms of lagged reaction of the money supply to changes in statistical indicators of the performance of the economy relevant to the main objectives of economic policy for most of the countries under study. If we assume that the money supply is the control variable the monetary authorities actually employ, empirical reaction functions suggest that during the period 1956–80, the main concerns of monetary policy in each country are as presented in Table 5.1.

The table suggests that several countries tend to concentrate their monetary policy on different objectives. The objectives of price stability and balance of payments receive a high score. It is also interesting to note that monetary authorities act as though various policy goals do

TABLE 5.1. Objectives of Monetary Policy in Ten Countries, 1956–80

Country	Price Stability	Economic Growth	Full Employment	Balance of Payments
Belgium	X			X
France	X			X
Germany	X	X	X	X
Italy	X	X		X
Netherlands	X	X	X	X
Sweden	X	X		X
United Kingdom			X	
Yugoslavia	X	X	X	X
Canada	X	X		
United States	X	X	X	X

Source: George Macesich and H. Tsai, *Money in Economic Systems* (New York: Praeger, 1982), Chapter 8.

conflict, while talking as though they do not. Moreover, unlike the situation in the 1920s when primary goals were price stability and balance of payments, some countries now give greater importance to the goal of employment. This seems to be the case in the United Kingdom during the period under review.

Some idea of the problems these countries have in pursuing the objective of price stability—assisted, to be sure, by the worldwide recession—is indicated by the movement in consumer prices in 1981 relative to 1980. Data available in *International Monetary Finance Statistics* show that the industrial countries as a group registered an inflation rate of 9.9 percent in 1981 compared with 11.9 percent in 1980. For countries presented in Table 5.1, the United States in 1981 registered 10.4 percent compared with 13.5 percent in 1980; Sweden 12.1 percent compared with 13.7 percent; the United Kingdom 11.9 percent compared with 18 percent; Yugoslavia 39 percent in 1980 to a further 52 percent in May 1981 declining in the six months to December 1981 to an annual rate of 23 percent;[5] Canada 12.4 percent compared with 10.1; Belgium 7.6 percent compared with 6.7 percent; Germany 5.9 percent compared with 5.5 percent; and Netherlands 6.8 percent compared with 6.5. The only country whose average rate of inflation remained unchanged in 1981 was France, with 13.3 percent. These goals to "promote maximum employment, production, and purchasing power" represent a significant departure in the monetary policies from those dominating the post-World-War-I period. Ambiguous and imprecise though they are, anything more specific would probably not be politically acceptable. During the prosperity of the 1920s, the chief roles assigned to monetary policy were to promote price stability and to preserve the gold standard.

Monetary policy in Sweden, for instance, remained largely passive in the early postwar years. The objective of monetary policy up to 1960 was to stabilize the interest rate level considered essential to rapid economic progress and full employment. During the 1960s such goals of monetary policy as price stability, internal or external balance, and stability or growth already prevailed in Sweden. The country then opted for growth and full employment relative to balance in international payments.

Postwar objectives of U.K. monetary policy are more difficult to grasp. It would appear that by 1969 and 1970, when some improvement occurred in the country's balance of payments and external balance, emphasis shifted to maintaining internal equilibrium to avoid both inflation and excessive unemployment. A major wage explosion shortly thereafter complicated the internal situation.

Nevertheless, there has been a change in stance regarding the objectives of monetary policy in the United Kingdom. This involves the Bank of England's withdrawal of automatic support for financial markets. Support of prices in financial markets made it impossible to use the price mechanism to limit the rate of growth of such monetary aggregates as bank advances, domestic credit, and the money stock. Any attempt by the monetary authorities to combine a deflationary monetary policy with continuing support for prices in financial markets would in fact require controls of one kind or another designed to ration available financial resources.

The shift in policy of providing automatic support for the gilt-edge securities market became apparent in late 1968. Official sanction was provided in 1971 when the vast and complicated structure of direct controls that had encumbered the U.K. banking system was finally removed. One would now expect the banking system to play a positive role in assisting the economy toward a freely competitive internal and external equilibrium. The monetarist policies of the Thatcher government certainly encourage such a move.

The goals of monetary policy in Yugoslavia focus on economic development, employment, price stability, and achievement of balance-of-payments equilibrium. Institutional and other changes after the 1965 reform have required significant adjustments in the pattern of monetary policy goals and have produced fundamental changes in the inter-relationship of individual goals and their conflicting effects and complementarities. The basic change in the pattern of monetary policy goals has been the increased importance of stabilization and balance-of-payments goals, so that they have become as significant as the previously dominating economic growth and employment goals. Thus, the list of basic goals of monetary policy was extended fundamentally after the reform. It is obvious that this change has made the problem of trade-offs far more complex and similar in difficulty to those in market economies. Moreover, a relatively easy monetary policy sustained a double-digit inflation in the 1970s (see note 5).

In Belgium, conflict between internal and external balance tilts in favor of the latter owing to the very strong influence of foreign trade and powerful economic neighbors. The country's foreign trade represents about 50 percent of its total economic activity. Over the long term, the country's balance of payments has had a surplus. One effect of such a surplus has been to increase the supply of money—much as though a specie-flow mechanism were in operation.

France shares in the goals of monetary policy outlined above, though at times in the postwar period it was not always clear that this was in fact the case. Since 1963 considerable emphasis has been placed on the goal of price stability. Rapid price rises, most notably in 1958–59, 1963–64, and 1969–70, have underscored the urgency for pursuing internal stability. Balance-of-payments problems were particularly acute in the period 1956 to 1958, when a pronounced deficit was registered. The situation improved in 1959–63 to the extent that France was able to repay borrowings from the International Monetary Fund, the European Payments Union, and the United States. Indeed, by 1963 French reserves were built up to almost 22 billion francs.

Price stability, economic growth, maximum employment, and balance-of-payments equilibrium are also goals of monetary policy in the Federal Republic of Germany. The Bundesbank was able to concentrate monetary policy on domestic goals through the revaluation of the deutsche mark in 1961 and 1969 as well as during much of 1971 when flexible exchange rates were in force. The strict orientation of German monetary policy to domestic requirements, however, is incompatible with the requirements of the Common Market. This also holds, of course, for other EEC members. If the Common Market is to work, it is necessary that its members pursue a common monetary policy in relation to the other countries of the world. Continuing difficulties with the European Monetary System (EMS) serve to underscore the difficulties of carrying out common monetary policies.

The stated goals of monetary policy in Italy are almost identical to those already discussed. In the past two decades monetary authorities achieved a rather rapid economic growth. Except for a period in the early 1960s when inflationary pressures threatened internal stability and monetary policy was focused on cooling the economy, the monetary authorities throughout much of the postwar period have provided the economy with liquidity to push the process of economic development. Indeed, the currency and bank deposits in public hands grew at a much faster rate than the value of the GNP.

The Social Economic Council of the Netherlands sets the goals of economic policy, including monetary policy. These goals are satisfactory economic growth, full employment, the greatest possible price stability, equilibrium in the balance of payments, and a reasonable income distribution. Monetary policy aims at establishing monetary conditions that will further economic equilibrium. This may result at times in monetary policy encroaching on the objectives of other policy instruments. The internal value of the currency and equilibrium in the balance of payments are the specific responsibilities of Netherlands Bank as laid down by the Bank Act of 1948.

The priorities assigned the various goals differ over time. For instance, the goals of monetary policy in Canada during the post-World-War-II period varied from combating inflation to reducing unemployment to defending the exchange rate of the Canadian dollar under fixed and flexible exchange rates. Moreover, the official view of monetary policy in Canada switched from a "quantity theory" to a "credit conditions" approach, with corresponding changes in the choice of appropriate targets and indicators of policy.

The repudiation of cheap money policies in the United States in 1951 with the Federal Reserve-Treasury accord, and formal abandonment of the pegging of government bond prices in 1953, led to a revival of belief in the potency of monetary policy. The goals of monetary policy are the promotion of full employment and economic growth while maintaining internal and external balance. The basic document in the area of macroeconomic objectives in the United States is the Employment Act of 1946. This act marks the government's acceptance of responsibility for the economic state of the U.S. economy.

Additional and more specific goals were given in the United States with the passage of the Full Employment and Balance Growth Act of 1978 (Humphrey-Hawkins Act Public Law 950523). This law requires the Federal Reserve to report its intended monetary policy for the year to the banking committees in the House and Senate; these committees then issue their own reports on the Federal Reserve report. Indeed, the House Banking Committee in March 1979 instructed the Federal Reserve that the specific goals of the Humphrey-Hawkins Act "would be promoted" by adopting given long-run money supply growth targets.[6]

INDICATORS AND TARGETS OF MONETARY POLICY

Given the goals of monetary policy, it is necessary to design a strategy for their achievement. In essence, a monetary policy strategy with explicit goals or objectives, intermediate targets, and operating targets must be available to the monetary authority. For the success of any given monetary strategy, the monetary authority must have policy instruments to hit operating targets that, in turn, affect the intermediate targets that change the ultimate goal variables. At the same time, a useful monetary strategy must also have a method of monitoring its effects on the economy.

Intermediate targets include monetary aggregates, credit aggregates, or capital market interest rates. Operating targets consist of such variables as bank reserve aggregates, "money market conditions" so indicated by the Treasury bill rate, free reserves, and, in the United States, the federal funds rate.

The monetary authorities cannot manipulate the money supply as directly as tax rates, nor can they determine the full structure of interest rates. As a result, they often choose a particular operating target that is easier to manipulate with the instruments available, but whose relationship to a particular intermediate target is reasonably well observed. Ready examples are the monetary base (currency plus the banking system's total reserves) in Switzerland and Italy. Short-term money market interest rates are traditional operating targets in the United Kingdom and Austria. Total bank credit is the operating target in France. In Germany some ratio of bank liquidity is used, although the relationship underlying the German operating target changed radically in the early 1970s. In the Netherlands and Spain this ratio usually means the difference between some compulsory ratio of assets to liabilities and the actual ratio.

In essence, the distinction between the operating and intermediate targets varies from country to country. The choice of operating target depends in good part on the monetary instruments available to the country's monetary authorities. Indeed, the distinction between instruments and targets may well be very narrow. For example, the central bank discount rate is an instrument, while short-term interest rates as a whole are the operating target. Moreover, the instruments available depend very much on the country's financial structure.

There are at least six categories of instruments that are important. One is central bank transactions in securities. If a well-developed money and capital market exists, central banks can influence interest rates by buying and selling (usually government securities). These open market operations must be legitimate. They conflict, however, with a central bank's efforts on behalf of debt management operations for the government.

Second, a central bank in its lending operations is important to monetary authorities. The manner in which central bank lending operates depends on the country and the level of commercial bank indebtedness. In the United Kingdom, for instance, the central bank does not lend directly to commercial banks. It carries on its operations with the discount houses. In France, on the other hand, the level of commercial bank indebtedness with the Bank of France is high. In any case, a central bank in its capacity as lender of last resort has a special role to play.

The third category of instruments deals with changes in minimum reserve requirements. Again, differences exist among countries. Reserve requirements may be fixed against all deposits or, as in Switzerland, only against special kinds of deposits. For instance, both the German and French central banks tend to make frequent changes in reserve requirements.

The fourth category of instruments deals with controls on bank lending. Many countries use direct controls of one sort or another. In France, controls are a central instrument of monetary policy.

The fifth category is direct control over interest rates. There is a trend toward eliminating such direct controls in most industrial countries. Nevertheless, banks still tend to take changes in the discount rate as a signal to change their own rates. France, Italy, and Yugoslavia still fix or subsidize rates for special categories of lending.

The final category is controls on the foreign transactions of banks in response to foreign exchange movements. These controls are, in essence, manifestations of the above categories. More straightforward controls prohibit certain classes of transactions abroad, or create special exchange rates for such transactions.

The monetarist preference for a money aggregate target rather than a money market target as the appropriate target for monetary policy is closely associated with their view of the control of nominal and real rates of interest. As noted earlier, monetarists hold that the authorities are at best able to fix the nominal rate of interest. Their theory on the real rate of interest emphasizes the importance of the link between the nominal market rate of interest and real rate of interest. Only if the expected rate of inflation is zero will nominal and real rates of interest be equal.

Furthermore, the choice in selecting a monetary aggregate target or money market target is conditioned on the relative importance of random disturbances occurring from the real and monetary sides of the economy.[7] If the real side of the economy is more unstable, then a money aggregate target is preferable. If the monetary side of the economy is more unstable, then an interest rate target is to be preferred. However, the rate of interest relevant for expenditure decisions, and therefore the position of the IS curve (in the IS-LM model for a closed economy), is the real rate of interest that the authorities cannot fix in any case.

The choice of an indicator that will quickly and accurately give the direction and magnitude of monetary policy is also closely associated with the monetarist preference for a monetary aggregate target.[8] A useful indicator must possess such characteristics as a high degree of correlation with the target variable; accurate and reliable statistics on the indicator must be quickly available to authorities; and it should be exogenous rather than endogenous—monetary authorities should be capable of controlling the variable. Indeed, Anna J. Schwartz eliminates the distinction between targets and indicators.[9] The ideal target, Schwartz argues, ought to be judged on three criteria: Is it measurable? Is it subject to control by central banks? Is it a reliable indicator of monetary conditions? On the basis of data for the United Kingdom, Canada, and Japan, Schwartz concludes that the money stock is the best "target-indicator." From a study of six countries (United States, Canada, Germany, Japan, United Kingdom, and South Africa), Keran concludes that the money stock is a good indicator.[10] A similar conclusion is reached by J. Ernest Tanner.[11] He reports that the money stock or monetary base meets his requirements for a good indicator. He finds the interest rate to be an unacceptable indicator. Like Keran, Tanner tests the closeness of the indicator to the goal variables. It is also a test of "monetary multipliers." He does not test whether the variables are exogenously determined or not.

We have discussed elsewhere the money supply and its sensitivity to interest rates in several countries.[12] Together with other studies, we now have a considerable amount of empirical evidence on the interest sensitivity of some reserve multipliers. If these multipliers are highly sensitive to interest rate changes, then it may be difficult to implement monetary control through the control of reserve aggregates. To judge from the evidence presented in these studies, the interest sensitivity of various multipliers is low. Accordingly, control of monetary aggregates through reserve control does not present a serious problem.

These issues have gained in importance in the United States, and in other countries as well, since the Federal Reserve changed its approach to implementing monetary policy. On October 6, 1979 the Federal Reserve shifted its focus from movements in short-run interest rates to movements in reserves held by the banking system. By early 1980 it had announced major redefinitions of monetary aggregates.

These changes in U.S. operating procedures and monetary definitions underscore once again the need to ascertain which of the new aggregates is the best indicator of monetary policy. R. W. Hafer presents test results relevant to both the indicator problem and the issue exogeneity of the new monetary aggregates with respect to the GNP.[13] That is, changes in GNP should be a direct result of monetary policy actions as evidenced by changes in the monetary indicator. Changes in GNP must not directly influence changes in the monetary indicator. Thus, a monetary aggregate can be used as an indicator but only if changes in GNP do not result in changes in the monetary aggregates.

Our discussion in Chapter 4 of the empirical tests conducted with the simple visions of the quantity theory of money and the income-expenditure theory focused in part on the predictability (or stability) of the relationship between various monetary aggregates as indicators and nominal income. The regression results indicate that M_2, a broad definition of money that includes currency, demand, and time deposits, is preferable in that it yields statistically superior results. Hafer's tests on whether the new monetary aggregates are exogenous of income are based on studies by C. W. J. Granger and C. A. Sims.[14] Using these tests, the empirical results for the period III/1961-II/1980 indicate that each of the new monetary aggregates (MIA, M1B, M_2, M_3, and L) is statistically exogenous to GNP. Accordingly, control of the money stock is important in influencing movements in GNP.

Hafer's test evidence does not determine which of the several monetary aggregates is the best indicator of monetary actions, but it does provide a useful basis upon which selection can be made. To be sure, it also suggests that further study would be useful. Hafer's work is consistent with monetarist views that influence of monetary actions are channeled to the economy via nominal GNP.

Table 5.2 presents a comparison between the new and old nontransactions-type monetary aggregates for the United States. In essence, these redefinitions by the Board of Governors of the Federal Reserve System represent a consolidation of the former M2, M3, M4, and M5 measures. The new M2 is similar in definition to the old M3; the new M3 is similar to the old M5. The new L aggregate is a broad measure of liquid financial assets and includes such items as term Eurodollars held by U.S. nonbank residents, bankers acceptances, commercial paper, U.S. savings bonds, and other liquid treasury obligations.

The new basic transactions measure is MIA. It is essentially the same as the old M1 measure except for the deletion of demand deposits

TABLE 5.2. Comparison of Old and New Nontransactions-Type Monetary Aggregates, United States

Component	Old M2	New M2	Old M3	New M3	Old M4	Old M5	L
Currency	X	X	X	X	X	X	X
At commercial banks:							
Demand deposits inclusive of deposits due to foreign commercial banks and official institutions	X		X		X	X	
Demand deposits exclusive of deposits due to foreign commercial banks and official institutions		X		X			X
NOW accounts[a]		X		X			X
ATS accounts[a]		X		X			X
Overnight RPs		X		X			X
Savings deposits	X	X	X	X	X	X	X
Small time deposits (< $100,000)	X	X	X	X	X	X	X
Large time deposits Other than large negotiable CDs	X		X	X	X	X	X
Including large negotiable CDs				X	X	X	X
Term RPs				X			X
At thrift institutions:							
Demand deposits		X		X			X
NOW accounts[a]		X		X			X
ATS accounts[a]		X		X			X
Credit union share draft balances		X	X	X		X	X
Savings deposits (mutual savings banks and savings and loan associations)		X	X	X		X	X
Small time deposits (< $100,000)		X	X	X		X	X
Large time deposits (> $100,000)			X	X		X	X
Term RPs (commercial banks and savings and loan associations)				X			X

TABLE 5.2 (continued)

Component	Old M2	New M2	Old M3	New M3	Old M4	Old M5	L
Other:							
Overnight Eurodollar deposits of U.S. nonbank residents[b]		X		X			X
Money market mutual funds shares		X		X			X
Term Eurodollars held by U.S. nonbank residents							X
Bankers acceptances							X
Commercial paper							X
U.S. savings bonds							X
Liquid Treasury securities							X
M2 consolidation component[c]		X		X			X

[a]These accounts were included previously in the savings deposit component of the definitions.

[b]Overnight Eurodollars issued by Caribbean branches of member banks.

[c]See Hafer, "The New Monetary Aggregates" Bulletin, Federal Reserve Bank of St. Louis (February 1980).

Source: R. W. Hafer, "The New Monetary Aggregates," Bulletin, Federal Reserve Bank of St. Louis, (February 1980): 27.

due to commercial banks and official institutions. The new M1B aggregate combines those financial items that have the dual characteristic of being held both for check-writing purposes and as savings accounts. Essentially, the new M1A and M1B aggregates focus on those items that are used privately as a means of payment.

The definitions most commonly used in international comparisons are of two kinds: a narrow definition of the money stock (called M1) and a wider definition. Some countries use M2, others M3, but the meanings of these broader money supply definitions also differ among countries. For this reason there is a tendency to call the broader category simply "M1 plus quasi money."

The evidence summarized in Tables 5.3 and 5.4 suggest that central banks only rarely succeed in hitting monetary targets. When they miss it is nearly always in overshooting, which creates "base drift." The base drift problem occurs if the supply of money ends up above its ceiling, raising the issue of what should be used as the starting point for the next

TABLE 5.3.   Target Practice: Monetary Targets and Overrun

Country	Monetary aggregate	Period	Target	Outturn
Britain	Sterling M3	Year to April 1977	9-13	7.2
		Year to April 1978	9-13	15.9
		Year to April 1979	8-12	10.9
		Year to Oct 1979	8-12	13.2
		June 1979-Oct 1980	7-11[a]	17.2
		Feb 1980-April 1981	7-11[a]	23.4
Canada	M1	2nd qtr 1975-Feb-Apr 1976	10-15	12.0
		Feb-Apr 1976 2nd qtr 1977	8-12	9.2
		June 1977-June 1978	7-11	8.5
		June 1978-2nd qtr 1979	6-10	8.1
		From 2nd qtr 1979	5.9[a]	6.3
France	M2	Year to Dec 1977	12.5	13.9
		Year to Dec 1978	12.0	12.3
		Year to Dec 1979	11.0	14.3
		Year to Dec 1980	11.0	10.0
West Germany	Central bank money	Average 1975-Average 1976	8.0	9.2
		Average 1976-Average 1977	8.0	9.0
		Average 1977-Average 1978	8.0	11.4
		Year to 4th qtr 1979	6-9	6.3
		Year to 4th qtr 1980	5-8	4.8
Italy	Total domestic credit	Year to Dec 1977	15.0	17.8
		Year to Dec 1978	19.4	20.6
		Year to Dec 1979	18.5	18.6
		Year to Dec 1980	17.5	21.5
United States	M1	Year to 4th qtr 1976	4.5-7.5	5.8
		Year to 4th qtr 1977	4.5-6.5	7.7
		Year to 4th qtr 1978	4.0-6.5	7.4
		Year to 4th qtr 1979	1.5-4.5	
		revised to	3.0-6.0	5.5
	M1B	Year to 4th qtr 1980	4.0-6.5	7.5

[a]At annual rate: to latest month at annual rate

Sources: BIS, IMF, OECD adapted from *Economist*, November 29, 1980, p. 13, and George Macesich and H. Tsai, *Money in Economic Systems* (New York: Praeger, 1982), Table 12.1, p. 304.

TABLE 5.4. Monetary Targets and Outturns

Country	Monetary aggregate	Period	Target	Growth to latest month[a]	Excess over targeted growth, 1975–1976 to latest (percentage points)
United States	M1B	Year to 4th qtr 1980	4.0-6.5	7.5	9.3
Japan	M2 and CDs	Year to 4th qtr 1980	10.0	9.5	1.0
		Year to 4th qtr 1981	9.5		
West Germany	central bank money	Year to 4th qtr 1980	5-8	4.7	3.0
		Year to 4th qtr 1981	4-7		
France	M2	Year to Dec. 1980	11.0	9.9	5.6
		Year to Dec. 1981	10.0		
Britain	M3	Feb 1980 to April 1981	7-11	23.4	19.6
Switerland	monetary base	Year to Nov. 1980	4.0	0	NA
		Year to Nov. 1981	4.0		

[a]At annual rate. Where ranges were set, their midpoints are assumed to be the target. Switzerland had no target in 1979.

NA: Not available

Source: *Economist*, December 6, 1980, pp. 70–71, and George Macesich and H. Tsai, *Money in Economic Systems* (New York: Praeger, 1982), Table 12.2, p. 205.

target. By unsettling financial markets, base drift creates additional difficulties for the monetary authority in its effort to achieve longer-term monetary goals.

We have already called attention to the issue of means and ends raised in several countries regarding the methods of monetary control. How can a central bank control monetary growth? One approach is through interest rates. The other is by controlling the monetary base directly. Interest rates affect the demand for money. But interest rate effects may be overwhelmed by other effects. This suggests that the central bank is better advised to operate more directly on the supply of money through the monetary base—cash and bank reserves held in the central bank. These magnitudes can be controlled. As a result, monetary growth can be affected in more predictable ways than through interest rates.

Methods and monetary targets differ in the several countries under review here. The German Bundesbank sets targets for central bank money fixed in such a way as to more or less reflect rather than influence overall monetary growth. In 1979 the U.S. Federal Reserve System switched from controlling interest rates to setting intermediate targets for the monetary base. The result has been greater fluctuations in interest rates; for example, the prime lending rate went from 11.5 percent in October 1979 to over 20 percent in January 1981. Great Britain also appears to be drifting toward the idea of monetary base methods.

Again, the target variable used in various countries differs. The evidence reported here suggests interest rates exert important influence on the movement of the general measures of the money supply (such as the movement between interest-bearing time deposits and demand deposits, which in the United States should be less important in the future owing to interest payment on demand deposits, which are also known as NOW accounts). The United States sets targets for several definitions of the money supply, from the narrow M1A to the broad M3. Great Britain, on the other hand, sets one target M3 defined as notes and coin plus sterling deposits of U.K. public and private sectors. Germany focuses on monetary base as the ultimate target, which is the same as its intermediate target. In France the broader definition of money M2 (cash plus demand and time deposits) is used as the target.

It is important to distinguish what central bankers say they do and what actually happens. A case in point is that since 1976 annual messages from central bankers intone that monetary growth is to be squeezed in the forthcoming year. In fact, what has happened is that monetary growth targets are informally raised. According to the *Economist*:

By letting monetary growth overshoot—and then not lowering next year's target to offset it—central banks have been much less tight-fisted than their statements suggest. Since the mid-1970's the cumulative overrun has been as much as 19.6% in Britain and as little as 1% in Japan.[15]

The evidence summarized in Tables 5.3 and 5.4 suggest that this is what happened, which is one reason for skepticism about monetary targets. Another is that the money supply definition used may not give a full picture of the situation in financial markets. There is divergence between such narrow definitions of money as M1 and central bank money and such broader definitions as M2 and M3. In fact, M3 has been growing much more rapidly than M1 thanks to rising interest rates, which encourage depositors to shift deposits. Not all divergence, however, can be so readily explained.

How seriously should governments react to such signals? If the monetary target is a single measure, there is little choice with which to judge policy. In low inflation countries this would not seem to be a problem (for example, Japan, Switzerland, and West Germany). Their narrow and broad definitions of money have been moving closely in line with each other. When they decide to change target rates the choice is clear. The United States uses several target definitions so as to assure itself that a broad thrust of policy is correct. If all targets are missed, then clearly something is wrong and presumably something else is required.[16]

There is a general consensus in Yugoslavia that changes in the money supply are used as targets of monetary policy. This consensus is based on the prevailing quantity theory of money approach and on empirical evidence suggesting that there is a close association between changes in the money supply and real developments (investment and such other developments as expenditures for goods and services, rate of increase in production changes in the price level, imports and exports).[17] Alternative indicators might be the monetary base (high-powered money), bank credit, and interest rate. Not all of these indicators can be used under specific Yugoslav conditions. Interest rates cannot be used since they do not reflect correct market conditions. High-powered money can be used as a subsidiary monetary indicator substituting for the money supply. This is possible because of the close association between changes in the monetary base and changes in money supply, at least in the long run.

Similar arguments hold for the choice between the money supply and bank credit. Bank credit has at least two advantages over high-powered money. First, it is related more closely to the money supply, as well as to expenditures for goods and services, than is high-powered money. Second, bank credit is conceptually and statistically simpler (at least under Yugoslav conditions). Thus, bank credit may be better than high-powered money as a substitution for the money supply as a monetary indicator. There is, however, a significant field of monetary action where bank credit serves as an independent indicator. This is the field of selective credit policy goals. In this instance bank credit, classified according to selective credit policy goals, presents the targets of credit policy that have to be implemented in supporting specific economic policy goals.

Declarations of the Yugoslav Federal Assembly on economic policy goals, which define monetary policy goals and targets, include the rate of increase in the money supply and in bank short-term credit. Changes in the money supply are considered a primary monetary target, whereas changes in bank credit are treated as a secondary target.

As to the efficiency of monetary policy in Yugoslavia, the evidence suggests that changes in money supply may deviate significantly from planned targets. Thanks to errors in the projection of monetary targets (a definite rate of change in money supply) as well as the uncertainties in the adjustment processes of demand to supply of money, monetary policy is less efficient in implementing the planned set of policy goals.

A strong monetarist tradition exists in Yugoslavia, which is in keeping with the ideological neutrality of monetary theory. The prewar quantity theory tradition is unbroken by Keynesian views. Keynesian monetary theory did not reach Yugoslav economists before World War II; after the war, the central planning framework was unsuited to Keynesian views.[18] By the end of the 1950s when Yugoslavia was more receptive, the rigid Keynesian views had already been substantially revised. At the same time, a revised and sophisticated quantity theory was rapidly gaining acceptance.

Moreover, the prewar quantity theory was not inconsistent with the dominant Marxist theory after the war. Both the theoretical and practical approaches to monetary problems are very close to the quantity theory views under conditions of noncommodity, fiduciary money. Indeed, even in the central planning system the quantity of money (currency in circulation) was strongly regulated by cash planning. Finally, one of the most decisive arguments for the prevailing monetarist approach has been the experience of strong inflationary impacts, which were produced by sharp monetary expansion.

As a result, there has always been a general consensus that "money matters" and that there is a need for an efficient monetary policy. This does not mean, however, that there has been complete agreement about the goals, targets, or efficiency of monetary policy. On this score it is possible to distinguish two views: "neutral money policy" and "easy money policy." The neutral money policy is related to the post-1965 reform developments, when stabilization goals became as significant as production and development goals. The easy money policy dominated monetary policy before the 1965 reform. It continues to exist and exert some influence. The rationale for it is that production and economic growth are the basic economic policy goals and that an easy money policy is presumably more helpful toward these goals. The risk of inflation apparently ranks lower than the risk of deceleration of production and economic growth. Although significantly different, the Yugoslav experience is useful for the insights it provides into the economies of East Europe.

SUMMARY OF THE INDICATOR AND TARGET PROBLEM: THE RECENT U.S. EXPERIENCE

According to some observers the Federal Reserve System has tried since the late 1970s to follow a monetarist policy in allowing a steady growth of the money supply as the best way to control inflation. Its strategic emphasis has shifted, presumably, from interest rates to the growth of the money supply. Indeed, it has set money supply targets for five years and attempted to meet them. Its operational targets, however, appear to be interest rates and particularly the overnight borrowing rate between banks known as the "federal funds rate." Open market operations have been conducted so as to assure a given federal funds rate.

Matters were not going well for the Federal Reserve. By 1979 it became clear that money markets in particular no longer believed in the Federal Reserve's ability to achieve its monetary supply targets. As a way of restoring its credibility, the Federal Reserve shifted its operational targets to bring them into line with the strategic emphasis on the money supply. The new operational target was to be a monetary aggregate and not interest rates. The target the Federal Reserve chose was the banks' weekly nonborrowed reserves (that is, those reserves provided for the most part through its own open market operations). Developments since 1979 are illustrated in Figure 5.1.

Put into place in October 1979, this change allowed the federal funds rate to fluctuate, which it has done along with other interest rates here and abroad. The apparent volatility of interest rate fluctuations since October 1979, however, was not expected. Neither the Federal Reserve nor other central banks are happy with the size of these

Figure 5.1

American Money Supply Targets
And Interest Rates, IV/1979-I/1982

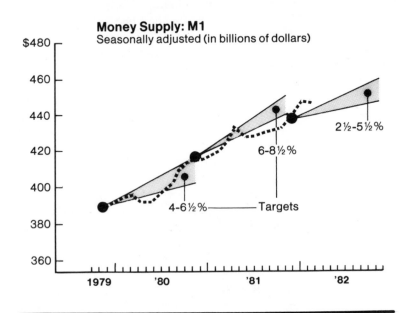

Money Supply: M1
Seasonally adjusted (in billions of dollars)

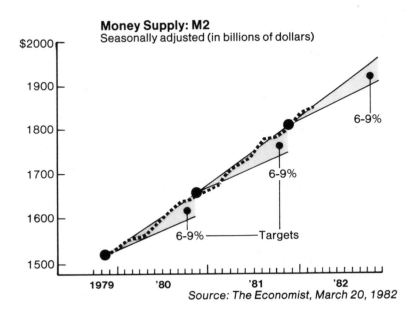

Money Supply: M2
Seasonally adjusted (in billions of dollars)

Source: The Economist, March 20, 1982

Figure 5.1, continued

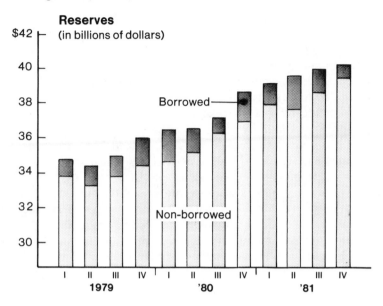

Reserves
(in billions of dollars)

Borrowed

Non-borrowed

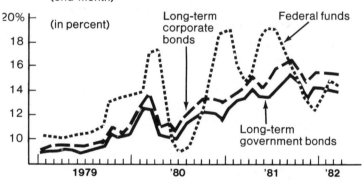

Short - and Long-term Interest Rates
(end-month)

(in percent)

Long-term corporate bonds

Federal funds

Long-term government bonds

Source: The Economist, March 20, 1982

fluctuations. Nevertheless, the Federal Reserve argues that by targeting nonborrowed reserves, it has chosen a target that minimizes the inevitable fluctuations in interest rates. It argues that through the borrowed reserves it lends to banks at its special discount rate it is able to cushion day-to-day savings in the financial system.

The difficulty with such cushioning is that a short-term rise in the money supply prompted by such a smoothing operation may be but the beginning of a significant monetary surge. Indeed, temporary increases in the money supply have become permanent. Thus, when the money supply started to increase in November and December 1981 and picked up tempo in January 1982, observers interpreted the change in tempo as permanent in nature. Monetarists argue that the evidence suggests that the Federal Reserve is not seriously committed to a monetarist doctrine. If committed it would change its operating practices to make sure that, whatever happened to interest rates in the short run, the money supply would stay on target.

Critics urge three operational changes in the Federal Reserve System.[19] The first is to target the monetary base (notes, coins, plus banks' total reserves) instead of nonborrowed reserves. The monetary base will not do as a strategic target, according to the Federal Reserve System, because movements in the monetary base are not as closely associated with those of the real economy as is the money supply. In any case, it argues that if there were need to change the present operating target, total bank reserves would be more useful than the monetary base. Neither total reserves nor the monetary base, argues the Federal Reserve, is as good as the current nonborrowed reserves target.

The second change pushed by critics is that the Federal Reserve System should shift to contemporaneous reserve requirements (CRR). Currently, a bank has two weeks from the time it receives any money in which to acquire the reserves to support it (that is, lagged reserve requirements). A bank can acquire these reserves by borrowing overnight from other banks with a surplus, through the federal funds market. As a last resort, it can also get them from the Federal Reserve System itself through the "discount window." The net result, according to critics, is that because the banks acquired the money two weeks ago, the Federal Reserve System had no choice but to accommodate the level of borrowing that the banks decided. In short, monetary control and initiative rests with the banks and not the Federal Reserve System under these circumstances. It is now expected that the Federal Reserve will adopt CRR in February 1984.

A third change deals with adopting a market discount rate by the Federal Reserve in place of the existing nonmarket rate. The Federal

Reserve does not charge a penalty rate for bank borrowing at the discount-rate window. In fact, it regularly keeps the discount rate two or three percentage points below comparable market rates. This is preferable, according to the Federal Reserve, for it allows for smoothing the uncertainties of economic life. Critics argue that money supply growth would be smoother if the Federal Reserve simply abandoned its central bankers' "pragmatic interference" and left markets to operate on their own.

NOTES

1. George Macesich and H. Tsai, *Money in Economic Systems* (New York: Praeger, 1982).

2. See, for example, Milton Friedman, "The Role of Monetary Policy," *American Economic Review* (March 1968): 1–17. See also the exchange of letters between Friedman and Chairman W. M. Martin on whether, in fact, the Federal Reserve System can control the nominal stock of money. Milton Friedman, "Monetary Policy: Theory and Practice," *Journal of Money, Credit and Banking* (February 1982): 106.

3. William G. Dewald and Harry Johnson, "An Objective Analysis of American Monetary Policy, 1952–1961," in Deanne Carson, ed., *Monetary Studies* (Homewood, Ill.: Irwin, 1963), pp. 171–89; Macesich and Tsai, *Money in Economic Systems*, Chapter 8.

4. Ibid.

5. The sharp acceleration in domestic prices in Yugoslavia in late 1980 and early 1981 is attributable to a number of factors, including the devaluation of the dinar, the large increases in domestic energy prices during 1980–81, the increase in turnover tax rates in the first part of 1981, sectoral imbalances between price controls in October 1980, and the uncertainty during the early part of the year over the criteria and targets for price policy for 1981. Taking advantage of both their increased freedom to set prices and the fluid situation at the end of 1980 and at the beginning of 1981, enterprises raised prices substantially.

6. See Robert D. Auerbach, *Money, Banking, and Financial Markets* (New York: Macmillan, 1982), pp. 337–39, for a useful discussion on a number of these and related issues. For a discussion of the Federal Reserve's failure to do so, see Friedman, "Monetary Policy: Theory and Practice," pp. 106ff.

7. The analysis underlying these conclusions is found in William Poole, "Rules of Thumb for Guiding Monetary Policy," *Open Market Policies and Operating Procedures—Staff Studies* (Washington, D.C.: Board of Governors of the Federal Reserve System, 1971), pp. 135–89; "Optimal Choice of Monetary Policy Instruments in a Stochastic Macro Model," *Quarterly Journal of Economics* (May 1970); Benjamin Friedman, "Targets, Instruments, and Indicators of Monetary Policy," *Journal of Monetary Economics* (October 1975): 443–93; Benjamin Friedman, "The Inefficiency of Short-Run Monetary Targets for Monetary Policy," in *Brookings Papers on Economic Activity*, Vol. 2, A. Okun and G. L. Perry, eds. (Washington, D.C.: Brookings Institution, 1975), pp. 293–335; Howard R. Vane and John L. Thompson, *Monetarism: Theory, Evidence and Policy* (New York: Wiley [A Halstead Press Book], 1979).

8. For a discussion of the complexity of issues surrounding discussions of targets and indicators, see for example Karl Brunner, ed., *Targets and Indicators of Monetary Policy* (San Francisco: Chandler, 1969); F. C. Schdrack, "Our Empirical Approach to the

Definition of Money," *Money Aggregates and Monetary Policy* (New York: Federal Reserve Bank of New York, 1974), pp. 28–34; F. J. Levin "The Selection of a Monetary Indicator: Some Further Empirical Evidence," *ibid.*, pp. 35–39; M. J. Hamburger, "Indicators of Monetary Policy: The Arguments and Evidence," *American Economic Review, Papers and Proceedings* (May 1970): 32–39; Richard Zecher, "Implications of Four Econometric Models for the Indicator Issue," in ibid., pp. 47–54; K. Holbrook and H. Shapiro, "The Choice of Optimal Intermediate Economic Targets," in ibid., pp. 40–46; M. W. Keran, "Selecting a Monetary Indicator—Evidence from the United States and Other Developed Countries," *Review*, Federal Reserve Bank of St. Louis (September 1970): 8–19; Keith M. Carlson and Scott E. Hein, "Monetary Aggregates as Monetary Indicators," *Review*, Federal Reserve Bank of St. Louis (November 1980): 12–21; R. W. Hafer, "Selecting a Monetary Indicator: A Test of the New Monetary Aggregates," in ibid. (February 1981): 12–18.

9. Anna J. Schwartz, "Short-Term Targets of Three Foreign Central Banks," *Targets and Indicators of Monetary Policy*, Karl Brunner, ed. (San Francisco: Chandler, 1969).

10. Keran, "Selecting a Monetary Indicator."

11. J. Ernest Tanner, "Indicators of Monetary Policy: An Evolution of Five," *Banca Nazionale del Lavoro Quarterly Review* (December 1972).

12. See for example Macesich and Tsai, *Money in Economic Systems*, Chapters 6 and 7; Robert H. Rasche, "A Review of Empirical Studies of the Money Supply Mechanism," *Review*, Federal Reserve Bank of St. Louis (July 1976): 11–19; Albert E. Burger, Lionell Kalish, III, and Christopher T. Babb, "Money Stock Control and Its Implications for Monetary Policy," *Review*, Federal Reserve Bank of St. Louis (October 1971): 6–22. A detailed presentation of the functional relationship of the multiplier concept to asset holdings of the nonbank public, banking system, and Treasury is given in Albert E. Burger, *The Money Supply Process* (Belmont, Calif.: Wadsworth, 1971).

13. R. W. Hafer, "Selecting a Monetary Indicator: A Test of the New Monetary Aggregates," *Review*, Federal Reserve Bank of St. Louis (February 1981): 12–18.

14. C. W. J. Granger, "Investigating Causal Relations by Econometric Models and Cross Spectral Methods," *Econometrica* (July 1969): 424–38; C. A. Sims, "Money, Income, and Causality," *American Economic Review* (September 1972): 540–52. For other citations see Hafer's study.

15. *Economist*, December 6, 1980, p. 70.

16. See for instance Milton Friedman, "A Memorandum to the Fed," *Wall Street Journal*, January 30, 1981, p. 20. According to Friedman, "the key defect in trying to control the [American] money supply by pegging the federal funds rate is that mistakes are cumulative and self-reinforcing, and lead to the kind of wide swings in monetary aggregates that we have experienced in recent years."

17. D. Dimitrijević and George Macesich, *Money and Finance in Contemporary Yugoslavia* (New York: Praeger, 1973), Chapter 10; D. Dimitrijević and George Macesich, *Money and Finance in Yugoslavia: A Comparative Analysis* (forthcoming).

18. Ibid.

19. See for example Friedman, "A Memorandum to the Fed"; and Friedman "The Yo-Yo Economy," *Newsweek*, February 15, 1982, p. 72; Lindley H. Clark, Jr., "Looking for Ways to Overcome Uncertainty," *Wall Street Journal*, March 23, 1982, p. 35; Milton Friedman "Churning at the Fed," *Newsweek*, August 31, 1981, p. 44; Milton Friedman, "The Federal Reserve and Monetary Instability," *Wall Street Journal*, February 1, 1982; Lawrence K. Roos, "The Attack on Monetary Targets," *Wall Street Journal*, February 3, 1982.

6

MONETARIST RULES
AND MONETARY POLICY

CENTRAL BANKS AND MONETARY RULES

The evidence summarized in the last chapter suggests that central banks only rarely succeed in hitting monetary targets. When they miss it is nearly always in overshooting, which creates base drift. By unsettling financial markets, base drift causes additional difficulties for the monetary authority in its efforts to achieve longer-term monetary targets.

Our discussion of rational expectations theory suggests at least one reason for the lack of better performance in target practice on the part of central banks. Another is the public's lack of faith in both the monetary authorities and the central bank to behave in a consistent fashion.[1] For these reasons, among others, monetary authorities are urged to abandon short-term stabilization attempts altogether and pursue instead a credible long-term steady state policy. One such policy is the constant money growth rule proposed by Milton Friedman and the monetarists. It is an idea that has been widely discussed for years. Since it is an important weapon in the monetarist arsenal, we shall trace its evolution.

Evidence also suggests why central banks have not adopted a fixed monetary rule. It may well be, as some economists argue, that discretionary policies serve the established bureaucracies. Such a policy permits them to take credit when economic conditions are good and allows for disclaimers of responsibility when economic conditions deteriorate.

Another reason for such reluctance may be in the degree of independence possessed by central banks in executing monetary policy.[2] Such independence is contingent on the method of appointment of governors; the length of time they serve; whether they have legislated objectives clear enough to be a barrier to government intervention; and whether their constitutions provide the bank or the government with the final authority for monetary policy. In practice, central banks may have rather less (or rather more) freedom than their charters suggest. This is likely to depend on tradition as well as on the personalities involved.

Only the German Bundesbank has final authority for monetary policy. The governor, moreover, is not directly appointed by the government. The National Bank of Yugoslavia is an independent federal institution, established by federal law. The bank is managed by the governor, who is appointed by the Federal Assembly on the recommendation of the Federal Executive Council. He is responsible to both of these institutions for the implementation of bank operations and targets. The Federal Assembly and the Federal Executive Council decide monetary policy targets and the National Bank is responsible only for their implementation. Nonetheless, in policy formation the National Bank plays a significant if not dominant role in monetary policy thanks to ready acceptance of its proposals by policymakers.

The central bank of the Netherlands has a clearly defined objective of price stability built into its constitution. On no other score could it be considered independent. In fact, the world's two oldest central banks, Riksbank of Sweden (1668) and the Bank of England (1694), are clearly subservient to their governments in the formation of monetary policy. In the United States and Germany, central bank control rests with a board composed of the heads of several regional banks, thereby allowing for greater "independence" from the central government.

Since they must meet the requirements of their governments, it is not surprising that central banks find themselves in the uncomfortable position where monetary and fiscal policies meet. This means ensuring that the government is able to function smoothly in meeting its financial obligation. In many countries government borrowing in the 1970s has resulted in regular deficits, and debt has risen as a proportion of gross national product.

Concern with inflation calls attention to the growth in the money supply. Governments have reacted by setting formal targets for monetary growth. Since central banks must now try to achieve monetary targets while at the same time financing much larger public sector borrowing, their job is made all the more difficult.

EVOLUTION OF MONETARY RULES

In a broad sense, an ancestral lineage could be established between today's proponents of a monetary rule and such time-honored challengers of convention as the "currency school" or the "bullionists." In a stricter sense, however, the origin of monetary rules is usually dated and personified more precisely: the year given is 1936, the author quoted is Henry C. Simons.[3]

Simons' 1936 proposal was not altogether new. In its underlying theoretical analysis, the importance of the development of the quantity theory of money from John Locke to Irving Fisher is clear. The proposal's affinity with the earlier "100 percent reserve plan" is also clear.[4] Simons' first mention of monetary rules is contained in a 1934 pamphlet, where a rule or rules are part of a larger program for bank reform better known today as the "Chicago plan" and economic reform in general.[5] Among five proposals presented "in a descending scale of relative importance," the proposal with reference to banking and currency ranks second only to the "elimination of private monopoly in all its forms":

> Establishment of more definite and adequate "rules of the game" with respect to money, through
> 1. Abolition of private deposit banking on the basis of fractional reserves
> 2. Establishment of a completely homogeneous, national circulating medium, and
> 3. Creation of a system under which a federal monetary authority has a direct and inescapable responsibility for controlling (not with broad discretionary powers, but under simple, definite rules laid down in legislation) the quantity (or, through quantity, the value) of effective money.[6]

At the same time, Simons states "that the adoption of one among the several definite and unambiguous rules . . . is more important than the choice among them,"[7] an observation most subsequent proponents of monetary rules have emphasized as well.

The kinds of rules Simons is referring to include, on one end of the spectrum, a constant quantity of money and, on the other end, a rule based on the stabilization of some price index. While Simons in his final position accepted a rule expressed in terms of a price index, he nevertheless felt "that his earlier persuasion as to the merits of the rule of a fixed quantity of money was fundamentally correct."[8] But the latter rule cannot be implemented, Simons argues, because we have not attained what he calls the "ideal financial structure."[9] This structure should include "a sharp differentiation between money and private obligations" in order to increase the power "of the central government . . . to create money and effective money substitutes."[10] In more specific terms, his argument against the rule of keeping the quantity of money constant in practice is based on what is today known as the "Gurley-Shaw Thesis":[11] the possibility "of sharp changes on the velocity side" due to "the perverse variability in the amounts of 'near-moneys'."[12]

The stabilization of some price index thus represents a second-best, unsatisfactory solution to Simons:

> If price-level stabilization is a poor system, it is . . . infinitely better than no system at all. And it seems now highly questionable whether any better system is feasible or possible at all within the significant future.[13]

On this score Simons agrees, at least in principle, with other economists and congressional committees of his time.[14] With them he sees one reason for the second-best nature of price stabilization in the difficulties presented by the definition of a particular index.[15] More important, according to Simons, is another disadvantage of rules in terms of some price index:

> All these schemes . . . define programs in terms of ends, with little discussion of appropriate means; they call for an authority with a considerable range for discretionary actions, and would require much intelligence and judgment in their administration; and they would leave us exposed to continuous legislative (if not administrative) tinkering.[16]

Here it becomes obvious that Simons' "underlying position may be characterized as severely libertarian or, in the English-Continental sense, liberal," with, he points out, the "emphasis upon liberty as both a requisite and a measure of progress."[17]

This is important since the major emphasis in Simons' political-economic program is not placed on specific or even quantitative economic targets, but on the ethical values of liberty or freedom. This inherent liberal persuasion thus entails one of the distinctive features of Simons' approach and argumentation.

Another early proponent of a monetary rule, though not talking in terms of rules, is Carl Snyder. He concludes from his empirical analysis:

> As trade and production as a whole grow at a fairly fixed and definite rate, then for the maintenance of price stability the volume of the media of exchange or bank credit must increase at the same rate.[18]

In contrast to Simons, Snyder derives his conclusion from a target-oriented, quantitative analysis. With this approach and his proposal in terms of "controlling the volume of bank credit, maintaining its increase at a fixed and predetermined rate per annum,"[19] he is in surprisingly close proximity to some of today's proponents of monetary rules.

Another contemporary and close colleague of Simons, Lloyd W. Mints, is usually associated with Simons in his ideas as to the proper management of monetary policy.[20] The existing differences between Mints and Simons are more a matter of emphasis than substance. Both believe in the inherent stability of the "free" economic system; both feel that some rule would be better than none; both mention the desirability (and at the same time similar difficulties) concerning a constant quantity of money; and both conclude that price-level stabilization may be the most feasible—even if difficult to implement—guide for monetary policy.

Some differences do exist in the valuation of objectives or targets. Mints seems to place greater emphasis on monetary stability per se as compared to Simons' ultimate objective of liberty. In the degree of special analysis concerning some details, Mints analyzes some of the questions under more technical aspects. He discusses, for example, various indexes in terms of stabilization and concludes that "an index of wholesale prices is probably the best guide for monetary action."[21] He then expands this discussion by also considering international aspects of the questions involved.[22] Mints analyzes the possible effect of lags, following a suggestion by Milton Friedman, to conclude tentatively that "the evidence . . . affords no confirmation of the contention that lags in the effectiveness of changes in the stock of money might accentuate fluctuations in the level of prices."[23] Again, however, there is no detailed description of how the guide of price-level stabilization may be translated into a simple monetary rule.

Starting from rather similar bases but different dispositions, Clark Warburton and Friedman both come up with at least superficially similar conclusions and proposals, the differences in which, though not trivial, are more a matter of specific detail than general substance.[24] Warburton, like Friedman, arrived at his final conclusion only after extensive empirical studies.[25] These studies led to two important findings. First:

> Scrutiny of . . . quarterly measures of quantity and circuit velocity of money, adjusted for trend, showed that the quantity of money led and its circuit velocity lagged at the turning points of business cycles. In fact, the departure in the quantity of money from a reasonable rate of growth occurred during the preceding boom phase of the cycle, and thus not only preceded a reduction in the rate of use of money but also the top of the boom. It was these observations which led to the emphasis . . . on an erratic money supply as the chief originating factor in business recessions and not merely an intensifying force in the case of severe depressions.[26]

And second:

> The influence of Federal Reserve action, together with monetary policies such as the Treasury price of gold, has been so overwhelmingly dominant that it is a realistic and truthful statement to say that the supply of money in the United States is the result of the *de facto* monetary policy of the United States government. The conclusion cannot be avoided that federal government agencies, particularly the Federal Reserve authorities, have been responsible for the drastic and erratic variability of the quantity of money in the United States since the close of World War I.[27]

From these findings and inferences, Warburton derives his conclusion and proposal for monetary policy: a constant rate of growth in the quantity of money.[28]

At least in principle, this is the same conclusion reached by Friedman. However, Friedman arrives at his proposal following a different road which, in its beginning, seems to have been staked out by Simons and Mints. Friedman is an early critic of discretionary monetary policy.[29] Through his research with Anna J. Schwartz at the National Bureau of Economic Research, he too arrives at the rule "that the stock of money be increased at a fixed rate year-in and year-out."[30] His subsequent research and studies helped to underpin his initial conviction and to enlarge and specify the proposal.[31]

A more precise delineation of the characteristics of the two proposals by Warburton and Friedman can best be achieved by comparing some of the major issues involved. The first issue is the general background of, or reason for, the proposal. As mentioned before, Friedman started out with a fairly strong inclination for some rule and against "the uncertainty and undesirable political implications of discretionary action by government authorities."[32] At the same time, however, he emphasizes a possible other, more pragmatic disadvantage of discretion—lags in response: "Long and variable lags could convert the fluctuations in the government contribution to the income stream into the equivalent of an additional random disturbance."[33] These initial premonitions about lags later became a conviction through his research on the lag in the effect of monetary policy, and the corresponding argument in favor of his proposal achieved importance. Friedman thus believes that the "contribution to economic stability" by the rule "is the most that we can ask from monetary policy at our present stage of knowledge," though, as he points out, "other forces would still affect the economy . . . and disturb the even tenor of our ways."[34]

Warburton, on the other hand, while not disregarding the possible effect of lags, places less emphasis on them "and their existence is not crucial to his proposal."[35] At the same time, he seems to consider—even more so than Friedman—"monetary . . . policy as the overwhelmingly important originating factor in serious economic disturbances."[36] Or as Richard T. Selden states: "Warburton comes close to accepting a monetary theory of business cycles, for mild and severe cycles alike."[37]

The second issue refers to the general framework surrounding the proposal. For Warburton, the only statutory change of major importance is the directive concerning the implementation of the rule itself. While he is in favor, for example, of retirement of the Federal Reserve stock, reduction in the number of members of the board of governors, abolishment of regulation Q, and some of the changes with regard to reserve requirements, he emphasizes "how admirably the central banking machinery, with the existing type of banking institutions, could serve . . . if given the proper directive by Congress."[38]

He therefore takes issue with Friedman, who regards the rule as the most important part, but as only one part, of desired changes in the monetary system. Among Friedman's many recommendations are the elimination of fractional-reserve banking, of the discount window, of the prohibition of interest payment on demand deposits, and of regulation Q.[39] As incisive as these changes may be, they are not indispensable:

> The problems of the organization of the Federal Reserve System are extremely important so long as . . . two guidelines . . . are not in effect. If these guidelines were put into effect, the problem of organization would become of little importance because the present power of the Federal Reserve System to introduce instability into the economy would be eliminated.[40]

The two guidelines Friedman is referring to here are a constant rate of growth of the money supply and competitively determined interest rates.

The third and last issue concerns the more pragmatic or technical aspects of the rule—the question as to the definition of money, seasonal adjustment, the specific rate of growth in the money supply, and the general flexibility of the rule. Both Friedman and Warburton are in favor of using an expanded version of the conventional definition of money. Whereas Friedman's proposal is in terms of currency held by the public plus adjusted demand and time deposits in commercial banks, Warburton considers several other concepts as well.[41]

Differences in emphasis seem to exist between Warburton and Friedman as to the question of whether allowance ought to be made in the proposal for seasonal variation. Warburton tends to favor seasonal adjustment while Friedman, after initial doubts, reaches the "tentative conclusion to dispense with seasonal adjustments because there is no seasonal to adjust until a decision is made what seasonal to introduce."[42]

The remaining two questions—the actual growth rate of the money supply and its flexibility—are closely related. In their respective answers, Friedman and Warburton have developed what appear to be rather marked differences. Friedman has suggested growth rates between 3 and 5 percent per year, and on more theoretical grounds, a growth rate of 2 percent.[43] However, in his own words: "I have always emphasized that a *steady* and known rate of increase in the quantity of money is more important than the precise numerical value of the rate of increase."[44]

Warburton has proposed similar growth rates with possible slight variations depending on the concept of money used. He arrived at these rates the same way Friedman did: by allowing for a certain percentage decrease in secular velocity.[45] But Warburton's emphasis seems to be more on an average range for the rate of growth in money than on its absolute constancy. When he states that, aside from seasonal adjustments, "adjustments . . . may be needed on acount of . . . any other conditions which have been demonstrated to require variations from the calculated line of growth in the quantity of money in order to maintain stability of prices of final products,"[46] he creates some uncertainty as to the specific content of his proposal. Compared to Friedman, who believes in a much more rigid application of the rule, Warburton seems to be closer to supporters of what might be called "formula flexibility."

In discussions of monetary rules, the proposal made by Edward S. Shaw is usually associated with Friedman's rigid rule, which has become known as the "Friedman-Shaw proposal." A reasonable degree of similarity exists with but one major exception: Shaw's preference as to the definition of money, though flexible, seems to lie with the conventional concept.[47] Two other supporters of what Shaw calls "the principle of look-Ma-no-hands in money management" are Robert L. Crouch and Leland Yeager.[48]

James W. Angell has suggested a monetary rule that may initially appear akin to Warburton's proposal, at least as far as the degree of flexibility is concerned.[49] However, Angell would apply the rule to the achievable money supply or indirectly to the commercial bank reserve base. Considering the additional proposals made by him, which include more frequent use of stronger selective controls, "it is obvious that Angell does not look with favor on the Warburton-Friedman proposals."[50] Phillip Cagan, on the other hand, seems to be in almost complete agreement with Warburton.[51]

Several other economists have suggested rules in terms of formula flexibility.[52] The element that all their various proposals have in common—as compared to Warburton's rule, for example, —is a built-in adjustment mechanism, which would lead to automatic adjustments in the rate of growth of the money supply whenever certain specified changes can be detected in the economy. These changes and the frequency with which they are to be considered represent the distinguishing elements of the proposals within this group.

For instance, Hosek favors a rate of growth of the money supply at "a rate that is equal to the expected rate of growth in potential GNP . . . after the money supply is initially raised to the full employment *level*."[53] Bronfenbrenner, on the other hand, suggests that "the growth rate of the money supply should equal the sum of the growth rates of the labor force and average labor productivity, less the growth rate of the velocity of circulation of money."[54] Adjustments based on observations of the past should be made every month or quarter. In addition, Bronfenbrenner also favors setting upper and lower limits to the annual rate of growth of the money supply in the vicinity of 8 and 1 percent, "regardless of the formula's occasional vagaries."[55]

It is this kind of a range or band that quite a few economists have adopted as a centerpiece of their proposals. Representatives of this group include Karl Brunner, Gregory C. Chow, Carl F. Christ, Thomas Mayer, Jacques Melitz, and the Joint Economic Committee.[56] Generally based on the observation of "wild gyrations in the growth rate of the money stock,"[57] the guidelines usually involve a range of about 2 to 6 percent per annum, sometimes with the possibility not only of adjustments in the band, but of exceptions to it as well. Some of these proposals seem to be supporting discretionary action more so than automaticity.

Finally, no two rules are alike. The range covers the complete spectrum from almost perfect rigidity to guidelines that come very close to supporting the existing degree of discretion. This diversity within the "Rules Party" may help to explain the sometimes almost scornful reception of some of these proposals by the opposition.

THE CRITICS

Consider now some of the major points against monetary rules raised by critics.[58] Two major points in dispute are the concept of money and the mechanism that links monetary and other economic variables.

The debate over the definition of money includes the issues of what is to be regarded as money now and the changing moneyness of assets, because "a fixed rule freezes the definition over time."[59] The first issue is debated not only between advocates of and opponents to rules, but also within each group and among monetary economists in general. As the proposals indicate, various concepts of money have been included and most advocates of rules are of the opinion that a rule applied to any definition is preferable to the existing degree of discretion. Thus, it seems that the definition of money per se is not really a vital issue in the theoretical debate. The issue of the flexibility over time of the concept of money may be more important, but it is obviously also a matter of the degree of specific flexibility built into the rule. No proposal is regarded "as the be-all and end-all of monetary policy for all time."[60]

The link between the stock of money and income is discussed in terms of the velocity of money and, more specifically, in terms of the variability or stability of the velocity. Proponents of rules believe in a relatively stable and predictable velocity, whereas opponents tend to regard velocity as subject to erratic variations.[61] Without analyzing all the details and individual differences, suffice it to say that these differences are no longer as sharp as formerly.

A similar statement could be made about time lags. This issue centers around three elements: the definition or measurement of lags, their length or distribution, and their variability. Typically, long and variable lags are associated with proponents of rules, while short lags are associated with opponents to rules.[62] Friedman is the only one among the proponents who makes explicit allowance for the variability of lags.[63] Also, while a few proponents seem to share the belief in at least the possibility of relatively long lags, any dividing line, if it is to be drawn, does not follow the established rules-versus-discretion discussion.[64] The haziness appears to be mainly a consequence of the lack of definitude in the theoretical issues. We have enumerated some of these issues elsewhere.

Another issue raised by critics concerns the best indicator of monetary policy. Analyzing monetary rules, Arthur M. Okun concludes:

> It takes . . . a big jump to go from the proposition that quantities deserve emphasis to the position that quantities alone should be the criteria of monetary policy. It is still another leap to the proposal that the only quantities that should count are those relating to one particular financial variable defined as money.[65]

It appears that for once Okun is not speaking for the majority. In a survey of more than 70 U.S. monetary economists, "by a more than 2 to 1 majority, respondents favored making the growth of the money supply or its cognate, base money, the target of monetary policy."[66] This question is presented at some length elsewhere in this study.

A similar issue raised by critics refers to the ability of the monetary authority to achieve a prescribed change in the money stock:

> The difficulty is that the money hinges on the willingness of business and individuals to borrow, the asset preferences of individuals and nonbank institutions—all of which are subject to only imperfect control by the Federal Reserve.[67]

Although the control of the money stock under the present system is subject to adequate forecasting by the Federal Reserve, the issue of effective control is not restricted to monetary rules. Once the money supply is accepted as an indicator or subtarget, any rational monetary policy implies effective control of the money supply as a prerequisite. Whether the present Federal Reserve System complies with this prerequisite is therefore a broader, much more basic question of monetary policy.

The essence of the differences between critics and proponents of monetary rules can be cast in another question: Can the target(s) be achieved more effectively and precisely by rules or by discretion? Two specific arguments can be usefully noted: first, the often heard critique that monetary rules are characterized by the "implicit precept: ignore fiscal policy";[68] and second, the obstacle to rules "is several ends are in complex and unstable rivalry or conflict with each other."[69]

The first argument appears overdrawn. Proponents of rules simply do not ignore fiscal policy. Whereas quite a few supporters rely more heavily on monetary policy, this cannot be interpreted as a subscription that "only money matters." On the other hand, as Selden points out, "even if it were true that money does not matter, we should nevertheless try to make it behave in the manner most consistent with economic stability."[70]

The second argument implies the hypothesis that conflicting objectives can be served more effectively by a monetary authority that is "to use its best judgment each time that a decision of some sort is called for as to the relative weight to be given to the objectives."[71] Aside from the question of whether this kind and degree of discretion is compatible with the economic and political system, the intuitive nature of the argument hinges on another, more institutional, issue: the relative fallibility or infallibility of the monetary authority.[72]

A LOOK AT THE EVIDENCE

The first attempts to compare the hypothetical performance of rules with other policy alternatives were made simultaneously with some proposals and their rebuttals.[73] Friedman, for example, compared the actual change in the quantity of money with his 4 percent rule. He scored the difference as being in the "right" or "wrong" direction using criteria such as "'leaning against the wind', namely, that the stock of money should grow at a slower than average rate during business expansions and at a higher than average rate during business contractions."[74] Applied to the United States on a monthly basis for periods of almost 32 years, the results show actual monetary policy as "right" or "better" than the rule in 40 to 55 percent of the months considered. Even before presenting the rather inconclusive results, however, Friedman declares the attempt a failure because of the difficulties in defining generally acceptable criteria of judgment.[75]

The first explicit tests of monetary rules were performed by Martin Bronfenbrenner.[76] His tests include four strategies of monetary policy: the "judgment" rule or actual monetary policy; two "inflexible" rules with an annual growth rate of the money supply of 3 and 4 percent; and a "lag" rule whereby the growth rate of the money supply is determined by the rate of change in real output and velocity during the past year or quarter. Defining the ideal growth rate of the money supply as the actual growth rate minus the rate of change in the price level, Bronfenbrenner explicitly assumes a constant aggregate income and velocity for each time interval. He also accepts price level stability as the only target and comparative criterion of monetary policy. The actual tests were initially performed using annual data for the period 1901 to 1958, excluding the years of World War II; further tests using quarterly data for the period 1947-I to 1958-IV were added later. The data include two concepts of money—the "conventional" and an "expanded" concept—and two price indexes—wholesale and consumer price. Though the results vary with different data and subperiods, they seem to suggest, according to Bronfenbrenner, the possible superiority of the inflexible rule (particularly the 3 percent rule using annual data) and the lag rule (using quarterly data) over the judgment rule.

Entirely different conclusions were reached by Donald P. Tucker when he repeated Bronfenbrenner's computations for the annual version excluding, however, the years of World War I as well.[77] The results so obtained show the judgment rule superior to all other rules. This indicates, Tucker claims, "how sensitive the conclusions are to changes in the underlying assumptions."[78]

Less obvious are the results obtained by Charles Schotta, who applied the Bronfenbrenner tests, with the exception of the lag rule, to annual Canadian data from 1927 to 1961, again excluding the years of World War II.[79] Overall, both the judgment and the 3 percent rule seem slightly superior to the 4 percent rule; but the margin varies and is hardly decisive. Schotta cites the possibility of different and changing objectives of Canadian monetary policy as perhaps the major reason for the difference in his result as compared to Bronfenbrenner's. He concludes by questioning "the applicability of American monetary history to the economic experience of other nations."[80]

Another test of monetary rules has been conducted by Franco Modigliani.[81] The basic procedure is similar to Bronfenbrenner's. Modigliani also tries to determine what he calls the "target money supply," considering not only price stability but full employment as a target as well. The determination of full employment income assumes a proportional relationship between income and employment. Full employment is defined as a 4 percent rate of unemployment, and price stability as no increase in the GNP deflator. Again, velocity is assumed to be constant for each time interval, in this case six-month periods.

Several concepts of money and various rules are examined. Aside from the conventional and expanded money supply, Modigliani also first adds time deposits in mutual savings banks and the postal saving system, and then outstanding deposits in savings and loan associations to the expanded definition of money. The main rule examined is a steady 3 percent annual increase in the respective money supply. Another rule first adjusts the money supply to the full employment level of the preceding period and then adds a fixed growth rate. A third alternative, the so-called switch rule, has the most inclusive concept of money growth at 3 percent whenever current income is greater than or equal to the previous peak level, and switches to the second rule with the conventional concept of money whenever current income is below the previous peak level.

Modigliani evaluates the performance of various monetary strategies by calculating the deviation of the actual money supply and the money supply according to the described rules from the target money supply for the period, beginning with the second half of 1947 and ending with the second half of 1962. The often quoted results state that overall discretionary policy has outperformed all rules, except the switch rule, no matter what concept of money is chosen. This is particularly true for the subperiod 1952 to 1960. The much poorer performance in the other subperiods stems from the fact, according to Modigliani, that during these periods the monetary authority was seeking to achieve other targets than price stability and full employment.

Concluding his study, Modigliani writes:

> As I see it, the inference to be drawn from the test is . . . that (1) on the whole the evidence supports the use of discretion over a rule, but that (2) there is room for some limitations in the use of discretion, particularly in the form of spelling out more precisely the goals to which the discretionary powers should be directed, and the procedures by which these goals are to be changed.[82]

Rather different results were obtained from two other tests conducted on the basis of Modigliani's approach. Richard Attiyeh changed two of Modigliani's assumptions: first, following Okun's research, Attiyeh chose a one-to-three relationship between employment and income rather than one to one; second, he defined price stability to be consistent with a 1.5 percent increase in the GNP deflator.[83] Using the same data as Modigliani, but restricting the tests to the subperiod 1952 to 1960, Attiyeh found the second rule to be markedly closer to the target than discretionary policy. He concludes that Modigliani's test results are very sensitive to the definition of the target money supply and evidently also to the period selected for analysis.

Introducing lags into Modigliani's procedure by letting the target money supply lead by one or two periods has been attempted by Thomas Mayer.[84] Again the results are distinctly different from Modigliani's and overall are more favorable for the rigid rule than for discretionary policy. Since empirical analyses "clearly suggest" the existence of a lag of at least one quarter, Mayer concludes that "Modigliani's claim to have established the superiority of discretionary policy must be rejected."[85]

In a recent study, Macesich and Tsai report test results on Bronfenbrenner's four monetary rules—judgment rule, 3 percent rule, 4 percent rule, and lag rule—as applied to Belgium, France, Germany, Italy, the Netherlands, United Kingdom, Sweden, Yugoslavia, Canada, and the United States, for the years 1956–80 (1958–80 for Yugoslavia) using annual data. We may draw on these results for the purposes at hand.[86]

The United Kingdom

To judge from the overall test results, the 3 percent rule performs best and the judgment rule poorest in the United Kingdom during the period 1951–80. The 4 percent rule and the lag rule perform equally well. The judgment rule aside, there are no clearcut results as to which might give the lower absolute deviations. An inflationary bias is revealed in all cases considered, irrespective of which price index or definition of money is used.

Sweden

The 4 percent rule performs best in Sweden during the period 1951–80. The 3 percent rule suggests a slight deflationary bias when a broader definition of money, together with either wholesale or consumer price, is used in the analysis. On the other hand, the judgment rule, the 4 percent rule, and the lag rule during the same period tend toward an inflationary direction. In all cases, the judgment rule is the poorest performer. The 3 percent is poorer than the 4 percent rule only when a broader definition of money together with wholesale prices is used. On the other hand, the lag rule is significantly poorer that the 3 percent and the 4 percent variants regardless of which price index or definition of money is used. Thus, the order of better performance is the 3 percent rule, the 4 percent rule, the lag rule, and the judgment rule.

Yugoslavia

In Yugoslavia the judgment rule does better than the 3 percent, 4 percent, and lag rules when wholesale prices are used, irrespective of which definition of money is used in the test. The 3 percent, 4 percent, and lag rules, in turn, are the better performers when consumer prices are used. The 4 percent rule performs slightly better than the 3 percent rule in all cases considered. However, there are no clear-cut results as to which might give the lower absolute deviations. On the other hand, the lag rule performs better than both the 3 percent and 4 percent rules in the case that uses a broader definition of money together with wholesale prices.

A deflationary bias is revealed in the 4 percent and 3 percent rules, while an inflationary bias is suggested in the judgment rule and the lag rule. However, the inflationary bias in the lag rule is relatively small compared to those of the judgment rule. The small negative algebraic deviation in the lag rule may be a statistical artifact as a result of fluctuation of annual data.

Canada

Looking at the overall test results, the judgment rule appears superior during the period 1951–80 when a narrow definition of money is used in the analysis. The average absolute value of the deviations for the judgment rule is consistently lower than the other three rules when a narrow definition of money is used. The judgment rule, however, has the larger average value of the deviations than these three rules when broader definitions of money and consumer prices are used in the test.

In the second set of tests, the results indicate a tendency toward an inflationary bias in the judgment rule, whereas a deflationary bias appears in the 3 percent and lag rules. The judgment rule aside, the absolute deviations tended to be smaller when consumer prices are used in the analysis. Again the judgment rule aside, the use of a broader definition of money yields the lower absolute deviations.

The United States

A look at the overall test results reveals that the judgment rule performs consistently poorer by comparison to the other three rules regardless of the definition of the money supply or price index used. The average absolute value of deviations for the judgment rule ranges from .0618 to .626. The use of consumer prices seems to yield lower absolute deviations in all cases considered.

In the second set of tests, the results indicate a strong tendency toward an inflationary bias in the judgment rule, while a deflationary bias appears only in the 3 percent rule when a broader definition of money is used. However, these deflationary biases are too small to be significant. This might be a statistical artifact. In order of performance, it is the lag rule that scores best in the United States, followed by the 4 percent, the 3 percent, and the judgment rules.

European Economic Community

What implication can we draw from this evidence with respect to the long-standing debate on "rules versus discretion" and a supranational monetary authority for coordinating stabilization policies? From the point of view of the individual member EEC countries, that combination of forecasting ability, political pressure, and administrative routine that passes as "judgment" or "discretionary" monetary policy has a slight edge. The individual records in these countries seem favorable to such policy, at least in comparison to the other three rules considered—provided, of course, that the monetary authority makes use of its discretion in the pursuit of price stability as the stated goal.

The evidence with respect to the other rules, though on balance not spectacular, is not irrelevant. On the contrary, in the experience of all six original EEC countries, the 3 percent and 4 percent versions of the inflexible rule came close to the record registered by the judgment rule. This is particularly significant for a supranational monetary authority. The formulation and implementation of a judgment rule by such authority for the entire community so that the rule is compatible for in all six countries may very well outtax the ingenuity of such an organization. It would probably lead to oligopolistic reaction on the part of each of the countries and to squabbles that would undermine EEC as an effective organization. A useful alternative would be the obligation on the part of the EEC monetary authority to adhere to, say, a 4 percent increase in the money supply designed to serve the goal of price stability. This rule does perform reasonably well in most member countries. Its adoption would serve to defuse the explosive nature of the situation by making it unnecessary for a central monetary authority to thrash about in search of a judgment rule acceptable to all member countries, individually and collectively.

To be sure, rules can provide only a rough guide to monetary management. Rules designed to serve specific goals nevertheless do focus attention on areas of conflict and lay open to public debate both the goals and means for reaching them. This is particularly important in such a multinational and multistate organization as the EEC. A given rule at least avoids one of the principal objections to discretionary policy, which is that such a policy may be used to serve goals other than those agreed upon by all participants within the community.

Events since the financial crisis in May 1971 underscore the difficulties of putting together a European monetary union and coordinating monetary policy. Indeed, it is doubtful whether any of the rules discussed would have been appropriate under the circumstances. French enthusiasm for and German opposition to exchange controls generated differences that even the Council of Finance Ministers failed to resolve. In the end, each country took its own separate road. Some countries resorted to exchange controls, while others allowed their currencies to find their own levels on the international exchange markets. These difficulties have been compounded by Great Britain's entry into the EEC and the Nixon administration's efforts on behalf of the dollar in the early 1970s.

By 1976 monetary turbulence divided Europe into weak and strong currency zones and compounded the problems of allowing EEC to function as an area of free trade and equal competition. Indeed, a question being asked nearly 20 years after the creation of the EEC is whether it can survive half submerged by currency turbulence, divisions between its rich and poor members, and mounting waves of protectionism. These problems become more pressing every year. We shall have more to say on this issue later.

NOTES

1. For a discussion of the credibility hypothesis see William Felner, *Towards a Reconstruction of Macroeconomics: Problems of Theory and Policy* (Washington, D.C.: American Enterprise Institute, 1976).

2. See for example *Economist*, January 28, 1978, pp. 91–93; George Macesich and H. Tsai, *Money in Economic Systems* (New York: Praeger, 1982).

3. Henry C. Simons, "Rules versus Authorities in Monetary Policy," *Journal of Political Economy* 44 (February 1936): 1–30. This chapter draws in part on Rainer Stuper, "An Empirical Analysis of the Debate over Rules versus Discretion with Special Reference to the Monetary Management of the German Bundesbank From 1958 to 1970" (Ph.D. diss., Florida State University, March 1973).

4. For a discussion of this and similar plans see Albert G. Hart, "'The Chicago Plan' for Banking Reform," *Review of Economic Studies* 2 (1935): 104–16.

5. Henry C. Simons, "A Positive Program for Laissez Faire: Some Proposals for a Liberal Economic Policy," *Public Policy Pamphlet*, No. 15, ed. H.D. Gideonse (Chicago: University of Chicago Press, 1934); reprinted in Henry C. Simons, *Economic Policy for a Free Society* (Chicago: University of Chicago Press, 1948), pp. 40–77.

6. Ibid., p. 57.

7. Ibid., p. 63.

8. Simons, "Rules versus Authorities," p. 16.

9. Ibid.

10. Henry C. Simons, "The Requisites of Free Competition," *American Economic Review, Supplement* 26 (March 1936): 69.

11. Cf. John G. Gurley, and Edward S. Shaw, "Financial Aspects of Economic Development," *American Economic Review* 45 (September 1955): 515–38.

12. Simons, "Rules versus Authorities," p. 5.

13. Ibid., p. 21.

14. See for example Irving Fisher, *Stabilizing the Dollar* (New York: Macmillan, 1920); U.S. Congress, House, Committee on Banking and Currency, Stabilization, Hearings, before Committee on Banking Currency, House of Representatives on H.R.

11806, 70th Cong., 1st sess., 1928; U.S. Congress, Senate, Committee on Banking and Currency, *Restoring and Maintaining the Average Purchasing Power of the Dollar,* Hearings, before Committee on Banking and Currency, Senate, on H.R. 11499 and S. 4429, 72d Cong., 1 sess., 1932.

15. Simons, "Rules versus Authorities," pp. 12–13, n. 11.

16. Ibid., p. 12.

17. Henry C. Simons, "Introduction: A Political Credo," *Economic Policy for a Free Society* (Chicago: University of Chicago Press, 1948), p. 1.

18. Carl Snyder, "The Problem of Monetary and Economic Stability," *Quarterly Journal of Economics* 49 (February 1935): 198.

19. Carl Snyder, *Capitalism the Creator: The Economic Foundations of Modern Industrial Society* (New York: Macmillan, 1940), pp. 220–21.

20. See for example Lloyd W. Mints, *Monetary Policy for a Competitive Society* (New York: McGraw-Hill, 1950), pp. 115–73; Mints, "Monetary Policy and Stabilization," *American Economic Review, Papers and Proceedings* 41 (May 1951): 188–93.

21. Mints, *Monetary Policy for a Competitive Society,* p. 136.

22. Ibid., pp. 143–59.

23. Ibid., p. 142.

24. For a comparative summary of the development of Warburton's and Friedman's proposal, see Selden, "Stable Monetary Growth," pp. 324–31. The following paragraphs partly rely on this study. An interesting and useful study by William Yohe, "The Intellectual Milieu at the Federal Reserve Board in the 1920's," presented at the Annual Meeting History of Economic Society, Duke University, May 25, 1982, sheds considerable light on the background of Federal Reserve policymaking during its formative years.

25. See for example Clark Warburton, "The Volume of Money and the Price Level between the World Wars," *Journal of Political Economy* 53 (June 1945): 150–63; Warburton, "The Misplaced Emphasis in Contemporary Business-Fluctuation Theory," *Journal of Business* 19 (October 1946): 199–220; reprinted in *Readings in Monetary Theory,* selected by a Committee of the American Economic Association (Homewood, Ill.: Irwin, 1951), pp. 284–318; Warburton, "The Secular Trend in Monetary Velocity," *Review of Economics and Statistics* 30 (March 1948): 128–34.

26. Clark Warburton, "Testing a Hypothesis" (March 1951) p. 12 (mimeographed), quoted in Selden, "Stable Monetary Growth," p. 327.

27. Warburton, "Misplaced Emphasis," p. 311.

28. See for example Clark Warburton, "How Much Variation in the Quantity of Money Is Needed?" *Southern Economic Journal* 18 (April 1952): 495–509; Warburton, "Rules and Implements of Monetary Policy," *Journal of Finance* 8 (March 1953): 1–21; U.S. Congress, House, Committee on Banking and Currency, *Compendium on Monetary Policy Guidelines and Federal Reserve Structure,* Pursuant to H.R. 11, Subcommittee on Domestic Finance of the Committee on Banking and Currency, House of Representatives, 90th Cong. 2d sess., 1968, pp. 634–44 (hereinafter referred to as *Compendium*).

29. See for example Milton Friedman, "A Monetary and Fiscal Framework for Economic Stability," *American Economic Review* 38 (June 1948): 245–64; Friedman, "Commodity Reserve Currency," *Journal of Political Economy* 59 (June 1951): 203–32; Friedman, "Price, Income, and Monetary Changes in Three Wartime Periods," *American Economic Review, Papers and Proceedings,* (May 1952): 612–25.

30. Milton Friedman, *A Program for Monetary Stability,* the Millar Lectures, No. 3 (New York: Fordham University Press, 1960), p. 90. Results of his research at NBER can be found in Milton Friedman and Anna J. Schwartz, *A Monetary History of the United States,* National Bureau of Economic Research, Studies in Business Cycles, No. 12 (Princeton, N.J.: Princeton University Press, 1963).

31. Cf. Milton Friedman, "The Lag in Effect of Monetary Policy," *Journal of Political Economy* 69 (October 1961): 447–66; Friedman, *The Optimum Quantity of Money and Other Essays* (Chicago: Aldine, 1969), Chapter 1.

32. Friedman, "Monetary and Fiscal Framework", p. 263.

33. Ibid., p. 254.

34. Milton Friedman, "The Role of Monetary Policy," *American Economic Review* 58 (March 1968): 17.

35. Selden, "Stable Monetary Growth," p. 331

36. Statement of Clark Warburton, *Compendium*, p. 634.

37. Selden, "Stable Monetary Growth," p. 331.

38. Warburton, "Rules and Implements," p. 17; see also for example Statement of Clark Warburton, *Compendium*, pp. 639–40.

39. Cf. Friedman, *Program for Monetary Stability*, pp. 100–02.

40. Statement of Milton Friedman, *Compendium*, p. 204.

41. Warburton, "How Much Variation?" pp. 495–98; Statement of Clark Warburton, *Compendium*, pp. 636–37.

42. Friedman, *Program for Monetary Stability*, p. 92.

43. Milton Friedman, "Should There Be an Independent Monetary Authority?" *In Search of a Monetary Constitution*, ed. L.B. Yeager (Cambridge, Mass.: Harvard University Press, 1962), pp. 242–43; Friedman, *Optimum Quantity*, pp. 45–48.

44. Ibid., p. 48.

45. Cf. Warburton, "How Much Variation?", pp. 498–500.

46. Warburton, "Rules and Implements," p. 7; as examples of such conditions, Warburton mentions changes in short-run velocity and changes in the rate of growth of population and productivity; see Warburton, "How Much Variation?" pp. 502, 506–08.

47. Edward S. Shaw, "Monetary Stability in a Growing Economy," in *The Allocation of Economic Resources: Essays in Honor of B.F. Haley* (Stanford, Calif.: Stanford University Press, 1959), pp. 218–35.

48. Ibid., p. 233. Statement of Robert L. Crouch, *Compendium*, pp. 119–27; Statement of Leland Yeager, *Compendium*, pp. 651–57.

49. James W. Angell, "Appropriate Monetary Policies and Operations in the United States Today," *Review of Economics and Statistics* 42 (August 1960): 247–52.

50. Selden, "Stable Monetary Growth," p. 333.

51. Statement of Phillip Cagan, *Compendium*, p. 106.

52. Martin Bronfenbrenner, "Monetary Rules: A New Look," *Journal of Law and Economics* 8 (October 1965): 173–94; Statement of William R. Hosek, *Compendium*, pp. 304–13; Statement of Allen H. Meltzer, *Compendium*, pp. 488–91; Statement of George R. Morrison, *Compendium*, pp. 493–501.

53. Statement of William R. Hosek, *Compendium*, p. 307.

54. Bronfenbrenner, "Monetary Rules," p. 179.

55. Ibid., p. 182.

56. Statement of Karl Brunner, *Compendium*, pp. 100–03; statement of Gregory C. Chow, *Compendium*, pp. 106–09; statement of Carl F. Christ, *Compendium*, pp. 109–15; statement of Thomas Mayer, *Compendium*, pp. 46–72; statement of Jacques Melitz, *Compendium*, pp. 479–88; U.S., Congress, Joint Economic Committee, *Standards for Guiding Monetary Action*, Report of the Joint Economic Committee (Washington D.C.: Government Printing Office, 1968), pp. 16–20.

57. Statement of Thomas Mayer, *Compendium*, p. 465.

58. See, for example, Abba P. Lerner, "Milton Friedman's 'A Program for Monetary Stability': A Review," *Journal of the American Statistical Association* 57 (March 1962): 211–20; reprinted in *Monetary Policy: The Argument from Keynes' Treatise to Friedman,*

ed. William Hamovitch (Boston: D.C. Heath, 1966): 102–17; Jacob Viner, "The Necessary and the Desirable Range of Discretion to Be Allowed to a Monetary Authority," *In Search of a Monetary Constitution*, ed. L.B. Yeager (Cambridge, Mass.: Harvard University Press, 1962), pp. 244–74; Daniel S. Ahearn, *Federal Reserve Policy Reappraised, 1951–1959* (New York and London: Columbia University Press, 1963), pp. 225–33; Paul A. Samuelson, "Reflections on Central Banking," *National Banking Review* 1 (September 1963): 15–28; Charles E. Walker, "Fact and Fiction in Central Banking," *Essays in Monetary Policy in Honor of Elmer Wood*, ed. P.C. Walker (Columbia, Miss.: University of Missouri Press, 1965), pp. 109–29; Lyle E. Gramley, "Guidelines for Monetary Policy—The Case against Simple Rules," *Readings in Money, National Income, and Stabilization Policy*, ed. W.L. Smith and R.L. Teigen (rev. ed.; Homewood, Ill.: Irwin, 1970), pp. 488–95; Erich Schneider, "Automatism or Discretion in Monetary Polilcy," *Banca Nazionale del Lavoro Quarterly Review* 23 (June 1970): 3–19.

59. Ahearn, *Federal Reserve Policy*, p. 226.
60. Friedman, *Program for Monetary Stability*, p. 98.
61. Cf. Samuelson, "Reflections on Central Banking," pp. 17–18.
62. Selden, "Stable Monetary Growth," pp. 347–52.
63. Milton Friedman, "The Lag in Effect of Monetary Policy," *Journal of Political Economy* 69 (October 1961): 447–66.
64. Thomas Mayer, "The Lag in Effect of Monetary Policy: Some Criticisms," *Western Economic Journal* 5 (September 1967): 324–42.
65. Arthur M. Okun, *The Political Economy of Prosperity* (Washington, D.C.: Brookings Institution, 1970), p. 116.
66. Staff Report, *Compendium*, p. 13.
67. Ahearn, *Federal Reserve Policy*, p. 226.
68. Okun, *Political Economy*, p. 116.
69. Viner, "Necessary and Desirable," p. 249.
70. Selden, "Stable Monetary Growth," p. 354.
71. Viner, "Necessary and Desirable," p. 259.
72. Charles R. Whittlesey, "Rules, Discretion, and Central Bankers," *Essays in Money and Banking in Honour of Richard S. Sayers*, ed. Whittlesey and J.S. Wilson (London: Oxford University Press, 1968), pp. 252–65.
73. See for example Shaw, "Monetary Stability," pp. 221–31; Mints, *Monetary Policy*, pp. 139–42; Walker, "Fact and Fiction," pp. 119–22.
74. Friedman, *Program for Monetary Stability*, p. 95.
75. Ibid., pp. 95–98.
76. Martin Bronfenbrenner, "Statistical Tests of Rival Monetary Rules," *Journal of Political Economy* 69 (February 1961): 1–14; Bronfenbrenner, "Statistical Tests of Rival Monetary Rules: Quarterly Data Supplement," *Journal of Political Economy* 69 (December 1961): 621–25. See also George Macesich, "Monetary Policy in the Common Market Countries: Rules versus Discretion," *Weltwirtschaftliches Archiv* 198, 1972, pp. 20–52; George Macesich, *Geldpolitik in einem gemeinsamen europaischen Market* (Money in a European Common Market) (Baden-Baden: Nomos Verlagsgesellschaft, 1972); Macesich and Tsai, *Money in Economic Systems*.
77. Donald P. Tucker, "Bronfenbrenner on Monetary Rules: A Comment," *Journal of Political Economy* 71 (April 1963): 173–79.
78. Ibid., p. 178.
79. Charles Schotta, Jr., "The Performance of Alternative Monetary Rules in Canada, 1927–1961," *National Banking Review* 1 (December 1963): 221–27.
80. Ibid., p. 227.
81. Franco Modigliani, "Some Empirical Tests of Monetary Management and of

Rules versus Discretion," *Journal of Political Economy* 72 (June 1964): 211–45.

    82. Ibid., p. 244.

    83. Richard Attiyeh, "Rules versus Discretion: A Comment," *Journal of Political Economy* 73 (April 1965): 170–72.

    84. Mayer, "Lag in Effect," pp. 331–35.

    85. Ibid., p. 334.

    86. Macesich and Tsai, *Money in Economic Systems*, Chapter 10.

INFLATION ENVIRONMENT

QUANTITY THEORY AND INFLATION: THE MONETARIST VIEW

Monetarists accept the quantity theory that emphasizes the role of money in inflation, with inflation generally defined as a process of continually rising general level of prices or continually falling value of money. They assume a stable demand for real cash balance when prices are expected to be stable. As discussed elsewhere, this is a reasonable theoretical and empirical assumption. The demand for real cash balances is cast as a function of several variables including income or wealth and the real rate of interest that is the opportunity cost of holding real balances.

This is also, more or less, a view that is shared by most Keynesians. They differ, however, in the role given to price expectations. Monetarists explicitly include price expectations in their analysis. Keynesians, on the other hand, assume expectations of zero price change. In effect, monetarists stress monetary factors while Keynesians emphasize nonmonetary phenomena as explanations of inflation.

As discussed in Chapter 3, these differences over the course of inflation are manifested in the manner in which the two theories provide a solution to the problem of the missing price level equation. The Keynesian solution reaches out to sociopolitical and institutional factors. Monetarists turn to the quantity theory of money.

In the quantity theory tradition, monetarists argue that the direction of causation is from monetary expansion to increases in the general level of prices. Others in the Keynesian tradition argue that monetary expansion per se is simply in response to inflationary "cost-push" pressures caused for the most part by nonmonetary sociopolitical factors.[1] For purposes of brevity, the traditional quantity theory will be called "monetarist," while the view that emphasizes sociopolitical factors will be called "Keynesian." Attempts to draw on both traditions shall be called the "eclectic" view of inflation.

In essence, the monetarist view attributes inflation to the increasingly favorable state of demand that permits a rise in the general level of prices. According to this view, inflation occurs whenever the general level of demand for goods and services exceeds available supply at existing prices. The emphasis is placed on changes in the general level of demand rather than on changes in the composition of demand. This emphasis is based on the assumption of reasonable price flexibility and a competitive nature of the economy as a whole. Thus, a change in the composition of demand with no change in its level means that the prices of goods and services that benefit from an increase in demand will rise, while prices of goods and services that suffer from a decline in demand will fall; so on balance, there will tend to be no change in the general level of prices.

A favorable demand-supply situation may appear from the demand side and supply side. Its source will depend on the nature of the changes in the given conditions underlying demand and supply. For instance, a favorable state of demand may be generated from the supply side owing to catastrophes, man-made or natural, and changes in production functions. A decline in the supply of goods and services owing to catastrophes may result in a higher price level until such time as conditions return to normal and prices decline. If we assume catastrophes aside on the basis of their random occurrence, changes in production functions may present sources of favorable state of demand so that price rises are permitted. However, changes in production functions over the years tended to increase and not to decrease supply. The notable exceptions are the supply rendering effects of OPEC price increases in the 1970s. More shall be said about these supply-reducing effects elsewhere.

We are thus left with increases in the level of demand as the most likely source for generation of a favorable demand-supply situation and hence inflation. An increase in the level of demand may occur owing to an increase in the supply of money or to changes in the given conditions underlying the demand for money (for example, an increase in the cost of holding money such as an increase in interest rates and expectations of a future price increase). Of these two sources, the traditionalist or monetarist view is that the most likely source is an increase in the supply of money. There are two main reasons for this view: first, the money supply variable is the most easily manipulated; and second, the historical record tends to support the view that countries that pursue easy money policies also experience rises in the general level of prices.

This relationship between movements of prices and money supply is indicated from readily available data. Table 7.1 provides a cross-country comparison of the rate of money growth and inflation over the 20-quarter period from IV/1975 to IV/1980 for the major industrial nations. The countries are ranked in descending order according to the rate of money growth experienced during the period. If the demand for money is relatively stable across countries, the analysis above predicts a positive relationship between money growth and inflation. This relationship can be clearly identified in Table 7.1. In particular, Italy had the highest rate of inflation; the United Kingdom experienced the second highest growth rates of money and prices, and so forth. In fact, if this comparison is continued, only West Germany violates the ordering of inflation with the rate of money growth. These results are extremely robust when one considers the heterogeneity of this group of countries.

TABLE 7.1.   Money Growth and Inflation in the Major Industrial Nations (IV/1975–IV/1980, percent)

Country	Annual Rates of Money Growth[a]	Annual Rates of Inflation[b]
Italy	20.5	17.1
United Kingdom	12.3	13.7
France	10.0	10.7
West Germany	7.8	4.1
United States	7.5	9.1
Canada	7.5	9.0
Japan	7.2	6.3
Netherlands	6.6	5.8
Switzerland	5.3	2.5

[a]M1 for all countries except the United States, for which M1B is used.

[b]Comsumer price indexes used as a measure of inflation.

Source: D. S. Batten, "Inflation: The Cost Push Myth," Review, Federal Reserve Bank of St. Louis (June/July 1981): 23.

KEYNESIAN THEORIES

The reasoning underlying many of the inflation theories based in the Keynesian tradition may be summarized by the now familiar term "cost-price spiral inflation."[2] Although there are many variations on the theme, their common thread is the assertion that the pricing mechanism is becoming progressively less sensitive. Whatever the alleged "cause" of inflation, the monetary preconditions must be satisfied so that the distinction among theories in the Keynesian tradition is between different mechanisms of inflation. Three variations on the theme, however, appear sufficiently important from a public policy viewpoint to warrant consideration. One is that union pressures for wage increases are the causal element in inflation. The second is that oligopolistic sectors administer prices and so are the causal element in inflation. The third incorporates elements of the first two and tangentially places the blame for inflation on the existence of both unions and oligopolistic industries.

The first variation argues that unions are responsible for inflation in that they fail to recognize that wage increases that go beyond overall productivity gains are inconsistent with stable prices. Thus, the argument is that unions push up wages, which raises costs and prices. In order to avoid a logical fallacy, the more sophisticated argue that since the monetary authorities are committed to a policy of full employment, they will expand the money supply so as to make possible the sale of the old output at the new price level.

The second variation argues that prices are set in a different way in those sectors of the economy that are composed of many firms than they are in industries where there are a few major producers.[3] Prices set by oligopolistic industries are "administered" so that they are excellent conductors of inflationary pressure. They are relatively immune to traditional anti-inflationary policies in that their prices, having once reached a high level, are stickier in declining than those of competitive industries when demand declines.

The third variation claims that both unions and oligopolistic industries are primarily responsible for inflation. Unions, so the argument goes, lodge themselves in oligopolistic industries and share in the "spoils" derived from the product side.[4] Thus, unions in such industries may take advantage of the inelastic or expanding demand conditions on the product market to obtain higher wages without fear that the entry of new firms will reduce union wage gains. According to this variation, the product market permitting, the oligopolist will grant a higher wage rate as a means of avoiding a more costly strike. Moreover, in contradistinction to more traditional views, such unions need not be old craft unions; they may be the new industrial unions that economists have tended to treat as relatively powerless in setting excessive wages. It is for this reason, presumably, that the advent of new industrial unions, when coupled with oligopolistic industries, has changed our economic system so greatly as to largely frustrate attempts to control inflation along traditional lines. In effect, the argument implicitly assumes that the pricing mechanism is becoming progressively less fluid or "automatic."

In place of traditional methods for coping with inflation, which some Keynesians consider largely ineffective or inappropriate, they advocate a "direct" assault on the problem of inflation.[5] Although such an assault may take many forms, three seem to be dominant. First, government should resort to "moral suasion" to induce business and labor to exercise their power in a socially desirable (noninflationary) way. Second, government could increase the degree of competition in the marketplace by a more vigorous enforcement of antitrust legislation. Some people argue that since labor unions are monopolies, they should also be subject to antitrust legislation. Third, government can participate more actively in or control the price-and-wage-setting process. Needless to say, these forms of control are not mutually exclusive.

Eclectics view the discussion of whether inflation is "demand-pulled" or "cost-pushed" as analogous to "Which came first, the chicken or the egg?" They attempt to synthesize, in varying degrees of sophistication, the two views of inflation. Of the several syntheses available, we shall consider only two. One, which draws heavily from the Keynesian tradition, turns on the assertion that we cannot empirically isolate inflation by types.[6] The other, which draws heavily from the monetarist tradition, asserts that we cannot conceptually isolate inflation by types.[7]

The synthesis that draws heavily from the Keynesian tradition asserts that it is impossible empirically to test for the existence of leads or lags from the cost or demand side, which is necessary if we are to classify inflation by types. For such a purpose, we need minute data on the cost and demand sides. Since such data presumably are not available, we cannot meaningfully classify inflation by types.

Even if such data were available, they would shed little light on the "causes" of inflation. Prices and wages, according to this view, are not set in the traditional manner. They are set with reference to some markup over the cost of living. Accordingly, inflation is generated whenever labor and management attempt to get more than 100 percent of the selling price. This is an impossible situation. Yet, it is on the very impossibility of the situation that the continuing process of inflation depends. Thus, each party increases the part he tries to take by increasing wages or by increasing prices. Since together they cannot succeed in getting more than 100 percent of the selling price, wages and prices are continually raised, thereby generating a continuing process of inflation. The process of inflation, though it may originate in the noncompetitive sector where market power is sufficient to raise prices and wages, will "spill over" into the competitive sectors, thereby gaining momentum.[8]

This may occur, it is argued, either from the demand side or cost side or both. Since the prices of the products and services of the noncompetitive sector rise, there will be a change in the composition of demand. Consumers will switch their demand to the products and services produced by the competitive sector so that prices rise in this sector. There is excess demand in the competitive sector and a deficiency of demand in the noncompetitive sector. The deficiency of demand will result in some unemployment in the noncompetitive sector. Owing to factor immobility, however, unemployment in this sector will not cause wages or prices to fall, so that unemployment persists. Attempts by the government to remove excess demand along traditional lines so as to check the overall price rise, while removing excess demand in the competitive sector, increases still further the unemployment in the noncompetitive sector.

The same situation will prevail even if the spillover occurs from the cost side. Thus, the spillover will occur because wage or price rises in the noncompetitive sector are signals for labor and employers in the competitive sector to do the same in order to protect, if not increase, their relative income shares. Accordingly, the government is confronted with the dilemma of either inflation or unemployment.

The other view, which borrows heavily from the traditional position, argues that we cannot even conceptually identify inflation by types, much less classify them empirically. In essence, this view turns on the proposition that while it is obvious that demand conditions influence costs, it is equally obvious that one cannot separate out the portion of the cost increase attributable to increased demand. Traditional monetarists and Keynesians accordingly have erred in attempting to establish rigid links between types of inflation and public policy.

The eclectic views essentially do not consider as practical the argument that the monetary authority, by refusing to expand the money supply, could "nip in the bud" an inflationary spiral.[9] The bases for such an assertion are, first, that velocity would increase, thereby frustrating the efforts of the monetary authority; second, even if velocity could no longer increase, the monetary authority could overcome the strong institutional forces making for rigidity in the pricing system only at the expense of a possible serious depression.

In order to control inflation, therefore, steps should be taken to remove institutional and other rigidities from within our economic system. It is only then that the control of inflation along more traditional lines would have effect.

We may turn now to an appraisal of the above views of inflation by drawing both on economic theory and on recent experience. Theoretical and empirical evidence, though not completely inconsistent with alternative views, tends to support traditional monetarists views of inflation.

The fundamental discovery of those de-emphasizing the traditional view of inflation is that prices and wages go up when somebody raises them.[10] There is general agreement as to the facts. We take it to be true that most sellers would always like to raise their prices. We also take it to be true that sellers will never raise their prices without limit. What are the limits and circumstances under which sellers will raise their prices? It is precisely to the answering of this question that economists have directed their labors.

The fruit of this labor has produced the consensus that the state of demand will set the limit and the circumstances under which sellers can raise or lower prices.[11] The state of demand permitting sellers can raise their prices without being penalized by a loss of sales and income and so they decide to "raise" prices. If, on the other hand, the state of demand permits a rise in prices only at the expense of losing net income, sellers will not raise prices. There is thus no conflict between the view that prices rise because somebody raises them and the view that somebody decides to raise prices because the state of demand permits such a rise without losing sales and income.[12]

The views that de-emphasize the traditional approach to inflation do not provide an alternate theory of inflation that is independent of the state of demand. Although not new, they gained currency in the postwar period when a favorable state of demand was assured by the existence of large liquid asset holdings by individuals and firms.[13] The assurance of a favorable state of demand permitted price increases without the loss of incomes, and so sellers decided to raise prices. In effect, the decision to raise prices is simply the form whereby a disequilibrium situation was brought into balance. In the absence of a favorable state of demand, however, such a decision may result in distortions in the relative price structure, or a one-time increase in the general level of prices coupled with a loss of sales and increased unemployment.[14] There is nothing in the process whereby sellers decide to raise prices that will assure a favorable state of demand.[15] It is essentially for this reason that these views have descriptive but not analytical validity.

Consider the view that unions are responsible for inflation in that they push up wages. In support of this view, evidence is presented that unit labor costs (in money forms) have risen faster than average productivity. Needless to say, in a period of inflation this observation is a truism. It does not help us to tell whether wages pushed up prices or demand pulled up wages.[16]

Rees has quite correctly pointed out that in the absence of a favorable state of demand, unions can cause either shifts in the relative wage structure, or a one-time increase in the general level of wages, together with increased unemployment. The flexibility of nonunion wages determines what will actually occur.[17] On the other hand, if the state of demand is favorable, union wage increases can be followed by inflation and continued full employment.

An important but unfortunately neglected point is that a necessary (but not sufficient) condition for unions to set off a "wage-price spiral" is that they need more than power to raise wages: they must have increasing power to do so. As Milton Friedman has noted:

> The existence of a strong union in one area simply means that wage rates in that area will be higher relative to wage rates elsewhere, and employment in that area lower relative to employment elsewhere than wages and employment would have been in the absence of a union . . . . Increasingly strong unions not simply strong unions are a necessary (though not sufficient) conditions for setting the wage-price spiral in motion.[18]

There is little serious scholarly evidence to substantiate the view that unions are becoming increasingly strong. Indeed, to judge from the size of union membership roles and recent unfavorable legislation, that power may be decreasing.

The above limitations similarly restrict the usefulness of the eclectic view that inflation is triggered and generated whenever labor and management attempt to get more than 100 percent of the selling price. It too depends on the existence or assurance of a favorable state of demand. At the same time, each party must be increasing its power as a necessary condition for setting off the wage-price spiral.

The positions that argue that union demands spillover into competitive sectors and so cause wages and prices to rise in this sector also depend, contrary to many of their adherents, on the existence of a favorable state of demand.[19] This state of demand occurs when union employers bid away more and better workers from other employers, and so lead these employers to raise wages in order to hold their employees.[20] Again, there is no conflict between the view that wages and prices rise because somebody raises them and the view that somebody raises them because a favorable state of demand for such a rise exists.

If the state of demand is not favorable to such a rise, a very different story will unfold and we may just as well talk in terms of a "spill-in" effect (movement of labor from union to nonunion activities). If owing to higher wages union employers curtail employment, the movement of general wages will depend upon two conditions. First, if wages elsewhere are flexible downward, the union workers will spill into nonunion activities and so nonunion wages will tend to fall. The movement in the general level of wages, if any, will depend, as Rees notes, "on the precise shapes of demand schedules of union and nonunion employers.[21] Second, if wages elsewhere are not flexible downward, the general wage level will rise but the resulting unemployment will check any further rise. Under these circumstances, nonunion employers are very unlikely to repeat the wage-rise experiment of union employers.

Consider now the view that oligopolies and monopolies, by administering prices, cause inflation. As noted previously, the assertion is that administered prices are more rigid than competitive prices, and so they are excellent conductors of inflationary pressures.

However, many economists, most notably Martin Bailey, argue that administered prices are not as rigid as they seem.[22] Insofar as these prices are rigid, their role in inflation is misunderstood. According to this interpretation, administered prices during periods when the state of demand is favorable do not rise as rapidly as competitive prices; so in effect, they may well be below levels that would clear the market, thereby creating waiting lists and gray markets. When administered prices do rise, however, they are apt to do so in large jumps, thereby attracting widespread attention and charges that they are responsible for inflation.

The converse argument—that administered prices are rigid on the downward side and so respond more slowly to an unfavorable state of demand than competitive prices—also leaves much to be desired. In the first instance, the evidence used to support this assertion is far from conclusive. Thus, the usual evidence cited is that after World War II, during periods (particularly 1957–58) when the state of demand was unfavorable, output and employment declined but prices, as judged by price indexes, did not. An examination of the past record, however, suggests that this is not a unique experience. Of the seven (other than 1957–58) recessions since 1920, in four of them the consumer price index rose in the early months.[23] Furthermore, these price indexes, among other limitations, do not pick up price changes that take the form of special discounts or other informal price concessions, such as freight absorption or advertising allowances. The effect is an understatement of actual price changes, and so overstates the actual degree of rigidity.[24] In the second instance, it should be noted that insofar as the administered price argument throws the blame for inflation on large corporations, available studies suggest little if any relation between concentration ratios and price rigidity.[25]

In the view of many economists, the source of price rigidity is not the market sector of the economy but, ironically, the government sector.[26] It is this sector that administers rigid prices through the medium of various regulatory agencies, price support programs, minimum wages, agricultural marketing programs, support of "fair trade," and restrictions on both domestic and foreign trade. Such policies are largely inconsistent with attempts to remove monopoly elements from the economy.

According to the view that incorporates unions on the factor side and oligopolies on the product market side, "large wage increases won by strategically placed unions may lead either to (a) distortion of the wage structure if other wages lag or (b) rising costs and upward pressure on prices if other wages rise equivalently," or a combination of the two. The net effect will be that the "economy will move between episodes of price plateaus (accompanied by a stretching of the wage structure) succeeded by periods of rising prices."[27]

But this view, as with others that de-emphasize the traditional approach to inflation, contributes nothing essentially new to our understanding of inflation. The traditional view does not deny that unions may "distort" wages or that unions may share in monopoly spoils. As noted elsewhere, in the absence of a favorable state of demand this may be one of the effects of a union wage rise. As the above view claims, "the precise proportion between wage-distorting and cost-inflationary forces depends upon the economic climate—in particular upon the level of national income." It simply re-asserts the traditional view with its emphasis on the favorable state of demand.[28]

The interesting point about this view is the implicit assertion that new industrial unions and oligopolies have, apparently, sufficiently changed the economic structure so that the pricing system lacks fluidity. Little evidence other than casual empiricism is offered in support of the above view.[29] Indeed, such evidence as we do have supports the opposite view—that the pricing mechanism is not becoming progressively less sensitive.[30]

Some consider the distinction between demand-pull and cost-push inflation useless. One view asserts that we cannot empirically identify inflation by types.[31] This view apparently turns on the question of the timing of demand-pull and cost-push types of inflation; that is, on the identification of the lead and lag series. If the inflation is of the demand-pull type, then presumably demand should lead the increase in costs. If it is cost-push, then costs should lead demand.

To put the distinction between the two types of inflation in this manner is to hopelessly confuse the issue. One would be hard-put indeed to identify the existence of leads and lags in the various relevant series. The consensus, however, seems to be that the essential difference between the two types of inflation is to be found not in the timing of the various series, but rather in their sensitivity to changes in demand.[32]

Thus, if the struggle to obtain more than 100 percent of the selling price is sensitive to sales losses and unemployment, then it is very unlikely that the struggle will continue in the absence of a favorable state of demand. On the other hand, if in the face of an unfavorable state of demand the struggle is such that substantial losses in sales and unemployment are the consequence, it does make sense to talk in terms of types of inflation.

Another view is that we cannot even conceptually classify inflation by type.[33] This view is interesting in that at times it is similar to the argument that raged in the latter part of the nineteenth century over the determination of value. The view states that we cannot identify that part of the price rise attributed to a cost increase and that part attributed to an increase in demand. The argument was settled, of course, when it occurred to economists that "each blade in a pair of scissors cuts." The analogy between the controversies breaks down because this view claims too much. Economists have long held that although each blade cuts, it make sense to distinguish between the blades. Changes in the price level may occur with shifts in either the supply schedules or the demand schedules or both.

To argue that we cannot conceptually identify which part of a price rise is attributed to costs and which to demand is to assert that we are always in a position whereby both schedules shift simultaneously and by about the same amount. It would not be difficult to conjure up cases in which either demand or supply is the dominant element in price rises.

Although arguments against traditional methods of controlling inflation take many forms, they do possess a common thread: we cannot expect high levels of employment and output and at the same time maintain stability in the general level of prices. This is the now familiar unemployment versus inflation dilemma. Owing to the lack of fluidity in our pricing system we cannot, so the argument goes, attempt seriously to use traditional methods against inflation because their use would simply add to unemployment. Inflation, accordingly, is the necessary price we must pay for avoiding unemployment and, presumably, for maintaining high levels of output.[34]

This represents another aspect of inflation views drawing on the Keynesian tradition. It attempts to rationalize the relation of wage and price movements to aggregate demand and supply through the Phillips curve, which argues a link between variations in employment (capacity utilization) and price changes. A critical question for this analysis is whether adjustments are made in money or real terms. The Phillips curve analysis is discussed in detail below.

There are a number of reasons why the lack-of-pricing-fluidity argument falls short of providing an adequate explanation. In the first place, less than a third of the workers are organized into unions, and many of these are in weak unions. As Rees and others have noted, even a strong union may temper its wage demands when confronted with the existence or possibility of unemployment. Furthermore, the idea of the spillover effect, whereby unions set a pattern for wage demands for nonunionized workers, is not independent of the state of demand. In the second place, the commitment by government to shore up the employment wall is not a commitment in particular occupations. Individuals and organizations are still free to price themselves out of the market. Finally, the argument tacitly assumes the existence of a period when prices and wages were flexible, and then proceeds to argue that the situation has now changed and prices and wages are no longer flexible—at least not in the downside. But we do not have studies that indicate that prices and wages were more flexible in the past than they are now.[35] Indeed, such studies as are available do not support the contention that the pricing mechanism is becoming progressively less sensitive; however, they do suggest continuing fluidity.

INFLATION TAX

Inflation is a method for raising revenues by a special kind of tax. This is a tax on the real money holdings, or, in the technical jargon of the economist, on the real cash balances of individuals.

When a government is either too weak or is unwilling on grounds of political expediency to enact adequate tax programs and to administer them effectively, it resorts to inflation as a method of raising revenue. This tax is often appealing because it does not require detailed legislation and can be administered very simply. All that is required is to spend the newly created money. The resulting inflation automatically imposes a tax on the real money holdings or cash balances of individuals. The tax rate is the rate of depreciation in the real value of money, which is equal to the rate of rise in prices. The revenue (in real terms) is the product of this base and the rate. The money-issuing authorities "collect" all the revenue. When prices rise in greater proportion than the quantity of money (demand deposits, time deposits, and currency in public hands), that is, when the real value of cash balances declines, part of the revenue goes to reduce the real value of the outstanding money supply. At the same time, inflation also reduces the real value of the principal and interest charges of debt fixed in money or nominal terms. Thus, total revenue for a period of time is the sum of two factors: first, the real value of new money issued per period of time; and second, the reduction in outstanding monetary liabilities, equal to the decline per period of time in the real value of cash balances. It should be noted, however, that the money-issuing authorities do not set the tax rate directly. They set the rate at which they increase the money supply, and this rate determines the tax rate through the willingness of individuals to hold and not spend the additional money supply.

Institutions other than the government have money-issuing powers. Insofar as these institutions exercise these powers, they share in some of the revenue from the tax, even though the initiating factor is government creation of money. However, in past inflations, these other institutions for the most part largely dissipated the revenue from their share of the tax. Banks, for example, largely dissipated their share by making loans at minimal rates of interest that did not take full account of the subsequent rise in prices. Thus, the real rate of interest received was on the average below the real return that could be obtained on capital. The revenue dissipated went to the borrowers.

The revenue received by the government consequently depends on the tax base, the tax rate, and the fraction of the revenue that goes either to institutions such as banks or to their borrowers. However, a higher tax rate will not yield a proportionately higher revenue because the tax base, or the level of real cash balances, will decline in response to a higher rate. As an increasing number of people begin to believe in the inevitableness of inflation, their money holdings will ultimately decline more than in proportion to the rise in tax rate, so that a higher rate will yield less revenue. It is at this point that inflation enters into a transition between the "creeping" and "galloping" varieties.

The productivity of taxation through inflation has been examined by Phillip Cagan. In his study of seven hyperinflations (galloping inflations), Cagan finds that the actual share of national income procured for different governments that used inflation as a means of taxation was 3 to about 15 percent, except in Imperial Rusia, which had an unusually low percentage of 0.5.[36] In almost all cases the revenue collected by the inflationary tax was lower on the average than could have been collected by other means of taxation, given that the respective countries had a stable growth in the money supply.

PHILLIPS CURVE

The trade-off between inflation and unemployment attracted considerable attention in the 1950s and 1960s. An article by A.W. Phillips appears to establish an empirical relation linking unemployment and the rate of change of money wage rates over almost a century in the United Kingdom.[37] Phillips fitted a curve to observations of the percent of unemployment and the percentage rate of change of money wage rates per year in the United Kingdom. Separate curves are also fitted for different subperiods 1861 to 1957. This has become known as "Phillips's curve." Its general appearance is presented in Figure 7.1. The interpretation of Phillips's curve suggests that money wage rates increased more rapidly at low levels of unemployment than at high levels of unemployment.

For the most part, Phillips's curve's contributions are in the Keynesian tradition and represent attempts to link real magnitudes and the rate of change in prices to their historically determined level. Subsequent studies substituted the rate of change of the price level for the rate of change of money wage rates. They purported to show that price stability had a calculable cost in unemployment and a low level of unemployment had a similar cost in inflation. Indeed, the issue spilled over into policymaking with the status of a near law. Paul Samuelson and Robert Solow argued, shortly after the publication of Phillips's study, that

> in order to have wages increase at no more than the 2 ½ percent per annum characteristic of our productivity growth, the American economy would seem, on the basis of twentieth century and postwar experience, to have to undergo something like 5 or 6 percent of the civilian labor force's being unemployed. That much unemployed would appear to be the cost of price stability in the years immediately ahead. . . . In order to achieve the nonperfectionist's goal of high enough output to give us no more than 3 percent unemployment, the price index might have to rise by as much as 4 or 5 percent, per year. That much price rise would seem to be the necessary cost of high employment and production in the years immediately ahead.[38]

Subsequent events, however, cast doubt on the relationship uncovered by Phillips's curve. By the end of the 1960s it became clear

Figure 7.1
Phillips' Curves

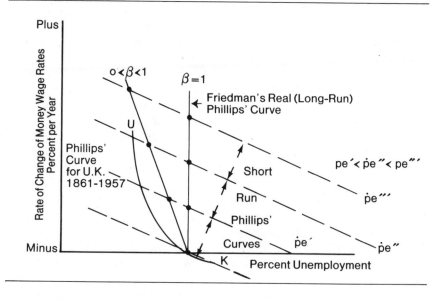

that ever higher rates of inflation are required to keep employment high. Albert Rees and Mary T. Hamilton report in their study of the U.S. experience over the period from 1900 to 1957 that

> the construction of a plausible Phillips Curve from annual data for a long period is a *tour de force* somewhat comparable to writing the Lord's Prayer on the head of a pin, rather than as a guide to policy. This is because it is highly probable that the relationship is changed during the period, because the data are of poor quality for much of the early part of the period, and because of the large changes in some of the variables that take place during the course of a calendar year and are blurred in annual data. If we are making policy recommendations we should prefer to test them on an analysis of monthly or quarterly data for the post War period . . . the authors of Phillips Curves would do well to label them conspicuously "Unstable—Apply with Extreme Care."[39]

These doubts are underscored by other studies as well, most notably by Friedman.[40] Essentially, if workers can correctly forecast current and future prices, there should be no relationship between the ratio of wages to prices and the rate of inflation. For instance, an increase in all prices and wages that leaves the ratio of wages to prices unchanged does not alter anyone's decision to employ more or less labor. In effect, when everyone's expectations about current and future prices are correct, unemployment will come to rest at a "natural rate." Fluctuations around the natural rate are the consequence of incorrect expectations about current and future events. Moreover, the natural rate of unemployment may itself change over a longer period. Thus, in the 1950s and early 1960s it may have been about 4 percent. It is likely that various institutional changes occurring since then may have pushed up the natural rate. Energy and raw material price increases during the 1970s may well have served to reinforce the movement.

Friedman and others point out that the relationship between unemployment and inflation depends on how individuals form these expectations about future inflation. If people believe that prices will rise at, say, 3 percent per year, any inflation above that level will be underestimated, and this will push the unemployment rate below its normal or natural rate. Conversely, any rate of inflation below 3 percent per year would push the unemployment rate above its natural rate. So long as the expected rate of inflation remains rigidly at 3 percent per year, there will appear to be a stable trade-off between inflation and unemployment.

For the 1950s and up to the mid-1960s, a 3 percent inflation rate is probably a reasonable expectation that would not have led to large forecasting errors. Since the mid-1960s the average rate of inflation is closer to 7-plus percent. A rigidly held 3 percent expectation of inflation will lead to very large forecasting errors. Moreover, deviations from the average rate of inflation are no longer random as in the earlier period. Their pattern is very different. Deviations from the average rate are now highly correlated. If one year's rate of inflation is over 7 percent, the following year's rate of inflation will probably be over 7 percent as well. In effect, when inflation rates are correlated, past rates of inflation contain a lot of information about future inflation rates. One consequence of this change in the pattern of inflation rates is that people now appear to use a weighted average of past rates of inflation to forecast future inflation. In effect, people no longer hold to rigidly fixed expectations regarding future inflation rates. To do otherwise is no longer rational.

This change in the way people form expectations undermines the long-run trade-off between inflation and unemployment. Thus, an increase in the rate of inflation will not permanently reduce the unemployment rate since people will revise their forecasts of inflation upward on the basis of past inflationary experience. As expectations of inflation adjust to the new situation, unemployment rises back to its normal or natural rate. If unemployment is to be kept below the natural rate, the actual rate of inflation must exceed the expected rate of inflation. Since expectations eventually adjust upward as a result of past inflation, an accelerating rate of inflation is required to maintain the gap between actual and expected inflation. To take account of the problem, Phillips's curve incorporates inflationary expectations; it is now called "expectations-augmented Phillips's curve analyses."

The requirement that prices rise faster and faster so as to maintain unemployment below the natural rate has come to be known as "the accelerationist hypothesis." It represents a significant change in emphasis from earlier formulations of Phillips's curve analyses. Earlier studies focus on the rate of change of prices as a function of the level of unemployment as well as other variables. The expectations-augmented Phillips's curve analysis makes unemployment a function of changes in the rate of change of prices and price expectations.[41]

We may present the above analysis more formally. Figure 7.1 presents short-run and long-run Phillips's curves. Two assumptions underlie the explanations offered by Phillips's curve. One is that even though workers and employers adjust to inflation equally rapidly, they have different pieces of information upon which to react. Employers are able to react more rapidly since they have fewer pieces to react to in determining whether or not it is profitable to take on additional workers. Typically, employers are concerned with a relatively limited range of prices of the goods and services with which their individual enterprises are associated. Workers typically take into account the general level of prices in determining their real wage and thus their reaction to price changes. The second assumption is that the natural rate of unemployment is basically stable and predictable, though it may change owing to changes in its basic determinants. These determinants include the structural characteristics of the commodity markets, including market imperfections, stochastic variability in demands and supplies, the cost of gathering information about job vacancies and labor availabilities, the costs of unemployment and mobility, and perhaps also upon the regional dispersion of employment. Indeed, the natural rate itself may be influenced by inflation which impairs the economy's resource allocative mechanism. Estimates of the natural rate of unemployment are between 5 and 6 percent for the United States according to James Tobin.[42] Estimates for other countries appear to be lower owing in part to differences in measuring unemployment and in the structure of the respective labor markets.[43]

Mathematically, the expectations-augmented Phillips's curve can be stated as

$$W = f(U) + \beta P^e \qquad (1)$$

where: W = rate of wage change
U = unemployment
P^e = expected rate of inflation.

Monetarists argue that $\beta = 1$ so that the expected rate of wage increase is equal to a component of excess demand plus the expected rate of inflation. Phillips's curve is vertical. The rate of increase in money wages is equal to the expected rate of inflation, if we have no excess demand. In the special case where the expected rate of inflation is zero, wage inflation would also be zero. Inflation in the monetarist view is the result of excess demand propelled by excessive monetary expansion and expectations regarding future price increases.

According to the monetarists, there is no long-run trade-off between unemployment and inflation. A short-run trade-off may be had, but only at the expense of faster inflation as postulated by the accelerationist hypothesis. This assumes, of course, that inflation is fully anticipated. If it is not, the coefficient β in equation (1) would be less than one. In this case, the slope of the long-run Phillips's curve is less than vertical, but steeper than in the short run. There is, thus, some permanent trade-off between unemployment and inflation in the long run, but less so than in the short run. If $\beta = 0$, the short run and long run would be the same.

To judge from recent studies, the empirical evidence offers support to the monetarist view that $\beta = 1$. There appears to be no trade-off between unemployment and inflation in the long run. Not everyone is convinced by the evidence, however. Indeed, Robert Solow (1969) produces results for the United Kingdom for $\beta = 0.4$; S. J. Turnovsky (1972) presents results for Canada for β not significantly different from one; R. B. Cross and D. Laidler (1975) report on results for 20 countries and find no evidence of a long-run trade-off for any country.[44]

In Chapter 2 we discussed the monetarist view of interest rates. It too distinguishes between nominal and real interest rates, which are determined by a multiplicity of factors traditionally summarized in productivity and thrift. The importance of price expectations is emphasized, as in the expectations-augmented Phillips's curve.

Mathematically, the relationship can be expressed as

$$r = i + p^e \qquad (2)$$

where r = market or nominal rate of interest
    i = real rate of interest
    p^e = expected rate of inflation.

In equilibrium, the real rate of interest is determined by real factors largely independent of monetary changes. During transitional periods, which can be quite long, changes in the money supply cause real rates of interest to change owing to slow adjustment of actual and expected rates of inflation to monetary changes. Recent studies support the relationship that inflation expectations play an important role in the determination of interest rates.[45] It is in fact a relationship underscored by Irving Fisher more than half a century ago.[46]

RATIONAL EXPECTATIONS

Explanations of Phillips's curve that focus on peoples' expectations of inflation owe much to Milton Friedman, Edmund S. Phelps, an earlier article by John F. Muth, and indeed even earlier contributions of Frank H. Knight and Irving R. Fisher.[47] The rational-expectations hypothesis is perhaps best understood in the context of our discussion of the expectations-augmented Phillips's curve. We noted that workers appear to adjust their expectations to inflation somewhat slower than employers. This delay on the part of workers produces a change in the unemployment rate from the natural rate and thus produces the real effects.

Now suppose that workers adjust their expectations without delay. Under these circumstances there will be no real effects. Wages and prices would increase simultaneously as a result of the new expectations. The real wage rate would remain constant and the unemployment rate would remain at the natural rate. There is, in effect, no trade-off. The rational-expectations hypothesis argues that this rapid adjustment in expectations may well be the case most of the time.

Monetarists have an affinity for the rational-expectations hypothesis. Instead of basing the formation of expectations of price level changes on past changes alone, monetarists focus on the rate of change of money supply as the most important element in the rational-expectations hypothesis. Accordingly, money supply changes that are not part of the trend in money supply growth and are not predictable lead to unexpected changes in the money supply. Such unexpected changes in the money supply lead to changes in such real variables as unemployment and output, among others. The argument is similar to the expectations-augmented Phillips's curve.

A major problem exists in assessing the credibility of the idea of rational expectations. According to some economists, it is the apparent lack of details on how one goes about quantifying the crucial learning curve for economic decisionmakers that takes into account their expectations of future prices rather than simply relying on extrapolation of past experience. In fact, Robert E. Lucas, Jr., one of its founders, doubts that rational expectations can ever be used to develop mathematically quantitative forecasts.

The restrictive monetary policy aspects of rational expectations have not been fully explored—possibly because the symmetrical aspect is not taken seriously by either the public or the government. Nonetheless, the idea of rational expectations is consistent with monetarist ideas. Both views argue against discretionary monetary policy; the monetarists because the stimulative effects are found to be lagging too far behind any action taken, and the rational expectationists because stimulative actions are believed to be self-defeating.

In any case, the impact of these ideas on central bankers and the public generally may mean that future changes in monetary policy will be less than in the past. In effect, monetary policy may not be as manipulative as some people in the Keynesian tradition believe.[48]

NOTES

1. These views are also highlighted in the papers submitted by economists and others in U.S. Congress, Joint Economic Committee, *The Relationship of Prices to Economic Stability and Growth, Compendium,* March 1958 (thereafter called *Compendium*) and U.S. Congress, Joint Economic Committee, *Staff Report on Employment, Growth and Price Levels,* December 24, 1959 (hereafter called *Staff Report*).

For various emphases on these views, see for example Yossef A. Attiyeh, "Wage-Price Spiral versus Demand Inflation: United States, 1949–1955" (Ph.D. diss., University of Chicago, December 1959); Albert Rees, "Do Unions Cause Inflation?" *Journal of Law and Economics* (October 1959): 84–94, and "Price Level Stability and Economic Policy," *Compendium*; Milton Friedman, "Current Critical Issues in Wage Theory and Price," Industrial Relations Research Association, Proceedings of the *Eleventh Annual Meeting,* Chicago, *Illinois,* 1959, and "The Supply of Money and Changes in Prices and Output," *Compendium*; Martin J. Bailey, "Administered Prices in the American Economy," *Compendium*; Walter Morton, "Trade Unionism, Full Employment and Inflation," *American Economic Review* 11 (March 1950): 13–40. This list is by no means complete, but it does give the flavor of the debate in the late 1950s and 1960s. See also J. R. Barth and J. T. Bennett, "Cost-Push versus Demand-Pull Inflation: Some Empirical Evidence," *Journal of Money, Credit and Banking* (August 1975); S. Lustgarten, *Industrial Concentration and Inflation* (Washington D.C.: AEI, 1975); D. S. Batten, "Inflation: The Cost-Push Myth," *Review,* Federal Reserve Bank of St. Louis, June/July 1981, pp. 20–26.

2. See Note 1 above.

3. See Martin J. Bailey's discussion on this view in *Compendium* and William J. Baumol's discussion in *Compendium* of J. K. Galbraith's "Market Structure and Stabilization."

4. See for example James R. Schlesinger, "Market Structure, Union Power, and Inflation," *Southern Economic Journal* (January 1959): 269–312.

5. Emmette S. Redford, "Potential Public Policies to Deal with Inflation Caused by Market Power," Study Paper No. 10 for *Staff Report*.

6. Gardner Ackley, "A Third Approach to the Analysis and Control of Inflation," *Compendium* and Abba P. Lerner, "Inflationary Depression and the Regulation of Administered Prices," *Compendium*.

7. William G. Bowen, "Cost Inflation versus Demand Inflation: A Useful Distinction?" *Southern Economic Journal* 26 (January 1960): 199–206.

8. Economic Research Department, *The Mechanics of Inflation* (Washington, D.C.: Chamber of Commerce of the United States, 1958), pp. 32, 37.

9. Ackley, *Compendium*; Lerner, *Compendium*; and Bowen, "Cost Inflation versus Demand Inflation."

10. That this idea as well as the reasoning underlying the cost-push theme was familiar as far back as at least the sixteenth century is indicated in the following quotation: "During the sixteenth century when prices were consistently rising because of an influx of gold from America, Bishop Lotimer (1548) put the blame on 'land lordes and rent raisers, step-lordes, unnatural lordes,' when it was the landowners who were being expropriated by the rise in prices because of long term leases." Morton, "Trade Unionism," p. 24.

11. See for example the following papers in the *Compendium*: Herbert Stein, "A General View of Inflation"; Bailey, "Administered Prices in the American Economy;" George L. Bach, "How Important Is Price Stability in Stable Economic Growth"; Baumol, "Price Behavior Stability and Growth"; Lerner, "Inflationary Depression and the Regulation of Administered Prices."

12. Stein, "General View of Inflation," p. 667..

13. According to John G. Gurley: "There was a tremendous growth of liquid assets during World War II . . . they rose from $95 billion in 1939 to almost $260 billion in 1946. U.S. Government savings bonds easily had the highest rate of growth during this period, followed by the money supply (demand deposits adjusted and currency outside banks), which tripled. There were roughly a doubling of time deposits, savings and loan shares. Smaller percentage gains were recorded for policy reserves and mutual savings deposits. . . . From this very high level, liquid assets continued to grow during the post war period reaching $430 billion in 1958. However, their annual rate of growth was lower in the post war period than in the war period."

14. Rees, "Do Unions Cause Inflation?" p. 68.

15. Ibid., p. 89.

16. Indeed, on the basis of existing evidence the *Staff Report* (p. 141) concludes that demand forces were the dominant explanation of the upward thrust of wages in the period before 1946–58.

17. Rees, "Do Unions Cause Inflation?" p. 88. The *Staff Report*, with regard to unionization and wage changes, finds no generally applicable relationship (p. 149). See especially Table 5-13, p. 148.

18. Milton Friedman, "Current Critical Issues in Wage Theory and Practice," in Proceedings of the Eleventh Annual Meeting of the Industrial Relations Research Association 1959, p. 213. See also Attiyeh, "Wage-Price Spiral," especially Chapter 4.

19. "Employers in less productive industries are caught in a price-cost squeeze—a

'spillover' of wage demands based on patterns set where productivity is rising more rapidly. Unless expensive monetary-fiscal policies allow these prices to rise, unemployment will result." *Mechanics of Inflation* (Washington, D.C.; Research Department, U.S. Chamber of Commerce, 1958.), p. 32.

20. Ibid., pp. 32, 37.

21. Rees, "Do Unions Cause Inflation?" p. 90.

22. Bailey, "Administered Prices and Inflation," *Compendium*.

23. Rees, "Do Unions Cause Inflation?" p. 91.

24. Bailey, *Compendium*; and Harold Wolozin, "Inflation and the Price Mechanism," *Journal of Political Economy* (October 1959) 67: 463–75.

25. Bailey, *Compendium*.

26. Ibid.

27. Schlesinger, op cit., pp. 309–10. Schlesinger uses as his case in point the steel industry.

28. Ibid., p. 310. See also *Staff Report*, pp. 141, 158–60.

29. See Note 27.

30. Wolozin, "Inflation and Price Mechanism," pp. 474–75.

31. The clearest statement emphasizing this view is contained in Ackley, *Compendium*.

32. Charles L. Schultz, "Recent Inflation in the United States," Study Paper No. 1 for the *Staff Report*.

33. The best statement perhaps is contained in Bowen, "Cost Inflation versus Demand Inflation," pp. 199–206.

34. See Lerner's discussion of this point in *Compendium*, p. 261.

35. Some insight into price flexibility in the nineteenth-century U.S. economy is provided in Macesich, *Political Economy of Money*, Chapter 5.

36. These occurred in Austria, October 1921 to August 1922; in Germany, August 1922 to July 1923; in Greece, November 1943 to August 1944; in Hungary, March 1923 to February 1924, and again in August 1945 to February 1946; in Poland, January 1923 to November 1923; and in Imperial Russia, December 1921 to January 1924. Milton Friedman, "The Monetary Dynamics of Hyper Inflation," in *Studies in the Quarterly Theory of Money* (Chicago: University of Chicago Press, 1956), pp. 25–117. See also Milton Friedman, "Government Revenue from Inflation," *Journal of Political Economy* (July/August 1971): 852–54 especially.

37. A. W. Phillips, "The Relationship between Unemployment and the Rate of Change of Money Wage Rates in the United Kingdom, 1861–1957," *Economica* (November 1958): 283–99; R. G. Lipsey, "The Relation between Unemployment and the Rate of Change of Money Wage Rates in the United Kingdom, 1861–1957: A Further Analysis," *Economica* (February 1960): 1–31.

38. Paul A. Samuelson and Robert M. Solow, "Analytical Aspects of Anti-Inflation Policy," *American Economic Review* (May 1960): 192, Samuelson and Solow also add: "A final disclaimer is in order. We have not entered upon the important question of what feasible institutional reforms might be introduced to lessen the degree of disharmony between full employment and price stability. These could of course involve such wide ranging issues as direct price and wage controls, anti-union and anti-trust legislation, and a host of other measures hopefully designed to move American Phillips curves downward and to the left" (pp. 193–94).

39. Albert R. Rees and Mary T. Hamilton, "The Wage-Price Productivity Perplex," *Journal of Political Economy* (February 1967): 70.

40. See for example Milton Friedman, "The Role of Monetary Policy," *American Economic Review* (March 1968); and Milton Friedman, Nobel Lecture, "Inflation and

Unemployment," *Journal of Political Economy* (June 1977); Milton Friedman, *Unemployment versus Inflation? An Evolution of the Phillips Curve* (London: Institute of Economic Affairs, 1975).

41. See for example Harry G. Johnson, *Macroeconomics and Monetary Theory* (Chicago: Aldine, 1967); Robert D. Auerbach and Ronald Moses, "The Phillips Curve and All That: A Comment," *Scottish Journal of Political Economy* (November 1974): 124–66; Thomas Sargent, "A Note on the 'Accelerationist' Controversy," *Journal of Money, Credit, and Banking* (August 1971): 721–24.

42. James Tobin, "Inflation and Unemployment," *American Economic Review* (March 1972).

43. George Macesich, *Comparative Economic Stability* (Belgrade: Beogradski Grafički Zavod, 1973).

44. For a discussion of a number of these empirical results see H. R. Vance and J. L. Thompson, *Monetarism: Theory, Evidence and Policy* (New York: Wiley, 1979), pp. 86–90.

45. See for example David Meiselman, *The Term Structure of Interest* (Englewood Cliffs, N.J.: Prentice-Hall, 1962); N. Gibson, "Price Expectations Effects on Interest Rates," *Journal of Finance* (March 1970); J. Foster, "Tests of the Simple Fisher Hypothesis Utilizing Observed Inflationary Expectations: Some Further Evidence," *Scottish Journal of Political Economy* (November 1977).

46. Irving Fisher, "A Statistical Relation between Unemployment and Price Changes," *International Labour Review* (June 1926): 785–92; Irving Fisher, *The Theory of Interest* (New York: Kelley, 1961), a revision of *The Rate of Interest* (1907); George Macesich, "Irving Fisher," *Dictionary of the History of American Banking*, G. T. Mills and D. A. Martin, eds. (Greenwood Press, forthcoming). Fisher's specification of the formulation of expectations made the expected rate of inflation a distributed lag formation of past rates of inflation with the most recent observation of inflation most heavily weighted. Fisher's expectations model leads to the conclusion that individuals will underestimate the current rate of inflation if inflation is accelerating. He also recognized the implications of this forecasting bias for the trade-off between inflation and unemployment as early as 1926.

47. John F. Muth, "Rational Expectations and the Theory of Price Movements," *Econometrica* (July 1961). Edmond S. Phelps, "Phillips Curves, Expectations of Inflation and Optimum Unemployment Over There," *Economica* (August 1967): 254–81; Thomas J. Sargent and Neil Wallace, "Rational Expectations and the Theory of Economic Policy," *Studies in Monetary Policy* 2, Federal Reserve Bank of Minneapolis, 1975; Robert J. Lucac, Jr., "Rational Expectations and the Theory of Economic Policy," *Journal of Monetary Economics* (January 1976); R. E. Lucas, Jr., "Rational Expectations," *Journal of Money, Credit, and Banking* (November 1980); George Macesich, *Political Economy of Money* (forthcoming).

48. See for example Robert F. Lucas, Jr., "Tobin and Monetarism: A Review Article," *Journal of Economic Literature* (June 1981): 558–67; L. Weiss, "The Role of Active Monetary Policy in a Rational Expectations Model," *Journal of Political Economy* (April 1980): 221–33. Franco Modigliani, on the other hand, argues that the rational expectations case against discretionary stabilization policies is incorrect. The goal, according to Modigliani, is to make stabilization policies even more effective in the future than they have been in the past. Franco Modigliani, "The Monetarist Controversy, or Should We Foresake Stabilization Policies?" *American Economic Review* (March 1977): 1–18.

8

FISCAL POLICY

THE RISE OF FISCAL POLICY

Economists usually define fiscal policy as the manipulation of government spending or taxes for the purpose of affecting aggregate demand. By fiscal policy multipliers we mean ratios of the change in real gross national product to policy-induced changes.

Fiscal policy emerged as a response to the practical and theoretical problems of the 1930s. Before that decade, the maxim of sound government finance had been the balanced budget, balanced annually. This rule was coupled with another—a sound money system, which meant the gold standard and a central banking system that confined itself to maintaining a supply of money sufficient for the legitimate needs of trade.

The change from the old to the new fiscal policy came during the 1930s. In the early years of the Great Depression, the United States as well as other countries attempted to combat the depression with cuts in government expenditures; by so doing, they may have made matters worse. Indeed, Franklin Delano Roosevelt campaigned in 1932 on promises to restore sound finance and a balanced budget in the orthodox tradition. Once in office, however, Roosevelt's policies included significant expenditures for public works and employment relief. At about the same time, John Maynard Keynes proposed deficit spending—that is, spending from borrowed funds—as a means for economic recovery in Great Britain. In 1936 Keynes published *The General Theory of Employment, Interest and Money,* which laid the foundation for the modern theory of fiscal policy. After several years of discussion and controversy, Keynes's theories came to be incorporated into the main body of accepted economic theory.

By the late 1930s the debates on Keynes's theories and the knowledge gained from reflection on New Deal policies of pump-priming and compensatory spending established the outlines of fiscal policy as it is now known. Alvin E. Hansen of Harvard University, among others, led the way in working out the theories of fiscal policy. Other economists at the University of Chicago fought a rearguard action, especially against the extravagances of some of Keynes's disciples, who like all disciples went further than the master.

During World War II economists continued to discuss fiscal policy and its uses in postwar stabilization. Economists now agree; and so do leaders in political life, that there should be a fiscal policy for stability. As illustrated in the monetarist-Keynesian dispute, disagreement continues over the emphasis to be given fiscal and monetary policy and on their appropriate policy mix.

The propositions of income theory are briefly stated elsewhere in this study. Rules of abstract fiscal policy need not be restated here; they are contained in most texts on the principles of economics. In any case, the real problems of concrete fiscal policy revolve about other matters.

How good a guide is abstract fiscal policy to concrete policy decisions that the U.S. Congress and parliaments of other countries have to make this year? Not good at all, is the monetarist answer. The gap between pure economic theory and usable policy recommendations exists everywhere and is by no means peculiar to fiscal policy. But this obvious reminder has to be given again, due to the overenthusiasm of some Keynesian economists for fiscal policy.

Abstract fiscal policy reaches its most exuberant expression in the writings of Keynesian economist Abba P. Lerner of Florida State University. He calls it "functional finance," and would have the government simply adjust the total of all spending so as to eliminate both unemployment and inflation. Just like that. Government expenditures and taxes and printed money would be manipulated so as to force businesses and consumers to spend the right amounts.

Consider some fiscal policy proposals not of the abstract sort, but of the kind intended for concrete action by Congress. These proposals were at first called compensatory—the federal budget would compensate for the deficiency of aggregate demand after allowing for private consumption and investment. Federal expenditures were visualized as filling a large gap. It was not very long into the postwar era that economists began to see that the problem was one of stabilization rather than secular stagnation, that the task of successful economic forecasting was proving to be disappointingly hard, and that some reliance could be placed upon built-in or automatic stabilizers.

One consequence was a search for a rule, which, when followed, would cause the volume of federal expenditures and taxes to behave in such a way as to stabilize the economy. To put fiscal policy on an automatic rule would provide it with greater acceptance, especially among monetarists. A case in point is the 1947 proposal by the Committee on Economic Development (CED) for fiscal policy by rule, where the rule would be fixed tax rates, not to be modified except as a response to a major change in national policy.

Other examples of fiscal policy rules include automatic flexibility and formula flexibility. The built-in stabilizers of the federal budget provide the automatic flexibility of tax revenues that fall and expenditures that rise when unemployment increases. The built-in stabilizers are not subject to recognition lags, let alone the administrative and operational ones. These automatic stabilizers cushion shocks and act as a first line of defense. They must be supplemented by additional measures of fiscal policy. Formula flexibility, on the other hand, is a modification of the rule concept. Under this concept, for instance, Congress would change the income tax laws so that rates (or exemptions or both) would move up and down in accordance with an appropriate economic index.

In 1949 economists from various shades of the political spectrum agreed that monetary policy in the United States and elsewhere was inoperative. It was not until 1951 (really 1953, at the end of the Korean War) in the United States, and later in other countries, that independent monetary policy began. Since that time there has been little agreement on stability policy. Keynesians look to a strong fiscal policy with monetary policy as an adjunct. The monetarists place their reliance on a strong monetary policy accompanied by a rule-bound fiscal policy.

MONETARY AND FISCAL POLICY MIX

How should monetary and fiscal policy be mixed? Milton Friedman discussed this issue at some length during the height of the Korean War in 1951.[1] This was a period of military buildup in the United States, which pushed inflation into double digits.

Friedman argued that "monetary and fiscal measures are the only appropriate means of controlling inflation." He ruled out any recourse to wage-price controls. According to Friedman, monetary and fiscal incomes are substitutes within a wide range. A large budget surplus would be consistent with no or, for that matter, any degree of inflation. In his view, a balanced budget would require tighter money to prevent inflation, and a budget deficit would require still tighter money. It is possible, according to Friedman, that budget deficits may get so large that they will simply overwhelm monetary policy. In fact, it may be impossible to design monetary policy that will prevent inflation. Consequently, there may not be a single best mix of monetary and fiscal policy and degree of inflation. According to Friedman, a good mix would be a roughly balanced budget (balanced over the business cycle) together with whatever associated monetary policy would prevent inflation. Moreover, no policy very far from this combination is likely to be appropriate.

As for high interest rates, Friedman in 1951 argued that while they curb investment expenditures, they also curb consumer expenditures, including spending on nondurable and durable goods. One reason, of course, is that high interest rates make saving more attractive. They also reduce the capital value of existing streams of wealth and thus reduce the ratio of wealth to income. In effect, high interest rates increase the desire on the part of the people to add to their wealth.

High interest rates in 1951 as today are not popular with many people for a variety of reasons. These reasons, however, are insufficient to overrule the requisite monetary policy to bring inflation under control. Interest rates remained high in 1982 at least in part because financial markets do not believe that inflation is under control. It could be, as pessimist argue, that financial markets believe that record U.S. budget deficits slipped into Friedman's worst-case scenario and became so large that they ultimately overwhelmed monetary policy.

President Reagan's economic program was originally thought to be what the financial markets ordered. This assumption proved to be premature. The debate is over interest rates and deficits. The key issue, according to some observers, is that long-term interest rates today have embodied in them the expectation of deficits three and four years out. Financial markets fear that deficits will either stifle a recovery or rekindle inflation later. The conventional wisdom on Wall Street is that uncertainty over the record-breaking deficits in excess of $100 billion Reagan has proposed is a major reason—if not the only one—why interest rates are high. Lenders are demanding a high premium for their money because they don't know what economic conditions will prevail when they get paid back.

Moreover, there is a feeling widely shared in the U.S. financial community that the Reagan administration is not paying attention to their views. Indeed, the Reagan administration argument that neither the Federal Reserve nor the government can do anything about the persistence of high interest rates is less than reassuring to the financial community. This pessimistic view is written into investors' expectations, and thus into high interest rates.

There is, indeed, a considerable distance between the political and financial worlds. One explanation for the gulf of misunderstanding between these two worlds is mutual suspicion. Wall Street looks upon the federal government as a "bloated monster loosed upon the land by vote-starved politicians." Washington, on the other hand, tends to think of Wall Street "as a tiny cell of conspirators secretly manipulating the markets of America to exploit Main Street."

In fact, deficits do matter. The U.S. economy can tolerate deficits less readily than most other countries because the U.S. economy is a comparatively low-saving economy. For example, in recent years in Japan personal saving, as a percentage of disposable personal income, was four times as large as in the United States. In the Federal Republic of Germany, it was about three times as large. As the business sector is, in most countries, a net borrower, one must look at personal saving as the main source of surplus funds. In short, countries that save a lot (such as Germany, Italy, and Japan) experience less difficulty in financing a given level of deficit, expressed as a share of Gross Domestic Product, than countries with lower rates of saving (such as the United States).

Although it is still a relatively low ratio to Gross National Product, the U.S. fiscal deficit accounts for a large share of available surplus funds and is of the same order of magnitude as total net outlays for new plant and equipment. When extra budgetary borrowing on behalf of other agencies is also taken into account, the current (1982) borrowing requirements of the federal government are such as to leave little of the surplus saving available for private sector borrowing. Unless the projected levels of fiscal deficits over the next two to three years can be reduced, only a very large expansion in private saving would prevent serious crowding out and a continuation of the present high rates of interest.

Moreover, if a recent National Bureau of Economic Research study for the United States is correct that there is a relatively fixed relationship between the total debt (both private and public) and GNP, the increase in public debt will imply a crowding out of private debt, with obvious implications for capital formation. In the United States, for example, total debt has averaged about 140 percent of GNP for several decades. In the 1960s, curiously, when the ratio of public debt to GNP in the United States was declining, the economy was growing at a lively pace. In the 1970s when that ratio was either stationary or increasing, the rate of growth slowed down.

In essence, high fiscal deficits accompanied by tight monetary policies (as measured in terms of the rate of growth of the money supply) may not generate inflation, but will nevertheless raise interest rates and thus bring about a reduction in private productive activities. This reduction itself will magnify the size of the deficit through its built-in negative effects on revenues and positive effects on public expenditures. The Federal Republic of Germany, Japan, and the United States are important examples of countries that have been pursuing tight monetary policies in the face of sizable fiscal deficits.

Suppose now that fiscal deficits are accompanied by an accommodating monetary policy. If the economy's productive capacities are fully utilized, the increase in aggregate demand will bring about increases in prices and wages. In the short run, the increase in the money supply may bring about a decline in nominal interest rates as a result of the liquidity effect discussed earlier. Consumption will rise at the expense of saving as inflationary psychology prompts people to anticipate purchases. The demand for financial assets will fall, while that for real assets will rise, leading to a process of disintermediation in the capital market. Imports will expand, leading to a deterioration in the balance of payments. If exchange rates are fixed, there will be a loss in net foreign reserves that will tend to reduce the initial acceleration in money supply growth. If exchange rates are flexible, the rate will depreciate, adding further to the domestic inflation rate. In short, high budgetary deficits accompanied by an accommodating monetary policy tend to aggravate inflation.

As an alternative to borrowing from the central bank or the private sector, governments can and do borrow abroad. For industrial countries where domestic capital markets are well integrated with those abroad, the process is direct if not always simple. Indeed, the evidence indicates that the practice of foreign borrowing to finance budget deficits has become prevalent since the mid-1970s along with the rapid expansion of international financial markets, as both industrial and developing countries incurred significantly larger deficits. In fact, during the latter part of the 1970s, estimates place foreign deficit finance as about one-sixth of industrial countries' budget deficits and one-third of those of developing countries. Indeed, if borrowing by public enterprises could be accounted for, these percentages would no doubt be much higher.

Moreover, the recent pool of international saving provided by OPEC countries unable to fully absorb their saving internally has become smaller. Though perhaps still sufficient to accommodate requirements of the smaller developing countries, the pool is inadequate to meet U.S. needs and other industrial countries over the next several years. High interest rates in the United States will no doubt attract many of these funds and thus contribute to financing the U.S. deficit. This will tend to aggravate the capital-needs situation in developing countries and elsewhere, who will thereby face much stronger competition and higher interest rates. The implications are ominous for developing countries. Deficits of large countries do indeed have implications for the rest of the world.

Given the present and persistent size of fiscal deficits in many countries, authorities are severely restricted in their ability to use fiscal policy in a countercyclical fashion. To regain their freedom, countries are best advised to pursue policies that reduce budget deficits. This will enhance the chances that the negative effects of restrictive monetary policy will be removed and countries will be able to enjoy growth without inflation. Under these circumstances, perseverance and political courage are required in dealing with the fiscal problem.

FISCAL POLICY AND CROWDING OUT

The monetarist view of fiscal policy is that pure fiscal expansion without monetary accommodation may influence national income in the short run.[2] In the long run, however, such government expenditures will "crowd out" or replace some elements of private expenditure so that real income remains unchanged. If reduction in private expenditure is identical in magnitude to the increase in government expenditure, the long-run fiscal multiplier is zero and crowding out is said to be complete. When the fiscal multiplier is greater than one, absence of crowding out is indicated. Crowding out is partial when the fiscal multiplier is between zero and one. In this instance, income rises by an amount less than the increase in government expenditure. Over-crowding is said to occur when the multiplier is negative. Private expenditure will fall by a greater magnitude than the rise in government expenditure.

The analysis of crowding out, moreover, can be done in real or nominal terms. This is illustrated in Figure 8.1. Panel A represents the market for the total output of goods and services in an economy. The intersection of aggregate supply (AS) and aggregate demand (AD) determines the equilibrium level of output X_0, and the price P_0 which will clear the market. We label this intersection and call it the initial equilibrium point.

Let us assume that the government, through its fiscal operation, increases the demand for goods and services financed by sales of its debt to the public. Now assume the net effect of the government's fiscal operations is an increased demand, as illustrated by shift of the demand

Figure 8.1
Definitions of Crowding Out

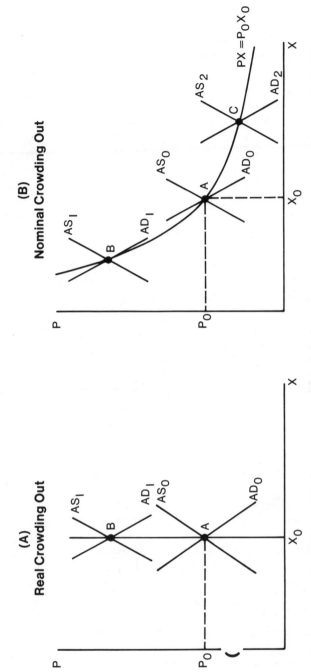

(A)
Real Crowding Out

(B)
Nominal Crowding Out

Source: Keith M. Carlson and Roger W. Spencer, "Crowding Out and Its Critics," Review, Federal Reserve Bank of St. Louis, December, 1975, pp. 2-17.

curve to AD. Suppose also that as a result of the expanded government sector, productive capacity and efficiency are adversely affected so that the supply curve shifts to AS_1. If the new equilibrium occurs anywhere on the vertical line through point A_1, say, at point B, then real crowding out has taken place. In effect, increased real government spending is completely offset by a decline in real private spending.

In panel B of Figure 8.1, the curved line drawn through point A is a rectangular hyperbola indicating that P times X (defined as nominal value of total output on GNP) is constant and equal to P_0X_0. What this states is that there is an infinite number of combinations of P and X besides P_0 and X_0 that give the same dollar value of total output as at point A. For instance, suppose that an expansionary fiscal action by government results in an aggregate demand and supply shift in various directions (according to various assumptions made) and the new equilibrium point is reached at B or C. An increase in government spending has been offset by a decline in the dollar amount of spending in the private sector. As a result, nominal crowding out is said to have occurred.

Since the one concept of crowding out does not imply the other, the distinction between them is important. Given expansionary fiscal operations on the part of government, various combinations of real and nominal crowding out are possible.

Presumably, the process also works in reverse. That is, reducing government expenditures may have the effect of "crowding in" private expenditures. This may have the effect, among others, of replacing "unproductive" government expenditures by productive private expenditures, thereby increasing the total output of goods and services in the economy. It is an implication that many monetarists and supply-siders would accept.

L. C. Anderson and J. L. Jordan (1968), with M. W. Keran (1969 and 1970) of the Federal Reserve Bank of St. Louis, reported on empirical results that appear to support nominal crowding out. Federal spending, whether financed by borrowing or taxes, while having an initial expansionary effect, is followed in about a year by off-setting negative effects. Their results appear to conflict with received theory and empirical evidence, and they have been challenged on both grounds.

J. Tobin argues that these results on nominal crowding out appear inconsistent with available studies on the interest elasticity of the demand for money. On the basis of a standard IS-LM analysis, the implication is that the interest elasticity of the demand should be nearly perfectly inelastic. That is, the LM curve in this instance is essentially vertical. As we noted elsewhere, most studies suggest that the interest elasticity of the demand for money is greater than zero.

In rebuttal, Friedman and others argue that the slope of the LM curve is irrelevant to the issue of crowding out. According to Friedman, the initial expansionary effect of increased government expenditures could eventually trigger a contraction as the economy attempts to finance the deficit.

Blinder and Solow challenge Friedman's explanation, arguing that it is not consistent with the stability of the economic system as portrayed by IS-LM framework. Essentially, a debt-financed increase in government expenditure in a situation of crowding out does not set in motion forces to return the IS-LM model to a new equilibrium once equilibrium is disturbed.

Carlson and Spencer, on the other hand, offer alternative explanations of how crowding out can occur in the IS-LM framework even if the interest elasticity of the demand for money is not zero. For illustrative purposes, their several cases are presented in Figure 8.2.

First is the classical case in panel A, in which the LM curve is drawn vertically, reflecting a zero interest elasticity of the demand for money. An increase in government spending shifts the IS curve to the right. Interest rates rise. The velocity of money, however, remains unaffected, since it is insensitive to interest rates changes. Aggregate demand does not change. Components of private expenditure are crowded out by an amount equal to the increase in government expenditures. As a result of the failure of aggregate demand to shift in response to an increase in government expenditure, crowding out occurs in both nominal and real terms.

There are, however, conditions under which government expenditures can crowd out private spending without assuming a vertical LM curve or lack of interest sensitivity in the demand for money. Indeed, Keynes in his *General Theory* considers a case in which government spending can adversely influence the expectations and confidence of the private sector and so of spending programs of the sector.[3] Carlson and Spencer demonstrate Keynes's case (panel B) within the IS-LM framework. Thus, an increase in government spending induces an increase in liquidity preference, a leftward shift in the LM curve, and a diminished marginal efficiency of investment schedule as reflected by a backward shift of the IS curve. They point out that if these shifts in IS and LM schedules result in no change in aggregate demand at the given price, both nominal and real crowding out will take place. Furthermore, the actual shift in aggregate demand could be positive, negative, or negligible depending on the relative shifts of the IS and LM curves.

Frank H. Knight and his many studies on capital and interest serves as an illustrative example of the horizontal IS curve in panel C.[4] Carlson

CROWDING OUT: FOUR EXAMPLES

Figure 8.2,
Panel A
Crowding Out: Classical Case

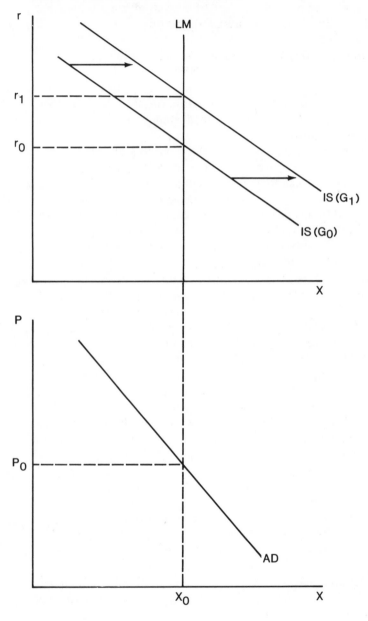

Figure 8.2 continued,
Panel B

Crowding Out: Keynes Case

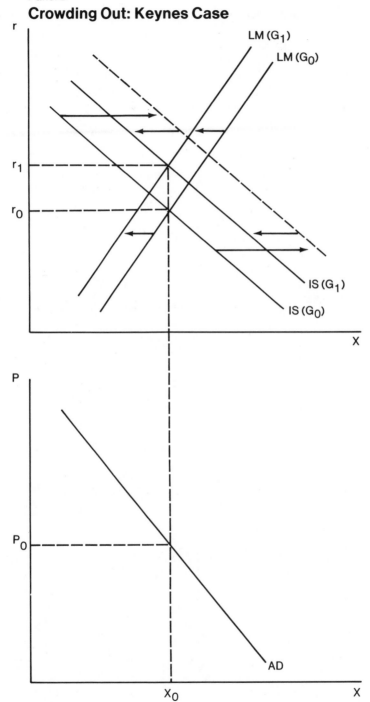

Figure 8.2 continued,
Panel C

Crowding Out: Knight Case

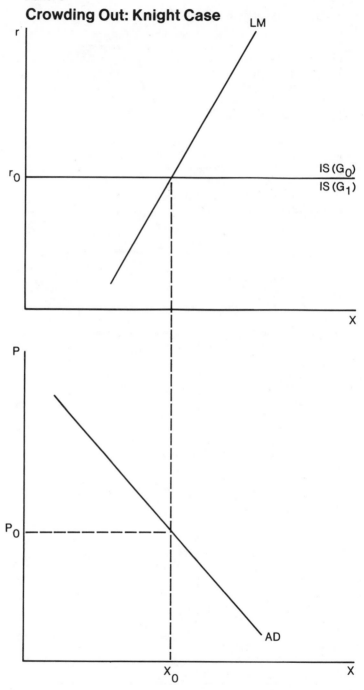

174

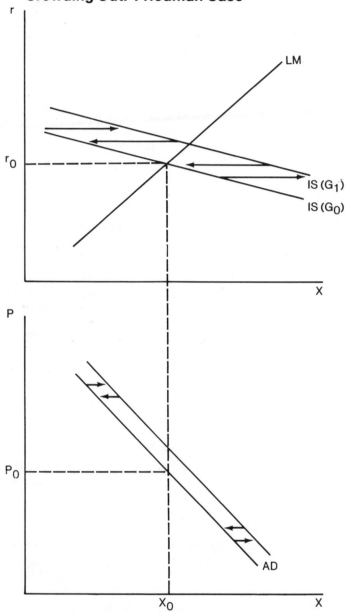

Figure 8.2 continued,
Panel D

Crowding Out: Friedman Case

Source for all four examples: K. R. Carlson and R. W. Spencer "Crowding Out and Its Critics," Review, Federal Reserve Bank of St. Louis, December, 1975, pp. 2-17.

and Spencer correctly interpret Knight's complex theory of interest and capital. (This is also my understanding of Professor Knight's lectures, which I attended while a graduate student at Chicago in the mid-1950s.) To be sure, Knight never conducted his analysis in terms of IS-LM curves.

In Knight's view, we should not expect diminishing returns from investment for several reasons. In the first instance, the quantity of capital is so large relative to additions to it that these additions will not significantly influence the yield on capital. Moreover, a declining marginal product of capital tends to be offset by technological advances. These advances themselves are promoted by research and development, which are investment spin-offs. The net effect is that an aggregate investment curve is drawn as almost horizontal with respect to the yield on capital.

In terms of the IS-LM framework, Knight's case of crowding out yields a perfectly horizontal IS curve, and fiscal actions on the part of the government are incapable of shifting the IS schedule. Increase in government expenditure absorbs savings, thereby reducing the amount available for private expenditures. There is a one-for-one displacement of private investment by government expenditures. Fiscal policy is thus ineffective.

Monetary policy, on the other hand, dominates output. This can be illustrated by assuming an upward sloping LM curve. Even so, monetary policy does not affect the interest rate, which is inconsistent with some of Knight's statements regarding capital and interest.

Panel D of Figure 8.2 attempts to summarize Milton Friedman's views on crowding out in terms of the IS-LM framework. Friedman focuses on the continuing effects of deficit finance and the basic distinction between stocks and flows. He underscores the point that monetarist propositions do not rest on the shape of the LM focus. These issues are discussed in his "Comments on the Critics" and other writings cited in this study.

According to Carlson and Spencer, their reading of Friedman permits an IS curve drawn quite flat. It reflects Friedman's view that "saving" and "investment" must be interpreted much more broadly than neo-Keynesians would have us believe. This is similar to Knight's view of a more inclusive investment that leads to a flatter IS curve. The effect also dampens fiscal actions. This is consistent with Friedman's view that monetary actions are more powerful than fiscal.

Friedman is quite pessimistic regarding the effect of the government's expansive fiscal activities on the economy's future ability to produce goods and services. Indeed, in his view, potential output in the future will be lowered relative to what it would otherwise be with the transfer of resources from private investment. According to Friedman, a transfer from the private sector produces or generates future capital stock to government spending, which absorbs the capital stock.

With these objectives in mind, Panel D illustrates that an initial shift of the IS curve may still be consistent with crowding out in the long run. A relatively flat IS curve for a given LM curve produces a modest shift to the right in aggregate demand. Since, as Friedman argues, government evidences of debt are largely in place of private securities in private portfolios, private expenditure is cut back. The net result may be to offset the initial increase in government expenditure. Whether the offset is full or partial, the IS curve and aggregate demand will shift leftward.

Though these may be the initial-round effects, Friedman expects the repercussion of deficits will continue to be felt. The IS curve will continue to shift leftward in the long term as private expenditures continue to be cut back as government debt is substituted for private debt. The net effect, on balance, will be a reduction in the stock of private wealth relative to what it otherwise would be because of reduced investment, thus reinforcing the shift to the left of the IS curve.

In reply to Friedman's concern over long-term effects of monetary and fiscal actions, papers by Alan Blinder and Robert Solow ("Does Fiscal Policy Matter?") and James Tobin and William Buiter ("Long Run Effects") argue that the crowding-out effect of fiscal actions is inconsistent with the assumption of stability of the economic system as envisioned in the standard IS-LM model. Carlson and Spencer discuss these papers at length, along with another by Karl Brunner and Allan Meltzer ("Money, Debt and Economic Activity"). None contributes significantly to our understanding of empirical results that imply the existence of crowding out.

The Blinder-Solow analysis incorporates the usual IS-LM model, treating the price level as fixed and abstracting from the existence of a banking system. The approach by Tobin-Buiter is similar. Both are marked by the stability requirement of a balanced budget process; both utilize more than one version of the basic IS-LM model; and both conclude that the stability considerations inherent in the balanced budget requirements generate a positive government-spending multiplier. Tobin-Buiter stress that their analysis is for periods when the economy is at less than full employment. In view of a positive fiscal multiplier in the Tobin-Buiter model, it is not a foregone conclusion that crowding out occurs at full employment.

The Brunner-Meltzer model differs importantly from the standard IS-LM model. In contrast with the other two models discussed above, this model allows the price level to be determined endogenously and includes a banking sector. As in the other models, stability considerations and a government sector issuing interest debt are features.

These common elements, according to Carlson and Spencer, account for the unusual results reached in the models. For instance, Brunner-Meltzer find that government spending financed by debt issuance is more stimulative than government spending accompanied by expansionary monetary actions. It is a result required by the need for a balanced budget for long-run equilibrium. This conclusion contradicts their earlier studies, a fact they recognize.

Carlson and Spencer correctly point out the curious result reached in all three models: namely, government spending financed by debt issuance is more expansionary than such spending accompanied by money creation. The expansionary effect is in terms of real output in the Blinder-Solow model and of prices in the Brunner-Meltzer model.

Blinder-Solow's insistence that the crowding-out hypothesis requires a negative fiscal multiplier is simply overdrawn. It is, indeed, as Carlson and Spencer note, that the crowding-out hypothesis does not require that a dollar of government spending unsupported by monetary expansion, lead to a reduction in private spending by more than a dollar as implied by a negative fiscal multiplier. Crowding out is a matter of degree rather than of absolute magnitudes. Moreover, the failure to include changing price levels in various IS-LM models contributes to these models' bias against the possibility of crowding out. The ability of such models to synthesize current reality with its generally rising world price levels is at best questionable.

SUMMARY AND CONCLUSION

To judge from recent studies surveying and testing several econometric models, results tend to confirm monetarist views that crowding out does indeed occur.[5] As Carlson and Spencer note, the question is no longer whether crowding out exists, but how much time it needs to occur. For instance, the Wharton Mark III model yielded a multiplier of minus 3 after 40 quarters, and the U.S. Department of Commerce model over the same period was minus 23. This is far in excess of a crowding-out effect as defined by a steady-state government spending multiplier of near zero.

The performance of small monetarist models, such as that of the Federal Reserve Bank of St. Louis, suggests that crowding out occurs in a much shorter period of time than in the earlier Keynesian-type models. Moreover, crowding out occurs in nominal rather than in just real terms. The reported results on the St. Louis model indicate that government spending, as measured by high-employment expenditures, exercises a relatively strong influence on GNP, assuming a constant change in the money supply in the current quarter and the next quarter, but it is approximately offset within a year's time.

All of this, of course, does not mean that government spending does not matter. Indeed, it matters very much, especially if government expenditures accelerate or decelerate rapidly. The reduced form results of the St. Louis model are all the more interesting since they do not follow from a structural model that constrains the channels of transmission from fiscal actions to economic activity. This is consistent with the monetarist view noted earlier that government expenditures cover a wide range of activities. They may substitute or complement private sector expenditures for consumption and investment. The very diversity of these effects is apt to render limited any model that severely restricts the transmission channels of fiscal actions to income and/or interest rates.. As such, the full impact of government expenditures on the private sector may well be missed.

These and other simulation studies serve as tools for policymakers, who use them along with other information to make public policy. The size and variability of monetary and fiscal policy multipliers that they yield leave much to be desired. Indeed, Michael Evans, a leading builder of large econometric models, now admits that econometric models built around Keynesian demand theories are seriously flawed, primarily because they ignore supply-side factors.[6] Moreover, failure to take into account recent data and changing economic structures (including legal and sociopolitical changes) limits the usefulness of these large econometric models for both simulation exercises and forecasting purposes. For instance, observers note that the parameters and multipliers of existing models are typically based on people's past reactions to government policies. As such, their utility for policy-simulation purposes has limited value to policy markets, though these models may still be useful for forecasting purposes.

Forecasting, however, has its own shortcomings. No matter how sophisticated the econometric model used, it depends on the political and economic assumptions about government policies on which it rests. If these assumptions change, the model's forecasts will very likely be erroneous. Furthermore, since we cannot attach probability statements to economic forecasts, the utility of these models is limited. What we can say is that if a forecaster could make the same forecast under the same conditions a very large number of times, he would be correct a certain percentage of the times—albeit within a certain range. Not very useful, unfortunately, if we wish to forecast turning points in the GNP.[7]

This inability to forecast accurately has serious implications for stabilization policies, as we noted elsewhere. Together with variability of leads and lags in stabilization policies, erroneous forecasts have pushed some policymakers to reject short-run stabilization policies altogether in favor of a policy of rules.

The finding of a strong empirical relationship between several measures of money and economic activity suggests that monetary policy can play a singularly important role in stabilization policy. Indeed, failure to recognize these relationships can have serious consequences on economic activity. These relationships to economic activity, moreover, appear more certain than fiscal actions.

Furthermore, the evidence provided in a number of Federal Reserve Banks of St. Louis studies is consistent with other evidence that suggests that the money stock is an important indicator of the total thrust of stabilization actions, both monetary and fiscal. In the first instance, changes in the money stock principally reflect discretionary actions of the Federal Reserve System as it uses open market operations, discount rate changes, and reserve requirements. Second, the money stock reflects the joint actions of the Treasury and Federal Reserve System in financing newly created government debt. These actions are based, in the final analysis, on decisions regarding the monetization of new debt by Federal Reserve actions, and Treasury decisions regarding changes in its balances at Reserve banks. Thus, changes in government spending financed by monetary expansion are reflected in changes in the monetary base and in the money supply.

As noted above, many economists argue that the major influence of fiscal actions results only if expenditures are financed by monetary expansion. In the United States, the Federal Reserve does not buy securities from the government. Its open market operations, along with other actions, serve to provide funds in the markets in which both the government and private individuals borrow.

Moreover, it is not easy to reverse a stimulative stance in fiscal policy—a result in part of the institutional context in which fiscal tools are used. To be sure, some fiscal tools, such as automatic stabilizers, can be redirected very quickly. These programs expand and contract more or less automatically in response to changes in the pace at which the economy is expanding. Such programs include unemployment compensation, welfare programs, leasing subsidies, and, in the United States, the progressive nature of the federal tax structure.

Some insight into how difficult it is to change quickly the posture of fiscal policy in either direction may be had by considering that all new programs in the United States require congressional approval.[8] This approval must be in a form that provides for the actions sought by the administration. Bills are sometimes changed in committee or on the floor of Congress in ways that significantly redirect their thrusts. Much the same is true in tax legislation. Political realities often intervene to make either raising or lowering taxes a long, drawn-out process. The political give-and-take may very well result in less than an optimal tax system.

Transfer payments, although they are outlays rather than taxes, are subject to the same forces that slow tax changes. Changes are likely to be a long time in coming, and temptation to embellish a proposed program is likely to be considerable. In fact, once recipients become accustomed to the payments, they and their political representatives will not be anxious to see them withdrawn when the need for stimulus passes. Discretionary changes in transfer payments thus tend to be one-way stabilization tools at best, for use when stimulus is needed.

J. de. Larosiere, director of the International Monetary Fund, argues forcefully that the "fiscal policy followed by many countries over the past decade has been a basic ingredient of stagflation. Rather than being the 'stabilizing factor' advocated by Keynes, fiscal policy has, in many countries, become one of the major destabilizing forces."[9] He underscores that many of these transfer programs and other benefits were introduced when their cost was low and their future fiscal consequences were ignored. In other cases, highly optimistic forecasts about important variables, such as growth, unemployment, and inflation, were made at the time the programs were introduced or expanded, mainly during the 1960s and early 1970s. Changed circumstances in the 1970s made it difficult for many countries to keep their commitments and still pursue a sound fiscal policy.

Readily available data suggest the impact of these developments on public expenditure for seven major industrial countries.[10] For these countries, the ratio of total public expenditure to gross domestic product rose from 29 percent in 1965 to around 37 percent in recent years. For some individual countries, these increases have been even more pronounced: in Canada, West Germany, Italy, Japan, Spain, and Great Britain, the ratio of total public expenditure to GDP rose by more than 10 percent between 1965 and the end of the 1970s. For some of the smaller industrial countries, such as Belgium, Ireland, Luxembourg, the Netherlands, Norway, Portugal, and Sweden, the increases were even more pronounced, exceeding 15 percent. In all of these countries, including France, the ratio of public expenditure to GDP now exceeds 40 percent. In all cases, concludes de Larosiere, entitlement programs and other transfers have been the main factor in this expansion.

NOTES

1. See for example Milton Friedman, ed., *Essays in Positive Economics* (Chicago: University of Chicago Press, 1953); see also H. Stein, *Fiscal Revolution in America* (Chicago: University of Chicago Press, 1969).

2. This section draws on the following studies: K. M. Carlson and R. W. Spencer, "Crowding Out and Its Critics," *Review*, Federal Reserve Bank of St. Louis (December 1975): 2–17 and Appendix; R. W. Spencer and W. P. Yohe, "Crowding Out of Private Expenditures by Fiscal Policy Actions," *Review*, Federal Reserve Bank of St. Louis (October 1970): 12–24; L. C. Anderson and J. L. Jordan, "Monetary and Fiscal Action: A Test of Their Relative Importance in Economic Stabilization," *Review*, Federal Reserve Bank of St. Louis (November 1968): 11–24; M. W. Keran, "Monetary and Fiscal Influences on Economic Activity—The Historical Evidence," *Review*, Federal Reserve Bank of St. Louis (November 1969): 5–24; M. W. Keran, "Monetary and Fiscal Influences on Economic Activity: The Foreign Experience," *Review*, Federal Reserve Bank of St. Louis (February 1970): 16–28; J. Tobin, "Friedman's Theoretical Framework," *Journal of Political Economy* (September/October 1972): 852–63; M. Friedman, "Comments on the Critics," *Journal of Political Economy* (September/October 1972): 906–50; K. Brunner and A. H. Meltzer, "Money, Debt and Economic Activity," *Journal of Political Economy* (September/October 1972): 951–77; A. S. Blinder and R. M. Solow, "Does Fiscal Policy Matter? *Journal of Public Economics* (November 1973): 319–37; P. A. David and J. L. Scadding, "Private Savings: Ultrarationality, Aggregation, and 'Denison's Law,'" *Journal of Political Economy* (March/April 1974): 225–49; A. Andro, "Some Aspects of Stabilization Policies, the Monetarist Controversy, and the MPS Model," *International Economic Review* (October 1974): 541–71; E. F. Infante and J. L. Stein, "Does Fiscal Policy Matter?" *Journal of Monetary Economics* (November 1976): 473–500; A. S. Blinder and R. M. Solow "Does Fiscal Policy Still Matter?" *Journal of Monetary Economics* (November 1976): 501–10; B. M. Friedman, "Even the St. Louis Model Now Believes in Fiscal Policy," *Journal of Money, Credit and Banking* (May 1977): 365–67; R. W. Hafer, "The Role of Fiscal Policy in the St. Louis Equation," *Review*, Federal Reserve Bank of St. Louis (January 1982): 17–22.

3. J. M. Keynes, *The General Theory of Employment, Interest and Money* (New York: Harcourt,Brace, 1936), pp. 119–20.

4. See for example F. H. Knight, "Capital and Interest," in *Readings in the Theory of Income Distribution* (Philadelphia: Blakiston, 1949), pp. 384–417. The case was suggested to Carlson and Spencer by William Dewald of Ohio State University. It is also a case that my colleague and one of Knight's former students, Professor Marshall R. Colberg, discussed with me.

5. See for example Gary Fromm and Lawrence R. Klein, "A Comparison of Eleven Econometric Models of the United States," *American Economic Review* (May 1973): 385–93; Lawrence R. Klein, "Commentary on the State of the Monetarist Debate," *Review*, Federal Reserve Bank of St. Louis (September 1973): 9–12; K. M. Carlson, "Monetary and Fiscal Actions in Macroeconomic Models," *Review*, Federal Reserve Bank of St. Louis (January 1974): 8–18; R. W. Hafer, "The Role of Fiscal Policy in the St. Louis Equation," *Review*, Federal Reserve Bank of St. Louis (January 1982): 17–22.

6. Michael Evans, "Bankruptcy of Keynesian Econometric Models," *Challenge* (January/February 1980): 13–19.

7. See for instance Victor Arnowitz, "On the Accuracy and Properties of Recent Macroeconomic Forecasts," *American Economic Review* (May 1978): 313–19.

8. For an evaluation of fiscal activities on the local level, see for example Bernard F. Sliger, Ansel M. Sharp, and Robert L. Sandmeyer, "Local Government Revenues: An Overview," in *Management Policies in Local Government Finance*, J. R. Aronson and Eli Schwartz, eds. (Washington, D.C.: International City Management Association, 1975), pp. 42–62.

9. J. de Larosiere, "Coexistence of Fiscal Deficits," High Tax Burdens Is Consequence of Pressures for Public Spending," *IMF Survey*, March 22, 1982, p. 82.

10. Ibid.

9

MONEY AND
ECONOMETRIC MODELS

Monetarists prefer small-scale econometric models. Since changes in the stock of money are dominant in explaining changes in nominal income, their focus is on the behavior of the demand for real cash balances. Keynesians, on the other hand, prefer large-scale econometric models that provide detailed information on various sectors believed to influence significantly the aggregative behavior of the economy.

This chapter investigates the role of money and monetary policy within several econometric models that illustrate the preferences of monetarists and Keynesians. The results of some of these studies serve as important inputs into public policy. As a consequence, they have been and continue to be important in setting the tone and influencing the environment under which monetary policy is formulated and implemented in the United States and elsewhere.

KLEIN-GOLDBERGER MODEL

Construction and use of econometric models have become so widespread in postwar years that in 1966 Mark Nerlove was able to survey and document 25 such models.[1] All the models he describes are basically Keynesian in nature and all are estimated on the basis of time-series data. Many of the models have at least one consumption function, one investment function, one liquidity-preference function, and one production function. The models considered are dynamic and most contain at least a few nonlinearities. The 25 models cover nine countries and time periods, spanning nearly 100 years. Several of the models contain no monetary or financial sectors. One of the first models for the U.S. economy was constructed by Lawrence R. Klein. This was a 12-equation model using data for the period 1921–41. The study itself was published in 1950. In a joint study with Arthur Goldberger, the original effort was expanded and published as a 21-equation model.[2]

Consider now the monetary aspects of several of the more important econometric models. First is the Klein-Goldberger model (1955) consisting of 20 equations, six of which are identities. In total, there are 39 distinct variables; of these, 26 also appear in lagged form. Hence, there are 49 predetermined variables, of which 19 are lag-endogenous, 17 are exogenous, and seven are lag-exogenous. Consider the monetary sector. Of the 15 equations to be estimated, a set of four relates to the money and securities market. The first of these describes the demand by households for liquid assets L_1 (endogenous) as a function of national income M (endogenous); wage taxes less transfers T_w (exogenous); corporate taxes T_C (exogenous); nonwage, nonfarm, noncorporate taxes less transfers T_N (exogenous); and the long-term interest rate I_1 (endogenous): thus the equation

$$L_1 = 0.14(M - T_W - T_C - T_N - S_C - T_r) + 76.03(I_1 - 2.0)^{-0.84} \qquad (1)$$

where S is composite savings (endogenous) and T_r is farm taxes less transfers (exogenous).

In effect, the L_1 consists of the transactions balances and idle balances, the former being proportional to disposable income and the latter a function of the long-term interest rate. The coefficient of the first variable is (.14). It is determined as the smallest ratio of the greatest personal holdings of currency in checking accounts deflated by disposal income in the sample period. For the year 1929 when the ratio is smallest, the assumption is that there were no idle balances in that year and that such balances in other years can be measured by the difference between L_1 and the first right-hand term, (.14). The equation states that the idle balances are a log-linear function of the long-term interest rate measured as a percentage per year in excess of 2 percent. The variable I_1 fluctuated between 2.7 and 6.9 in the sample period. Clearly, this equation is nonlinear. The standard error of the −0.84 estimate is .03.

A similar equation describes business demands for liquid assets as a function of the private wage bill, a short-term interest rate, a change in the price level variable, and liquid assets held by businesses during the previous period:

$$L_2 = -0.34 + 0.26W - 1.0211_S - 0.26(P - P_{-1}) + 0.61(L_2)_{-1} \qquad (2)$$

Here the first variable shows that the larger the operating expense measured by the private wage bill, the greater the need for cash. The second indicates that when the short-term rate rises, there is a tendency to substitute securities for cash. The third shows that if prices are increasing, they are presumed to increase even further so that it is advantageous to have a large amount of liquid assets. The fourth, with its large coefficient, shows that L_2 is subject to considerable inertia over time. The third and fourth equations representing the money supply sector are indicated in terms of long-term and short-term interest rates:

$$I_1 = 2.58 + 0.44(I_S)_{-3} + 0.26(I_S)_{-5} \qquad (3)$$

$$100I_S - (I_S)_{-1} = 11.17 - 0.67L_b, \qquad (4)$$

where L_b is the percentage excess reserve (exogenous). The fourth equation shows that with large excess, reserves banks can lend easily and are forced to accept lower interest rates to get rid of their excesses.

The statistical properties of the 1955 version are perhaps best described as follows. The actual number of nonzero coefficients in the 1955 version (of which 98 are based on accounting identities) was 151; of these, 51 were estimated coefficients expressing net relationship between economic variables. The statistical method used to estimate the 51 parameters was that of the limited information maximum likelihood method. This approach is one in which an equation may be estimated knowing merely the general form of the equation in question and the variables that enter the model as exogenously given. Fox has shown, however, that a cogent argument can be advanced in support of the belief that the use of this technique in such cases as this has little result in the way of additional economic input.[3] That is, in this case, he shows that the ordinary least-squares technique yields the same parameter estimates.

Seven of the estimated 15 limited information equations for 1929–52 show significant measures of autocorrelation of the disturbance terms as indicated by a low von Neumann ratio. The Klein-Goldberger model can be subjected to criticism on many scores, which is only to be expected. It is, after all, an early attempt at modeling an economy. Foremost is the fact that some of the equations finally decided upon for inclusion in the model do not adequately reflect theoretical economic considerations. That is, in some cases equations that were more consistent with conventional economic theory were discarded—in favor of relationships little grounded in economic theory—because they did not fit the data well enough. A case in point is that long-term interest rates are expressed as a function of short-term rates, lagged three and five years, a relationship that is yet to be supported in economic theory.

The degree of aggregation in the model is also very high. This has implications, of course, for the use of the model in a policy context. It is very difficult to determine in the highly aggregated model the effect of certain specific policies on some or all of the crucial variables in the model as fully representative of the policy in question. One of the noteworthy features of the Klein-Goldberger effort is that the model contains lags of up to five periods, distributed lags of the Koyck and dynamic adjustment types, and was the first model to treat imports endogenously and to contain a separate endogenous agricultural sector in an essential way.

What about the monetary sector? If we examine the model, it is indicated that the real sector affects the monetary sector, but that the monetary sector does not affect the real sector in the same year since L_1, L_2, I_1, and I_S occur in the real sector only in lag form. This is unrealistic.[4] In effect, the monetary sector may be considered as inadequately represented here.

BROOKINGS-SSRC MODEL

A model as highly aggregated as the Klein-Goldberger one has major drawbacks if used for policy purposes. Much detailed information on individual sectors of the economy is discarded, and thus lost. Further, interaction between various sectors is poorly expressed and the major channel of communication among sectors is inadequately outlined.

Assuming we desire the coordination of economic policies as a whole, it is obviously most efficient to use the detailed knowledge of specialists in specific economic sectors, and to build an internally consistent model that reflects the interaction among these sectors. For this reason, in 1960 Klein and James Duesenberry organized a major research effort that brought together a number of economists for the purpose of building a much larger and more sophisticated model of the United States economy than had ever been attempted. This is known as the Brookings-SSRC model. Its initial development was sponsored by the Social Science Research Council in 1961–63, through a grant from the National Science Foundation that was later transferred to the Brookings Institute.

In order to reduce some of the problems discussed above, the SSRC model divided the initial research work among approximately 20 economists. Each major block of equations in the model was the responsibility of an economist with special expertise and previous research work in that area. Many of these sectors, including the monetary and financial ones, are treated in greater detail than in the previous model, and thus a clear definition of policy instruments occurs.

The system is a block recursive one—that is, one in which blocks of simultaneous equations feed into one another in a recursive causal chain.[5] The endogenous values are determined in each block by the equation parameters, predetermined variables in the lower order blocks, and exogenous variables.

The model contains about 275 equations, of which 125 are of a stochastic nature, 50 are a priori, and 100 are definitional. The number of variables exogenous to the model is approximately 100. The model was estimated on quarterly data and some annual data, mainly seasonably adjusted, for the period 1953–62.

The financial sector created for use in the Brookings project was designed by Frank DeLeeuw.[6] This model of financial behavior deals with demand and supplies in seven U.S. financial markets—markets for bank reserves, currency, demand deposits, time deposits, U.S. securities, and savings in public insurance and private insurance, with the participants in these markets being banks, nonbank financial institutions, the Federal Reserve, the Treasury, and the public.

The model contains 19 equations, of which four are identities. Most of the equations also contain nonfinancial variables, the main ones being personal and business income and capital expenditures. The model thus portrays the behavior of financial markets given certain crucial real variables. The model itself, of course, does not deal with the effect of interest rates on nonfinancial behavior, but it is within the financial sector that the levels of interest rates (and dollar stocks and flows of financial variables that affect other variables) in the other sectors are determined.

Demand and supply relationships for components of reserves of money involve interest rates and dollar amounts in several other financial markets, and thereby lead directly to a wider group of financial markets.

Underlying most of the equations in this model are several assumptions. First, financial institutions, households, and nonfinancial institutions have in mind long-run desired relationships between the composition of their balance sheets and the level of interest rates in order to maximize net worth. Second, changes in stocks of assets and liabilities by the public and financial institutions are assumed to depend in part on the differences between actual and desired amounts. Third, portfolio adjustments are influenced by short-term constraints as well as actual and desired stocks (that is, adjustments are contingent upon readily available funds). Thus, for example, current income acts as a constraint on portfolio changes by the public, just as wealth constrains the level of stocks. Fourth, all relationships are homogenous of degree one and all are in dollar magnitudes.

A disturbance in one market of a financial model rapidly affects behavior in all seven markets. For example, an increase in the supply of unborrowed reserves and currencies first affects either bank holdings of excess or required reserves, or the public's holding of currency, or combinations of the three. In order for banks to desire to hold more excess reserves, one of the equations says that either the Treasury bill rate must fall, deposits must increase, or bank lending must fall. No matter which occurs, effects spread until all the financial systems and endogenous variables are changed. Effects then continue beyond the financial system, since changes in the interest rates and asset positions affect markets for goods and services.

The financial sector estimated by DeLeeuw has many equations dealing with several types of financial assets and asset holders. In the aggregate version of the model, attention is focused on three financial variables: short- and long-term rates of interest and total cash holdings.[7] These three variables can be estimated fairly well from a compact system of four equations and some definitions. DeLeeuw condensed the model into such a form for use in the aggregate model, with all the effects of the economy included.

In this condensed form, the monetary sector consists of two demand functions: the first for demand deposits and time deposits, and the second for money supply functions for time deposits, interest rate determinants, and the long-term government bond interest rate determinant. Variables endogenous to this sector are holdings of currency, demand deposits, and time deposits, long-term interest rates on government bonds, and required reserves as a function of the ratios of time and demand deposit levels. Exogenous variables include the federal government debt total and short and long maturities, total of all maturities outside the Federal Reserve System, municipal bond yields, and required reserve ratios.

The model attempts to deal with the term structure of the United States security yields in a single equation that is a combination of separate demand for different classes of securities. This equation encompasses the behavior of financial sectors as well as that of the nonfinancial public. The dependent variable in the equation is the difference between the long-term rate and the Treasury bill rate—a single variable presumed to reflect a good deal about the maturity structure of rates. Consider now the econometric aspects. On an exploratory basis, most stochastic equations were estimated by the ordinary least-squares techniques. But since there exists some simultaneity among endogenous variables, consistent methods of estimation are called for when looking at the model as a whole. Thus, for the most part, after all these sectors had been joined together to form the model, limited information maximum likelihood information was used wherever possible. These, however, are very sensitive to multicollinearity and other complications. Therefore, in cases where limited information and estimates were "bad" because of these problems, two-stage least squares was used. In those equations with but one unlagged endogenous variable, ordinary least-squares estimates were retained.

In many of the equations, the lag level of the dependent variable appears as an independent variable. This implies, at the very least, that estimates of these parameters gleaned from the use of ordinary least squares are biased estimates and perhaps inconsistent as well—depending on the pattern of disturbance terms.

In the two-stage procedure, the following eight variables were used as predetermined variables: the New York federal discount rate; an exogenous open market variable equal to unborrowed reserves divided by a fixed-weight combination of required reserves and currency; this variable lagged; current population; current defense spending; real stock; real capital stock at the start of the quarter; GNP lagged one quarter; and new orders for durable goods lagged one quarter.

Two-stage least-squares results are here generally similar to the ordinary least-squares results. Serial correlation is often present in the residuals, but no attempt was made to transform the data in order to increase the efficiency of estimation. The evaluation of the model suggests that, owing to the piecemeal fashion in which the model was constructed, each equation specified by the individual differs from those of the model synthesizers would select, but there also is a tendency for incompatibilities in variable definitions and data sources to arise. Much effort was put forth to minimize any biases, inconsistencies, and inefficiencies resulting from these possibilities.

Some of the model's noteworthy features include: first, this is an extremely elaborate model in which major emphasis has been placed upon government sectors; second, ingenious use of input-output information has been made in relating categories of the final demand conductors sectors; and third, the investment equations distinguish between intentions and realizations, and thus make use of further information in a favorable way.

The monetary-real sector links suggest that, in DeLeeuw's condensed form, the short interest rate is determined; this appears in equations for housing construction, demand, and government interest income. The long-term interest rate is in the investment function and business interest income equations, and cash balances affect consumer demands. These are, in effect, the monetary-real sector links produced by DeLeeuw.

FEDERAL RESERVE-MIT ECONOMETRIC MODEL

The major purpose of the construction of the Federal Reserve-MIT econometric model was to be able to say more than in previous models about the effects of monetary policy instruments. No previous model had as its purpose the quantification of monetary policy and its effects on the economy. Existing models did not satisfactorily serve the needs of those responsible for stabilization policy, for these models did not incorporate adequately policy instruments such as Federal Reserve credit, the discount rate, reserve requirements, the various federal tax rates, and other tax provisions. Thus, in the FRB-MIT model, efforts have been concentrated on treating financial markets and on the links between these markets and the markets for goods and services.

In the model, lags and the demand for money are found to be shorter than estimated elsewhere. Further, the short-term effect of open market operations on interest rates is bound to be smaller than implied in some other models. The financial sector also differs from some others in its inclusion of a model for bank commercial loans as an integral part of the determination of money stocks and interest rates, and by inclusion of a wide range of interest rates.

The results here suggest that both monetary and fiscal policy have significant effects upon the economy, with monetary policy operating with the longer lag. It is also found that the effects of policy on money income are stronger than what is applied in other models.

The model consists of four large blocks of equations.[8] The first block is the financial block, containing demand and supply equations for financial claims. The second block is a fixed investment block, dealing with housing, plant, and equipment, and the behavior of state and local governments. The third block is the consumption inventory block, covering income shares, imports, federal personal taxes, as well as consumption and inventory investments. The fourth block is a price and labor market block, showing a fair degree of rigidity in the short run under conditions of moderate slack in labor and product markets. The model is of intermediate size, containing 65 to 70 stochastic equations estimated on quarterly aggregate data. The financial sector in this block of equations depicts the behavior of financial markets given both GNP and its components and a number of Federal Reserve policy-determined variables. Here the central equation of the block relates an exogenous open market variable on borrowed bank reserves to deposits, reserve requirements, and free reserves. Then three demand equations for these various uses of reserves depend mainly on the interest rates and the components of GNP, with interest rates rising or falling in the short run to bring the quantities demanded and the balance with the exogenous supply. Each of these equations contains a lag value of the dependent variable. Thus, deposits and free reserves adjust but gradually to changes in their determinants, with large jumps in interest rates being implied in order to clear markets in response to a change in unborrowed reserves or reserve requirements.

Six equations in this block show that slower-moving interest rates (for example, the dividend yield on common stocks) are complex distributive lags of the more volatile short-term rates or of the corporate bond rate, which itself depends on short-term rates. Thus, the various rates are closely interrelated and, in turn, so are the various financial markets (for example, the stock market and the bond market).

Monetary policy's effects on the investment block are felt through interest rate changes that affect demand for producer's durables and nonresidential construction in the way suggested by the neoclassical theory of the firm. Mainly, this effect comes through changes in the desired capital output ratios, through "cost of capital" considerations that will be discussed below. Housing inventory, too, starts and depends on consideration of rates of return relative to mortgage rates.

Now consider the money market and interest rate determination equations. Short-term interest rates are determined here by the inter-action of: the demand equation for demand deposits and for currency by the public; demand for earning assets and the resultant supply of demand deposits by commercial banks; and federal government cash balances.[9] This interaction is modified by the central bank through the effects of its policy variables on the commercial banking sector. Further, the demand and supply of commercial loans must be dealt with to complete the model. Commercial bank behavior is significantly influenced by the volume of commercial loans outstanding.

The total money supply in the model consists of the sum of currency and demand deposits. The supply of currency is entirely controlled by the demand for currency. The supply of demand deposits by commercial banks is a function of their demand for earning assets, with the latter being expressed as a function of free reserves, the reserve requirements, unborrowed reserves, changes in time and savings deposits, demand deposits, net at member banks, and the Treasury bill rate. The demand for free reserves is thought of as an inventory held because of uncertainty about changes in deposits and loans to regular customers that affect banks' reserve positions. Demand is here a function of the Treasury bill rate, opportunity cost variable, and the discounting rate representative of the cost of increasing reserves, in addition to changes in bank commercial loans, lag, free reserves, and changes in unborrowed reserves.

Since the commercial paper rate is the short-term rate used in the money demand equation and the Treasury bill rate is the one used in the money supply equations, the model contains an equation relating to two: namely, the commercial paper rate is expressed as a function of the current and lag values of the Treasury bill rate.

The long-term rate is determined via the term structure hypothesis developed by Modigliani and Sutch.[10] The estimated coefficients and equations imply that an equilibrium rate in the long-term interest rate is somewhat higher than the short-term interest rate, a phenomenon that cannot be accounted for by a pure expectations hypothesis.

The econometric considerations are as follows. With regard to simultaneous equation difficulties, simultaneous equation techniques (or transformation of an equation) were used in an attempt to neutralize bias only when it was especially likely to be important. Most parameter estimates were derived by ordinary least-squares procedures with appropriate corrections where necessary for serial correlation of residuals. In general, heavy emphasis was placed on a rather detailed examination of the lag patterns involved, relying largely on Almon-Lagrange interpolation techniques.

The actual specifications of the model reflect the judgment that there were few if any periods of demand inflation (aggregate demand greater than the short-run productive capacity of the economy) in the United States since the Korean War. The structure of the model therefore is built on an explanation of the demand for a constant dollar gross private domestic business product. Prices and wages are largely determined by lag variables. The model is characterized by heavy emphasis on the role of the instruments of economic policy, particularly monetary policy. Implicit in the model structure is that the full effect of monetary policy is felt immediately only in the short-term money market. The effect of monetary policy on long-term bond yields and the cost of capital comes only with a considerable lag; its full effect takes even longer. But the long-term effects of monetary policy seem to be quantitatively important. The time length of this transmission process suggests that the current level of aggregate demand is largely unaffected by current interest rates, except perhaps for housing demands. Thus, given aggregate demand, current interest rates are determined by the supply of Federal Reserve bank credit, currency plus unborrowed reserves, and by other monetary policy instruments.

Fiscal policy effects on aggregate demand come through varying levels of government spending and taxation. The debt management of the Treasury has no impact on this model since the relationship between interest rates on various maturities of debt is taken to be independent of maturity composition of publicly held federal debt. This result might be attributed to the fact that the maturity composition changed little over the period.

The channels of monetary policy, which concern the influence of financial variables on the real economy, are one of the most perplexing macroeconomic problems. Studies by Friedman, Meiselman, Macesich, the staff of the Federal Reserve Bank of St. Louis, and others find monetary variables to be decidedly more important than fiscal variables in explaining movements in money income. Yet several of the large econometric models—the Wharton School model, the Michigan model, and to some extent the Brookings model—give evidence that monetary forces are rather unimportant in influencing total demand. This evidence comes mainly from the fact that in these models, monetary forces influence the real sector through but one channel: an interest rate that effects tangible investment in goods and structures.

The FRB model, with its emphasis on monetary possibilities, encompasses three channels through which the real sector can be affected by financial policy variables: the cost of capital, the wealth effect, and the credit-rationing channels. The cost of capital channel operates on four categories of final demand—equipment, plant, single family housing, and multiple family housing—and also upon state and local construction spending in consumable and durable goods. In the producer category of final demand for plant and equipment, producers are assumed to make plant and equipment decisions so as to maximize expected future profits given product prices, expected future output, and the cost of capital. Demand for equipment is seen to depend on an industrial bond rate and the dividend price ratio on common stock. Housing demand is a function of the mortgage rate. Similarly, a relative (to consumer nondurables) cost term for consumer durable goods is taken as a function of relative price and past interest rates on corporate bonds, the latter serving as a proxy for unobserved rates and other credit terms on credit installment contracts. The capital stock the government desires to hold is assumed to be a function of relative prices and interest rates (measured by rates on state and local bonds), among other variables.

The second channel of monetary policy is through the net worth of consumers. There are two crucial relationships here: the length between household net worth—one component of which is the value of common stock equities—and consumption, and the length between financial rates of return and the stock market rate of return (and hence the value of equities). Involved here is the life-cycle hypothesis of saving or consumption in which total consumption depends on current and lagged disposable income and net worth (which is defined to include capital gains along with accumulation due to past savings). With the net worth dependent then upon the volatile stock market in the form of the dividend price ratio, long swings in this market can have important effects on the economy.

The third channel is consumer rationing, which refers to the failure of the interest rates on loans to adjust rapidly enough to clear financial markets, so that lenders ration credit by various nonprice terms, such as changes in downpayment terms and other nonrecorded devices. These effects show up empirically more transparently in the mortgage housing market than in any other credit market.

ST. LOUIS FEDERAL RESERVE BANK MODEL

The St. Louis model is designed to analyze economic stabilization within a monetarist framework, focusing on the influence of monetary changes on total spending.[11] The model is very small in comparison with other models that incorporate a large number of behavioral relationships. It attempts to focus on certain strategic variables and their response to monetary and statistical action.

The St. Louis model consists of eight endogenous variables to be determined in the model's eight equations, five stochastic variables, three definitions, and three nonlagged exogenous variables, though other variables do enter in lagged form. The variables exogenous to the model are: changes in money stocks; changes in high employment federal expenditures; and potential (full employment) output. The eight endogenous variables are: first, the change in total spending, which is specified as a function of current and past demand pressures and anticipated price changes; second, the change in the price levels, which is specified as a function of current and past demand pressures and anticipated price changes; third, demand pressure, which is defined as the change in total spending minus the potential increase in output; fourth, the change in output, which enters the structural form of the model as the variable in both a total spending identity and the interest rate equation (its value is determined from the former, given other variables' determined values); fifth, the market rate of interest, which is specified as a function of current change, changes in the money stock, and past changes in output, current price change, and anticipated price changes; sixth, the anticipated price level change, which is specified as a function of past price changes; seventh, the unemployment rate, which is a function of the current and past GNP gaps; and eighth, the GNP gap, which is specified as a function of the potential full employment output and actual current output. The crucial relationship in this model is the first specification given—total spending as determined by monetary and fiscal actions—though this gives no direct explanation as to how these actions affect spending. The change in total spending is combined with potential output to provide a demand pressure measure, which comes with an anticipated price change measure to determine changes in the price level. Given this change in the price level, the change in output can be determined from the total spending identity. The changes in output prices, anticipated prices, and money stock determine market interest rates. The unemployment rate is determined by combining the change in output with potential change to determine the GNP gap, which is then transformed into an un-employment rate.

The significant differences are as follows. In most econometric models, output and prices are determined separately and then are combined for a measure of total spending or nominal GNP. The St. Louis model first determines the change in total spending, and from this the division of the change into output and price change. The market interest rate does not play a direct part in the model in determining spending, output, and prices, owing to the lack of any kind of investment demand function. This, of course, is a significant departure from those models stressing belief in the efficiency of fiscal actions as stabilization measures. The econometric considerations are that the data used in estimating the various relationships mentioned above are quarterly, seasonally adjusted data for the period 1953–69. The "best" empirical specification of each equation was chosen on the basis of minimization of standard error or estimate, elimination of serial correlation of the residuals, correct sign, and statistical significance of the estimated coefficients. Various lag structures were tested before selection of the various equations.

In general, it can be said that the estimated coefficient change in the money stock and Federal Reserve expenditures is in agreement with the monetary view of the response of total spending on these variables. These coefficients show that monetary actions have a large and rapid influence on total spending relative to the fiscal operations, which have some short-run effects. The spending equations indicate that about half of the total response of change in monetary growth occurs in the first two quarters, about 80 percent in the first three quarters. The effect of a change in total spending is reflected first in output, later in price.

Although interest rates have no explicit role in the model in transmitting changes in the money stock to changes in output and prices, the estimated long-run market interest rates play a crucial role in the calculation of price anticipation measures. The long-term rate is measured by the rate on seasonally adjusted AAA corporate bonds.

The empirical results showing the best equation explaining the long-term rate to be a function of change in output and prices lagged from 17 periods reflect the view expressed by monetarists that a change in the rate of monetary expansion influences market interest rates in three stages. First, the liquidity effect of an increase in the rate of change in the money stock on interest rates is negative. Next, there is an influence in the rate of monetary expansion on the rate of change in output. This in turn has a positive influence on the rate of change in prices, which has a positive effect on market prices.

Econometric models are useful. But in realizing their potential, it is also important to understand their limitations. Many of these models are the results of the increased interest in the postwar period of applying Keynesian economic theory to the practical problems of governmental policies, the buildup of an economic data base, and the rapid growth of computer technology. The expectations of these economists and others was that such models were the answer to the challenges of economic forecasting and policymaking. These economists were to be disappointed, as was discussed in Chapter 8.

This is not surprising. Data shortcomings in both quality and quantity are serious. Large-scale econometric models of the type preferred by Keynesians are particularly vulnerable because they require so much data. Even more serious errors are those resulting from the failure to properly describe relationships between variables. For instance, as discussed earlier, the relative roles of monetary and fiscal policies are not always adequately portrayed.

Furthermore, the evidence suggests that a mechanical use of available models cannot be relied upon for accurate prediction, since inflexible mathematical formulas cannot automatically adjust to changes in the economy they describe. For instance, many of these models badly underestimated both the speedups and the slowdowns in the inflation rate during the 1970s. Indeed, the construction of ever larger and more complex econometric models may have been pushed too fast in recent years. This movement may well have left behind efforts to test each model's analytical foundations and to evaluate its performance.[12]

NOTES

1. Mark Nerlove, "A Tabular Survey of Macro-Economic Models," in *International Economic Review* (May 1966): 127–75. See also George Macesich, "Money, Monetary Policy and Econometric Models," *Jugoslovensko Bankarstvo* (December 1973): 14–25, and W. Allen Spivey and William J. Wrobleski, *Econometric Model Performance in Forecasting and Policy Assessment* (Washington, D.C.: AEI for Public Policy, 1979).

2. L. R. Klein and A. S. Goldberger, *An Econometric Model of the United States, 1929–1952* (Amsterdam: North-Holland, 1955).

3. Carl A. Fox, *Intermediate Economic Statistics* (New York: Wiley, 1968).

4. H. Theil, *Principles of Econometrics* (New York: Wiley, 1971).

5. L. R. Klein and Gary Fromm, "The Brookings-SSRC Quarterly Econometric Model of the United States: Model Properties," *American Economic Review* (May 1965): 348–61.

6. Frank DeLeeuw, "A Model of Financial Behavior," Chapter 13 in *The Brookings Quarterly Econometric Model of the United States*, James Duesenberry et al., eds. (Chicago: Rand-McNally, 1965), pp. 465–532.

7. Duesenberry et al., eds., *The Brookings Quarterly Econometric Model of the United States*, pp. 726–27.

8. Frank DeLeeuw and Edward Gramlich, "The Federal Reserve-MIT Econometric Model," *Federal Reserve Bulletin* (January 1968): 11–40; idem, "The Channels of Monetary Policy," *Federal Reserve Bulletin* (June 1969): 472–91.

9. Robert H. Rasche and Harold T. Shapiro, "The FRB-MIT Econometric Model: Its Special Features," *American Economic Review* (May 1968): 123–49.

10. F. Modigliani and R. Sutch, "Innovations in Interest Rate Policy," *American Economic Review* (May 1966): 178–97.

11. L. C. Anderson and T. M. Carlson, "A Monetary Model for Economic Stabilization," *Monthly Review*, Federal Reserve Bank of St. Louis (April 1970): 7–25.

12. Spivey and Wrobleski, in *Econometric Model Performance*, present a useful guide to the current status of the evolution of forecasts made with the use of large-scale econometric models. Various descriptive measures of quarterly forecast errors of the Wharton, Data Resources, Inc., Chase Econometric Associates, and BEA econometric models are examined, as well as the inherent limitations of all published studies of forecast errors. The authors conclude with a brief critique of some studies of the policy multiplier performance of econometric models.

10

THE MONETARY APPROACH AND THE BALANCE OF PAYMENTS

MONETARY STANDARDS AND EXCHANGE RATES

Three different types of monetary arrangements can be usefully distinguished.[1] One is a single commodity standard such as gold or silver; a domestic fiat standard with agreed upon exchange rates between countries such as existed during the postwar Bretton Woods arrangement; and a fiat standard with flexible (or floating) exchange rates among national currencies in existence since 1973.

Consider the gold or specie standard that served much of the trading world for many years. As a monetary standard, the international gold standard dominated the pre-1914 world economic scene. The necessary operation of the standard required participating countries to observe certain rules:

A country must take steps to fix the specie value of its national currency.

There must be a free import and export of specie into and out of each country making up the gold standard system.

Each country must make arrangements for its own money such that the supply of that money goes up when there is a persistent inflow of gold into its territory, and such that it goes down when there is a persistent export of gold out of its territory.

These three rules are sufficient to ensure external balance between the countries on a gold standard. But in order to ensure what we call "internal balance" as well, a further rule must be observed:

In each country there must be a reasonable degree of price flexibility.

Although a relatively minor part of the nineteenth- and early twentieth-century trading world, the United States along with other countries participated in the operation of the international gold standard. This required the United States and others to observe the four rules enumerated above. In accordance with these rules, the exchange rate was fixed. To a first approximation the internal price level in the United States was determined by the external price level; it had to be whatever was necessary in relation to the external price level to keep payments, including capital flows, in balance. This means that there is a special domestic problem to explain only insofar as internal prices move differently from external prices. It does not mean that domestic conditions cannot affect the internal price level. They can insofar as they affect the conditions of external balance. For example, suppose internal monetary expansion threatens suspension. This will promote a capital outflow that will be deflationary—that is, suspension will be avoided only by an internal price level sufficiently low relative to the external price level to create the surplus to finance the capital outflow.

If a country is not on the gold standard and fixed exchange rates, the situation is different. Internal monetary changes affect the price level and through it the exchange rate, so the price level is no longer rigidly linked to price levels abroad.

This link with external conditions under fixed exchange rates is important because internal disturbances may be simply a manifestation of a disturbance more fundamental in nature. This is, in fact, one link emphasized by monetarists in their discussions of balance-of-payments problems. It is a view that evolves from classical theory. Accordingly, money used as a standard of value consists of coin (or notes redeemable in coin or bullion) and the coins circulate at their value as bullion. This money is assumed to be convertible into gold and silver bars and to be freely exchangable either as coin or as bullion between countries. Its value is fixed at its bullion value, and the rate of exchange between two countries is easily calculated by comparing the intrinsic value of the precious metal in their coins. In these conditions, the supply of precious metals would internationally adjust itself to the needs of trade in each country.

Ricardo, Mill, and others believed that there is nothing a government can do about a country's money supply. If a government issues paper money beyond the amount that the public would accept in the belief that these notes could at any moment be converted into gold, the surplus issue would be cashed and the government would have to redeem it with gold or silver from its reserves. If the notes are made inconvertible, their value would fall and the price of gold/silver and all commodities as measured in the paper money will rise in proportion to their overissue. Moreover, money accommodates itself to the needs of trade. True money is gold and silver, and is beyond government control. There is thus no place in classical economics for positive or manipulative money policies.

Neoclassicists adopted a more flexible approach to the control of money and monetary policy. In fact, they assign to monetary policy a major role in preserving economic stability through proper management of the supply of money. This is done by a central bank acting as proxy for government. The criterion for such control, however, is to limit monetary expansion to the legitimate needs of trade. In practice, banks are to restrict themselves to short-term, self-liquidating commercial loans. In effect, the real-bills doctrine provides the guideline, albeit an unsatisfactory one, for monetary control.

The contemporary world differs radically from the world of the early nineteenth century, whose revolutions were aimed at assuring political and economic liberty by breaking through the outworn controls of a preceding age of regulation. For the most part, the revolutions of our time have been protests against the philosophy and institutions of the system of individualism based on natural rights. They have aimed at the opposite values of social control, and they have created myths and utopias that differ radically from the nineteenth-century utopias of individual liberty. The impersonal forces of the market on which classical (and neoclassical) economists relied to bring about a maximum of production and distribution (which, if not equitable, would at least be effective in maintaining high production) tend now to be displaced as political ideals by such other objectives as full employment and various social safety-net programs.

These interventionist ideas are not new. They have been evolving in the history of economics for more than a century. The only mechanism presently available for pushing these ideas into practice is the nation-state. The evidence for this is found everywhere, and nowhere is it more conclusive than that in the field of domestic and international monetary affairs. Monetary policies directed toward various goals, including stabilizing the national income, constitute a formidable reinforcement of nationalism in the economic sphere. Whatever may be thought of the wisdom or practicability of such intervention, the fact must be recognized that the nineteenth-century integration of market processes has been impaired by the emergence in every country of a greater measure of state intervention, particularly in monetary affairs.

Moreover, the days of the gold standard and fixed exchange rates were not as golden as its advocates claim. Between 1815 and 1914 there were 12 major crises or panics in the United States, which pushed up interest rates, created severe unemployment, and suspended specie payments (conversion of the dollar into gold), in addition to 14 minor recessions.[2] To be sure, between 1879 and 1965, a period when the United States was on some sort of gold standard (the dollar's final links with gold were not cut until 1971, during Nixon's administration), the consumer price index rose by an average of only 1.4 percent a year. On the other hand, severe bouts of inflation were followed by deep deflation in which prices actually fell. For instance, in the 1921 world recession when production fell for only a few months, there were 30 to 40 percent cuts in manufacturing wages in some countries over the the period 1920–22.

A fiat or paper money standard coupled with flexible exchange rates takes into account varying political, economic, cultural, and historical conditions of the world community of nations, thereby avoiding friction over conflicting issues of national sovereignty. The International Monetary Fund (IMF) has never become the international central bank that some of its founders hoped it would, though it has brought a measure of discipline to the fluttery currency exchanges. Flexible exchange rates provide an automatic trade-balancing mechanism, thereby eliminating the necessity for exchange and trade controls.[3] At the same time, individual nations are freed from having to coordinate monetary (and fiscal) policies and economic development programs with other nations. Encroachment into the delicate area of national sovereignty is minimized.

A system of flexible exchange rates would also help compensate for the "stickiness" of wages and prices brought about by different stages of economic development among member states of the world community. By promoting what would partially deputize for competitive price flexibility, flexible exchange rates would increase the effectiveness of the price mechanism and thus contribute to legitimate world economic integration. Such an arrangement provides a means for combining interdependence among countries through trade with the greatest possible amount of internal monetary and fiscal independence; no country would be able to impose its mistakes of policy on others, nor would it have others' mistakes imposed on it. Every country would be free to pursue policies for internal stability according to its own appraisal of possibilities. If all member countries succeeded in their internal policies, reasonably stable exchange rates would prevail. Effective intercountry coordination would be achieved without the risks of formal but ineffective coordination.

On the other hand, critics of a system of flexible exchange rates argue that an exchange rate left to find its own level will not necessarily trace out an optimum path through time. An optimum, however, is very difficult to define since its criteria hinge on medium- and long-term expectations that can never be guaranteed.[4] Nevertheless, there is no necessity that the market per se will yield such a reasonably satisfactory rate. Moreover, in small, undiversified, and less-developed countries, a lack of sophisticated individuals with a heterogeneous outlook and sufficient capital may impair the working of a competitive market in foreign exchange.

Another criticism is that exchange rate adjustments will not necessarily insulate the level of domestic activity while correcting an internal imbalance. Exchange rate adjustments are particularly desirable where price levels have moved out of line. The exchange rate correction will restore the terms of trade to their original position and leave the volume and balance of trade and real income in each country at their original levels. The units of measurement will simply be changed. This is no longer true where the sources of disturbance are structural changes in trading countries, different rates of full employment growth, and cyclical income fluctuations. In effect, repercussions on domestic employment and output can be reduced, but apparently they cannot be eliminated by flexible exchange rates.

THE THEORY

The monetary theory of the balance of payments interprets surpluses and deficits as results of excess demands and supplies of money in a country.[5] The theory argues that international or inter-regional money flows eliminate the surpluses or deficits and so create balance-of-payments equilibrium and monetary equilibrium at the same time. It stresses the stability of the money demand and supply functions. The theory is, in fact, an extension of the monetarist quantity theory discussed earlier. It encompasses the gold standard or gold-exchange standards of years past as well as contemporary fiat money standards with regimes of floating or flexible exchange rates such as have existed since 1973.

To be sure, the "law of one price" or the Purchasing Power Parity Theory (PPP) is an important (if not necessarily critical) element in the monetarist approach to the balance of payments. What is important is that after allowing for transportation costs, tariffs, and similar items, prices of identical goods will be equalized in the long run. There may very well be departures in the prices for these goods in the short run. In the long run, however, arbitrage will ensure equality. The analysis is more complicated by the existence of traded and nontraded goods. This does not, however, invalidate the results.

The Purchasing Power Parity Theory combines with the monetary approach to the balances of payments to explain movements of international exchange rates between national currencies over both the short and long run. The essential proposition of the theory is that, in the long run, exchange rates adjust to the relative purchasing powers of different national currencies. As noted above, internal purchasing powers of currencies are determined by relative demands and supplies of domestic currencies. Exchange rates are, in the final analysis, determined by factors that affect the demand for money such as interest rates, real income, and the money supply in each country. The PPP theory thus argues that, as a consequence, monetary authorities have little direct influence on exchange rates.

Inflationary expectations play an important role, especially in the short-run theory. For instance, we discussed earlier Irving Fisher's argument that nominal interest rates equal the real interest rate and the expected rate of inflation. By the extension of the law of one price to international capital markets, and except for differences in risks and cost of transporting loanable funds between markets, competition for borrowing and lending should equalize the real rate of interest.

Nevertheless, people will not readily lend abroad if they expect a high rate of inflation abroad to erode the purchasing power of the principal sum of their loans. As a result, nominal interest rates will adjust so as to reflect expected rates of inflation in each country. These expectations are reflections of traders in international money and capital markets and their expectations of excessive monetary growth in various countries.[6] The higher the expected excess monetary growth (other things being equal), the higher will be the expected rate of inflation and the higher will be nominal interest rates relative to those elsewhere.

We can express the monetary approach more formally as follows: assume full employment in each country so that national income stays fixed at Y at home and Y* abroad. Domestic and foreign price levels are P and P*, nominal money supplies are M and M*. Assume also that the velocity of money, V and V*, is given and independent of the interest rate. Then the domestic and foreign demands for money are respectively:

$$M = (1/V)PY \text{ and } M^* = (1/V^*)P^*Y^* \tag{1}$$

Rearranging these expressions, the price levels are

$$P = V(M/Y) \text{ and } P^* = V^*(M^*/Y^*) \tag{2}$$

If E is the exchange rate that is the price of foreign currency, and absolute PPP holds, then $P = EP^*$, or $E = P/P^*$. Substituting, we get:

$$E = \left(\frac{M}{M^*} \right) \left(\frac{V}{V^*} \right) \left(\frac{Y}{Y^*} \right). \tag{3}$$

Domestic currency depreciates (that is, E rises) if the domestic money supply grows faster than that abroad, domestic real income grows more slowly than that abroad, or the domestic velocity coefficient increases relative to that abroad.

The theory may be extended so as to take into account that velocity (reciprocal of the demand for money) depends on real income and the alternative cost of holding money:[7]

$$V = Y^{n-1} \exp(\theta r). \tag{4}$$

where r is the nominal rate of interest. The functional form is a matter of expositional convenience and monetary tradition.

Substituting (4) into (3) and taking logs, we obtain the standard equation of the monetary approach:

$$e = m - m^* + \lambda(y - y^*) + \theta(r - r^*) \tag{5}$$

where e, m, and m^* are logarithms of the corresponding capital letter variables.

Equation (5) says that an increase in domestic money stock or a decline in domestic relative income will lead to a depreciation, as would a rise in domestic interest rates. The conclusion that a rise in interest rates will lead to depreciation is contrary to received doctrine, which holds that the exchange rate will appreciate. The explanation is as follows: an increase in interest rates reduces the demand for real cash balances. Given the nominal stock of money, the price level must increase to reduce the real stock of money to its lower equilibrium level. Since domestic prices are rising and thus out of line with those of other countries, a depreciation is required to restore PPP.

A LOOK AT THE EVIDENCE

How consistent is the monetary approach to the balance of payments with available empirical evidence? The answer to this shall draw briefly on the studies of Putman, Zecher, and Wilford on international reserve flows and Macesich and Tsai's investigation of the United States, Canada, and Mexico.[8]

The model developed by Putnam and Wilford is also examined by Wilford and Zecher for Mexico. This model is also tested by Macesich and Tsai against the floating exchange rate experience of the United States, Canada, and Mexico. The basic reserve flow equation is:

$$\left(\frac{R}{H} \right) gR = b_o + b_1 gY + b_2 gr + b_3 gP + b_4 ga$$

$$+ b_5 \left(\frac{D}{H} \right) gD + u \tag{6}$$

where: $gX = dlnX/dt =$ the rate of growth in country j of $X:X=R_1$ Y, P_1 r, a, D and:

P = price level
r = interest rate
Y = real income
u = a log normal distributed disturbance term
a = the money multiplier
R = the stock of international reserves
D = domestic credit

The annual data for the period 1973–80 are from the IMF's *International Financial Statistics*. Interest rates are comparable for Canada, Mexico, and the United States, and the price variables are the individual consumer price indexes. The real income variable is nominal GNP deflated by the consumer price index. Money supplies are narrowly defined.

In addition to estimating equations specified solely with domestic prices and interest rates as proxies for the world price level and interest rate, the purchasing power parity and interest rate parity assumptions are integrated directly into the reduced form tests as suggested by Putnam and Wilford. Thus, U.S. price level and interest rates that also serve as proxies for world variables are substituted for domestic variables. This specification follows from the hypothesis that "the world's financial markets ensure interest arbitrage such that movements in any interest rates (the U.S. rate specifically) reflect the underlying real factors which cause a portfolio holder to demand money.[9] Results for the floating exchange rate regime, 1973–80 are summarized in Table 10.1, where U.S. prices and interest rates are used as "proxies" for world variables.

Further, the stock of high-powered money H_j in country j is defined in two different ways:

H_j = international reserves (foreign exchanges) + domestic credit

or

H_j = net foreign assets (monetary survey) + domestic credit

For the floating exchange period 1973–80 results are less satisfactory than reported by Wilford, Putman, Zecher and others for the fixed exchange rate period. Most of the F-values are not significant at the 0.05 level. However, when high-powered money is defined as a sum of net foreign assets and domestic credit, the results for Canada and Mexico are superior. All F-values are highly significant at the 0.05 level. The R^2's range from .9491 to .9980. Most of the regression coefficients are significantly different from zero for Canada and Mexico. However, the signs of coefficients for most of the variables are not in conformity with the theory. These results may be due to drastic changes in the Mexican economic structure and its foreign economic policy during the period 1973–80. There is additional evidence in the fact that U.S. prices and interest rates seem to have a rather significant effect on the Mexican and Canadian balance-of-payments equilibrium.

Additional insight into the exchange rate issue may be had by testing a simple static equilibrium model of exchange rate determination proposed by Humphrey and Lawler.[10] The model states that the bilateral exchange rate between any two national currencies is determined by relative money stocks, relative real incomes, and relative nominal interest rates—the last variable reflecting expectational influences that enter into exchange rate determination. In other words, the interest rate

TABLE 10.1. International Reserve Flows Canada, Mexico, and United States: (U.S. Prices and Interest Rates) 1973–80—Flexible E/R Period

Country	No. of Eq.	R^2 / F	DW / R	SEEB / SEE	Constant t-ratios	Real Income	Interest Rate	Price Level	Money Multiplier*	Domestic Credit
High-powered Money = International Reserves (Foreign Exchange) + Domestic Credit										
Canada	1	.7837	2.0476	.0046	.0006	.1364	.00003	-.0041	.1148	.1180
		1.4491	.8853	.0023	.0360	2.1420	.0051	-.0553	2.3352	1.3855
Mexico	2	.8764	1.4549	.0471	.0315	.1518	-.0102	-.1112	-.5642	.3743
		2.8355	.9361	.0235	.1912	.2240	-.1176	-.1171	-2.1575	.4274
United States	3									
High-powered Money = Net Foreign Assets + Domestic Credit										
Canada	4	.9905	2.0361	.0029	-.0387	.2163	-.0231	.1233	-.1139	.0850
		41.5816	.9952	.0014	-4.0585	4.7179	-5.5930	2.8109	-3.9201	1.8966
Mexico	5	.9995	3.7356	.0981	2.6640	-62.8310	1.9209	9.7313	10.7864	3.3659
		798.4199	.9997	.0491	9.8017	-41.0841	9.3720	3.1162	16.9863	2.6821
United States	6									

*Calculated on basis of M_1.

Source: International Financial Statistics (Washington, D.C.: International Monetary Fund, May 1980–September 1981).

variable reflects relative expectations regarding national inflationary prospects.

The following reduced-form exchange rate equation is estimated and used by Macesich and Tsai to explain the behavior of the United States/Canada, United States/Mexico, and Canada/Mexico exchange rates, respectively, over the post-1972 period of generalized floating:

$$\ln X = a_0 + a_1 \ln(M/M^o) - a_2 \ln(Y/Y^o) + a_3 \ln(r/r^o) \qquad (7)$$

where X = the exchange rate (defined as the domestic currency price of a unit foreign currency)

Y = real income

M = nominal money stock (assumed to be exogenously determined by the central bank)

r = nominal rate of interest

o = omicrons used to distinguish foreign country variables from home variables

a_i = coefficients to be estimated from the statistical data.

It is noted that a priori expected values of the coefficients attached to the money and income variables are unity, whereas the coefficients attached to the interest rate variables should lie between zero and unity. Annual data for the period 1973–80 are used in the analysis. The results are shown in Table 10.2.

The empirical results are, in general, consistent with the theoretical model. All of the coefficients on the explanatory variables have the expected signs, except the coefficients on United States/Canada interest rate. All coefficients on Mexico/United States money stock, real income, and interest rate variables are statistically significant at the 0.01 level. The coefficients on Canada/Mexico money stock and interest rate are also significantly different from zero at the 0.01 level. However, the Canada/Mexico coefficient on real income is not significantly different from zero at the 0.01 level. The results for Canada/United States exchange rate are less satisfactory. Only the coefficients on money stock and real income (when M_1 is used) are significant at the 0.01 level. Thus, the empirical results obtained by Macesich and Tsai seem to support the simple model of exchange rate determination developed by Humphrey and Lawler. These results suggest that the model is a fairly accurate description of floating exchange rate regimes, at least, for the Mexico/United States and Canada/Mexico exchange rates.

Additional insights into our discussion are provided in a recent National Bureau of Economic Research study of how inflation was transmitted among countries during the Bretton Woods fixed exchange

TABLE 10.2. Exchange Rates, 1973–80, Flexible E/R Period

Eq. No.	Exchange Rates	M_q^s	R^2 / F	Constant t-ratios	$\ln(M/M^0)$	$\ln(Y/Y^0)$	$\ln(r/r^0)$
1	CA$/US$	M_1	.7735	3.5505	1.6905	1.6535	-.7222
			4.5536	3.5759	3.0327	2.1567	-3.1265
2		M_2	.9366	.3333	.5311	-.2366	-.1477
			19.7021	.7392	6.5694	-.4806	-1.3115
3	PESO/US$	M_1	.9235	1.0794	1.7378	-4.0886	.5080
			16.0980	4.5579	3.4854	-2.0326	2.6778
4		M_2	.9614	1.5641	1.4767	-2.7918	.3197
			33.2461	16.0843	5.2947	-2.5432	2.6910
5	CA$/PESO	M_1	.9447	-1.3125	1.1884	-.9381	.9580
			22.7933	-1.9354	5.0994	-.8980	4.8477
6		M_2	.9058	-.6237	1.3438	.2619	.7290
			12.8169	-.7991	3.6874	.2249	3.0974

Source: International Financial Statistics (Washington, D.C.: International Monetary Fund, May 1980–September 1981).

rate period.[11] For the most part, the study covers the period 1955–76 and includes the United States, United Kingdom, Canada, France, Germany, Italy, Japan, and the Netherlands. According to the study, monetary factors are responsible for the worldwide inflation during this period. Such special factors as OPEC-induced oil price rises in 1973–74, the monopoly power of business and unions, and the substantial rise in commodity prices account for only a small part of the inflation.

The inflation of the 1960s and 1970s was a monetary phenomenon. A key role was played by the United States. Its excessive monetary growth was exported abroad via the fixed exchange rate system in existence de facto until 1973. This is, in fact, consistent with monetarist ideas discussed earlier.

The oil-shock hypothesis advanced by some people receives limited empirical support in this study. Increased oil prices can affect the general price level either by decreasing the real quantity of money demanded or by increasing the nominal quantity of money supplied. Indeed, the oil shock appears to account at most for 1 percent of the 3.5 percent increase in the average 1971–75 inflation rate over 1966–70.

If acceleration of money growth is the major cause of the worldwide inflation, the evidence points to the United States, the reserve country, as the culprit. In the first instance, international factors accounted for little in the Federal Reserve's money supply reaction function. Indeed, variations in the United States' money growth were a cause of its balance-of-payments flows, which affected domestic money growth in the seven other countries but not in the United States.

Moreover, growth in real money demanded in the United States is stable over long periods, even though it is responsive to money and other shocks in the short run. According to the reported results for four-year averages, variations in nominal money growth explain some 97 percent of the variations in postwar U.S. inflation. In effect, the acceleration of the trend rate of U.S. inflation is domestic and not international in origin.

Evidence is also provided by Darby et al. as to whether induced reserve flows were completely or partially sterilized during the Bretton Woods era. Monetarists argue that sterilization is impossible in the long run. The level of foreign currency reserves provides a limit to the duration of time a deficit country can finance a deficit and therefore sterilize the monetary effects. However, it is not clear that there are similar pressures on a surplus country that is continually acquiring reserves. To be sure, it is irrational for a country to pursue a long-run policy of achieving continuous balance-of-payments surplus, for it means that it is willing to trade goods and services for foreign balances without limit.

According to Darby et al.'s evidence, which is based upon three separate investigations of sterilization, partial or complete sterilization appears to have been a general practice for the set of industrialized nonreserve countries studied. Their finding is consistent with short-run sterilization and a pattern of lagged adjustments. They consider as well an important conclusion of the monetary approach to the balance of payments—that nonreserve central banks are unimportant with respect to their domestic money supplies and interest rates, but can attain any desired balance of payments via their actions. This conclusion is based on the following assumptions: goods are perfect substitutes internationally, and assets are perfect substitutes. Darby et al. add a third assumption—that expectations of depreciation are also responsive to variations in the balance of payments. Any one of these three conditions, along with others, precludes effective monetary control. As such, it is difficult to test conclusively the importance of nonreserve bank control with respect to their money supplies.

Nevertheless, the authors conclude that nonreserve central banks did in fact exercise monetary control under pegged exchange rates. They argue that the direct evidence on the two major conditions indicated that neither goods nor assets were perfect substitutes internationally. According to their interpretation, the evidence was incontrovertible that the actual growth in the money supply was determined, in part, by domestic policy goals.

As a result, Darby et al. conclude that the adjustment process under the Bretton Woods System can be characterized roughly as follows: first, international factors as such played a minor role in the U.S. monetary and inflationary trends. These were determined largely by domestic factors. Second, the proximate determinant of inflation in the nonreserve countries was found to be in their own past money supply growth. Third, changes in money growth in the United States did not lead to significant capital outflows. Trade-flow effects built up as a result of inflation shifted price levels. Fourth, these balance-of-payments flows did not significantly impact on the nonreserve country money growth. Their cumulative lagged effects could be very important.

In fact, they argue, it is this long cumulative lag from U.S. money growth to an increase in inflation in nonreserve countries that can explain the failure of the Bretton Woods System. According to the study, the increase in U.S. inflation at the onset of the 1966–70 period had little impact on inflation rates in the nonreserve countries. As the U.S. inflation continued, however, relative price levels shifted by some 8 percent. The nonreserve countries responded with a lag, and their money growth rates began to rise in response to growing balance-of-payments surpluses.

The inflation rates of these countries responded only with an additional lag. Eventually the large surpluses of the late 1960s and early 1970s generated a money growth that was sufficient to outpace U.S. inflation in 1971–75. The inflation so generated offset about half of the 8 percent change in relative price levels that had occurred in 1966–70. These surpluses, however, became so large as to produce speculative capital flows and a breakdown of the Bretton Woods System.

To make matters worse, the inflation rate targets of the Federal Reserve System and nonreserve banks were not in harmony. Had they been so, the lagged adjustment process outlined above might have been equal to the relatively small stress implied by once-and-for-all shifts in purchasing power. As Darby et al. point out, however, the strong upward trend in the U.S. money supply reaction function was closer to such countries as Great Britain and Italy, which preferred faster money supply growth. Furthermore, the United States at the same time parted from such countries as Germany, which preferred a lower money supply growth and lower rate of inflation.

The essential message Darby et al. underscore is that controlling inflation reduces to the problem of controlling the money supply. This is technically possible, although central banks were not directed to do so by any constitutional requirement establishing a specific money growth rule or fixing the exchange rate between money and either a commodity or the currency of a country fixed in terms of such a commodity.

The special position of the United States as a reserve currency country also suggests the asymmetry of the Bretton Woods System. The feedback from the reserve currency country (in this case the United States) and its balance of payments to its money supply is broken. Other countries were willing to acquire certain liquid assets drawn on the United States and to regard these as reserve assets. An expansionary monetary policy by the reserve country may have no effect on its balance of payments; its trading partners will register a surplus in their balance of payments, leading to an inflow of foreign exchange reserves. One result is that the money supply becomes controllable by the monetary authorities in the currency reserve country. In effect, monetary policy has a domestic impact for a reserve country under fixed and flexible exchange rates, both in the short and long-run. Monetary policies in nonreserve countries have limited value since they are compelled, at least in the long run, to accept the rate of monetary expansion originating in the reserve country if they wish to remain on fixed exchange rates.

Since 1973 the world has passed over to a system of managed floating, which is somewhere between a fixed and flexible exchange rate system. As a result, monetary policy effects both a country's balance of payments and its exchange rate. The important issue is the degree of government intervention. If government intervention is limited to "extreme circumstances" (which is, in fact, what the Reagan administration has adopted), the situation is similar to a flexible exchange rate system. On the other hand, if government intervention to manage the exchange rate is more than an occasional venture, then the situation is fairly close to a fixed exchange rate regime.

The United States is under considerable pressure to "pay more attention to the dollar's foreign exchange rate."[12] A group of 30 leading world commercial and central bankers and government officials (including Henry Wallich, a governor of the Federal Reserve Board, and Anthony M. Solomon, president of the Federal Reserve Bank of New York) signed a statement that the "time has come for the U.S., in both its own and the common interest, to pay more attention to exchange-rate considerations in framing its domestic policies and in particular, to avoiding an unbalanced mix of monetary and fiscal policies." The Reagan administration, however, contends that governments and central banks should stay out of foreign exchange markets. The United States is prepared to intervene in the market to counter only "severe disorders."

NOTES

1. See, for example, Milton Friedman, "Monetary Policy: Theory and Practice," *Journal of Money, Credit and Banking* (February 1982): 98–118; Milton Friedman and Anna J. Schwartz, *A Monetary History of the United States, 1867–1960* (Princeton: Princeton University Press, 1963); George Macesich, "Sources of Monetary Disturbances in the United States, 1834–45." *Journal of Economic History* (September 1960): 407–34; George Macesich, "International Trade and United States Economic Development Revisited," *Journal of Economic History (September 1961). Reprinted in Stanley Cohen and Forest Hill, eds., American Economic History: Essays in Interpretation* (Philadelphia: Lippincott, 1966); Phillip Cagan, "The First Fifty Years of the National Banking System: An Historical Appraisal," in Deanne Carson, ed., *Banking and Monetary Studies* (Homewood, Ill.: Irwin, 1963); J. Earnest Tanner and Vittorio Bonemo, "Gold, Capital Flows, and Long Swings in American Business Activity," *Journal of Political Economy* (January/February 1968): 44–52; T.W. Willet, "International Specie Flows and American Monetary Stability," *Journal of Economic History* (March 1968): 28–50; George Macesich, *The Political Economy of Money* (forthcoming.)

2. *Economist*, September 19, 1981, pp. 17–18.

3. Milton Friedman "The Case for Flexible Exchange Rates," in M. Friedman, ed., *Essays in Positive Economics* (Chicago: University of Chicago Press, 1953), pp. 157–203;

Harry G. Johnson, "The Case for Flexible Exchange Rates, 1969" *Review*, Federal Reserve Bank of St. Louis (June 1969): 12–24. See also James E. Meade, *The Balance of Payments* (London: Oxford University Press, 1951).

4. See George Halm, "The Case for Greater Exchange Rate Flexibility in an Interdependent World," and Albert G. Hart, "Commentary" in G. Pontecarvo et al., eds., *Issues in Banking and Monetary Analysis* (New York: Holt, Rinehart and Winston, 1967), pp. 169–88.

5. In addition to references cited in Chapter 3, see also Thomas H. Humphrey, *Essays on Inflation* (Richmond: Federal Reserve Bank of Richmond, 1980); Anne O. Krueger, "Balance of Payments Theory," *Journal of Economic Literature* (March 1969): 1–26; Donald S. Kemp, "A Monetary View of the Balance of Payments," *Review*, Federal Reserve Bank of St. Louis (April 1975): 14–22; M.E. Kreiner and L.H. Officer, *The Monetary Approach to the Balance of Payments: A Survey* (Princeton: Princeton Studies in International Finance No. 43); L.H. Officer, "The Purchasing Power Point Theory Exchange Rates," I.M.F. *Staff Papers* (March 1976); R. Dornbusch, "Exchange Rate Economics: Where Do We Stand?" *Banking Papers on Economic Activity* 1 (1980): 143–85.

6. See Jacob A. Frenkel, "A Monetary Approach to the Exchange Rate: Doctrinal Aspects and Empirical Evidence," in Jacob A. Frenkel and Harry G. Johnson, eds., *The Economics of Exchange Rates* (Reading, Mass.: Addison-Wesley, 1978), pp. 1–25; John F. O. Bilson, "The Current Experience with Floating Exchange Rates: An Appraisal of the Monetary Approach." *American Economic Review* (May 1978): 392–97; Frenkel, "The Forward Exchange Rate, Expectations and the Demand for Money: The German Hyperinflation," *American Economic Review* (September 1977): 653–70; Frenkel, "Purchasing Power Parity: Doctrinal Perspective and Evidence from the 1920's," *Journal of International Economics* (May 1978): 169–91; Frenkel, "Exchange Rates, Prices and Money: Lessons from the 1920's," *American Economic Review* (May 1980): 235–42; John F.O. Bilson, "Profitability and Stability in International Currency Markets," Working Paper No. 664, April 1981, National Bureau of Economic Research. In addition to the Bilson paper cited above, see also Peter B. Kenan, "New Views of Exchange Rates and Old Views of Policy," Norman C. Miller, "Monetary vs. Traditional Approaches of Balance of Payments Analysis," and the discussion by Rudiger Dornbusch, Jacob A. Frenkel, and Marc C. Miles in *American Economic Review* (May 1978): 398–416.

7. For this account see Rudiger Dornbusch "Monetary Policy Under Exchange-Rate Flexibility," in *Managed Exchange Rate Flexibility: The Recent Experience*, J.R. Artus et al. (Boston: Federal Reserve Bank of Boston, 1978), pp. 90–122.

8. Bluford H. Putnam and D. Sykes Wilford, "International Reserve Flows: Seemingly Unrelated Regressions," in *The Monetary Approach to International Adjustment*, Bluford H. Putnam and D. Sykes Wilford, ed. (New York: Praeger, 1978) pp. 71–84; George Macesich and H. Tsai "A North American Common Market: The Issue of Independent Monetary Policy," a paper presented at the NAESA in Washington, D.C., December 27–29, 1981; D. Sykes Wilford and J. Richard Zecher, "Monetary Policy and Balance of Payments in Mexico, 1955–75," *Journal of Money, Credit and Banking*, August, 1979, pp. 340–48. The reader is referred to the Putnam, Wilford, and Zecher studies and, specifically, for the fixed exchange rate period before 1973.

9. Putnam and Wilford, "International Reserve Flows."

10. Thomas M. Humphrey and Thomas A. Lawler, "Factors Determining Exchange Rates: A Simple Model and Empirical Tests," in *The Monetary Approach to International Adjustment*, Bluford H. Putnam and D. Sykes Wilford, eds. (New York: Praeger, 1978), pp. 134–45.

11. Michael Darby, James R. Lothian, Arthur Gandalfi, Anna J. Schwartz, and Alan

C. Stockman, *The International Transmission of Inflation* (forthcoming, National Bureau of Economic Research). See also Bluford H. Putnam and D. Sykes Wilford, "Money, Income and Causality in the United States and the United Kingdom: A Theoretical Explanation of Different Findings," *American Economic Review* (June 1978): 423–27; Terry C. Mills and Geoffrey E. Wood, "Money-Income Relationships and the Exchange Rate Regime," *Review*, Federal Reserve Bank of St. Louis (August 1978): 22–27; Thomas D. Willet, *International Liquidity Issues* (Washington, D.C.: American Enterprise Institute for Public Policy Research, 1980); Lance Girton and Don Roper, "A Monetary Model and Exchange Market Pressure Applied to the Postwar Canadian Experience, *American Economic Review* (Sept. 1977): 537–48; Stephen P. Magee, "The Empirical Evidence on the Monetary Approach to the Balance of Payments and Exchange Rates," *American Economic Review* (May 1976): 163–70.

12. John M. Leger, "US Is Urged to Watch Dollar Exchange Rates: Group of Monetary Experts Advocate Readiness to Intervene in Markets," *Wall Street Journal*, May 10, 1982, p. 4.

11

MONETARISM AND THE INTERNATIONAL ECONOMY

IS MONETARISM TOO COSTLY?

What may look useful in theory, argued the eighteenth-century British philosopher Edmund Burke, may be ruinous in practice. In practice, its critics insist, monetarism is simply too costly. It imposes on the economy excessive burdens of huge losses in real output and prolonged high unemployment. Monetarists respond that the burden must be borne for there is no other way to restore the economy to price stability or economic stability.

Even so, there is disagreement within neoliberal thought as to how inflation should be controlled. For instance, F.A. Hayek argues that inflation can be cured only by reducing the rate of growth of credit so peremptorily and definitely as to cause a severe recession that may last a year or two. Any gradual attempt to reduce inflation would only prolong the agony and tempt politicians to reinflate. Milton Friedman, more alert to the U.S. political scene, argues for a gradual approach.[1]

In fact, criticism comes from many points of the geographic and philosophic compass.[2] Central bankers warn the United States to downplay monetarism or the world will suffer the consequences— perhaps even a 1930s-style collapse of the global economy. This is the solemn message from the Bank of International Settlements' (BIS) 1981 annual report. The bankers argue that the U.S. administration and other monetarist-minded governments like Great Britain must temper their rigid interest rate policies and put more emphasis on such fiscal cures for inflation as budget cutting and wage-and-price policies. Persistent fiscal deficits are of singular concern to the BIS.

The report stresses that the consequence of overdependence on monetarist measures is bound to be persistent unemployment. This could unleash social and political pressures that would force governments to abandon prematurely their anti-inflation strategies. Indeed, the BIS echoes U.S. domestic critics that even with improved procedures, the Federal Reserve may find it impossible to smooth out short-term fluctuations in money supply growth. As a result, warns BIS, U.S. interest rates will probably continue to gyrate, breeding instability in the exchange markets, which could have very serious effects on foreign trade. Other countries also experience troubling quarter-to-quarter fluctuations in money growth.

In sum, the BIS faults the Reagan administration's monetarist doctrines and the Federal Reserve's new monetary techniques, which have contributed a "host of new problems." These include "far too volatile conditions in the exchange markets." As in the 1970s, according to the BIS, the markets have experienced wide exchange rate movements. However, there is now a significant difference. It is now the less-inflationary countries that depreciate their currencies, while the currencies of the more-inflationary countries have become stronger. This cannot go on because, argues BIS, exchange rate fluctuations induced by broad short-term interest rate movements, for which the United States is responsible, may mask the influence of powerful underlying factors, chiefly relative inflation.

Thus, excessive reliance on monetary policy in one country can present acute problems for its trading partners. The 1981 increase in U.S. interest rates and the appreciation of the dollar in world currency markets have brought the United States' trading partners face to face with a dilemma. They must either impose interest rates that are high in real terms, thus risking worsening unemployment, or suffer higher inflation.

The *Economist* basically agrees.[3] It adds that guarantees by the Federal Reserve's Paul Volcker that high U.S. deficits will not be monetized as they were during Lyndon Johnson's administration leaves something to be desired. Cautious people note that Volcker's term expires in September 1983. If he is replaced by someone more cooperative, the way will be clear for Reagan to finance his military budget the way Johnson did—by inflation. According to the *Economist*, that is the biggest shadow hanging over Wall Street. This issue must be resolved either by budget cuts, tax increases, or both, if interest rates are to drop. It is the key to faster economic growth and smoother currency adjustments.

John F. Brothwell writes:

> From May 1979 onward the Thatcher experiment with monetarism greatly aggravated the U.K.'s economic problems. The return to free collective bargaining and the jettisoning of price controls could only accelerate cost inflation, accentuated in turn by increases in indirect taxation. The tight monetary policy and higher interest rates could only deepen the depression . . . heavy disinvestment in stocks further reduced demand and unemployment rose to 11 percent (July, 1981). . . .
> It is true that the huge rise in unemployment has begun to dampen down wage push. According to monetarist principles this should automatically raise employment, but there is little sign of an upturn, and the government's obsession with the size of Public Sector Borrowing (PSBR) prevents it from undertaking the degree of reflationary fiscal policy necessary to engineer a sustained recovery of demand and output. It is tragic that, as unemployment again approaches the level of the Great Depression, the government should be repeating the perverse economic policies of the interwar period (which Keynes so trenchantly attacked) based upon a neoclassical theory which Keynes struggled to demolish in the General Theory.[4]

On the other hand, in France under the new Socialist government

> Monetarism implies nothing more than monetary targeting, and monetary targeting as such implies nothing whatever about the techniques of monetary control, the zeal with which control is pursued, or the political ramifications both within and between organs of government and on the wider world.[5]

In Western Europe, unemployment in the first half of 1982 averaged 8 to 9 percent of the work force, a rate far higher than the continent has known in decades. In a few countries joblessness ranges up to 13 percent. Business investment has all but stopped. Though a modest recovery is forecast, analysts do not attribute Europe's problems to monetarism. Indeed, the opposite seems to be the case. The continent's weakness stems from such factors as obsolescent industrial plants, tight government restrictions in business, and heavy business dependence on government help.[6]

For instance, the failure of Europe's industry to modernize has left many firms unable to compete without costly government underwriting.

To judge from available estimates, these subsidies amount to 7 to 9 percent of output in Sweden, Belgium, Italy, and Ireland. Sweden in spending $60,000 per job per year to subsidize shipbuilding jobs that typically pay workers $30,000.

European government involvement has made private decision making in some industries very difficult. Planners have recognized that Western Europe must phase out excess steel-making capacity, but in Belgium the law requires that shutdowns must be negotiated among companies, the unions, the government, and the Common Market. To this may be added the rigidity of worker attitudes and local customs in Europe that make for difficult labor mobility.

Moreover, Europe has never really recovered from the first oil-price shock in 1973–74. Industries that once formed the backbone of Europe's economy continued to decline. Thus, while the United States added 24 million new jobs in the 1970s, Europe gained only two million. In addition, those out of work in Europe stay jobless longer than in the United States. In some European countries 30 to 50 percent of the jobless remain unemployed for six months to a year; by contrast, the median duration in the United States is about eight weeks. (To be sure, one reason for this difference may be the more liberal unemployment insurance arrangements in Europe.)

In Canada, where the jobless rate rose to a postwar high of 9.6 percent in April 1982, Finance Minister Allan MacEachen told the House of Commons: "The key to world recovery at the present time, for the U.S. and for other countries, is a change in the monetary policy that is being pursued in the U.S."[7] MacEachen goes on to argue that France attempted to ease unilaterally its fiscal and monetary policies but was forced to backtrack and raise its short-term interest rates to protect the value of the French franc. According to MacEachen, the "key solution at the present time doesn't rest with France or Canada. The key solution rests with the main economic partner we all have and that is the United States of America."

Not all Canadians share these views. Peter Anderson argues that there are a number of "made-in-Canada factors" that contribute to Canadian economic contraction.[8] These include the government's national energy policy, which had slowed growth in the oil-producing province of Alberta. The government's last budget removed various incentives for risk taking and for capital investment. Moreover, government policy on foreign investment made foreign investors less than welcome in Canada.

After the Cancun conference of October 1981, when representatives of the rich and poor held a 22-nation summit, the North and South retreated to their earlier positions.[9] Promises for exploratory talks to pave the way for later compromise negotiations were never fulfilled. In place of the U.S. proposal for "global negotiations" within the IMF, the World Bank, and Gatt, where industrial nations feel they have some protection, in December 1981 the Group of 77, the third world's U.N.-based organization, staged an end run in the General Assembly to force the start of "global negotiations" on its own terms. The third world representatives asserted that the Reagan administration, with its supply-side economics and monetarism, is not ideologically in tune with the developing world.

Rhetoric aside, many analysts find the "third world stance disappointing since it is eroding a rare opportunity. Cancun was the first time in the long North-South dialogue that industrial countries offered developing countries a serious proposal: Cast aside earlier demands of massive transfers of income and limit the talks to giving developing nations a larger share of global economic growth. This was not accepted by the third world.

In the face of the current world economic slump, the industrial nations' patience is rapidly wearing out. Many analysts consider the old North-South economic model obsolete. They argue that the main change may well be not just to single out what the developing countries need and try to help them, but to see what the whole world economy needs and try to deal with that. Pitting North against South no longer reflects reality. What is needed is a common platform.

Nowhere is the need for a common world platform greater than among the United States and its allies in dealing with Eastern Europe and the Soviet Union. The differences among the Western alliance members have both political and economic causes. The United States wants to protect its technological advantages over the Soviet Union, largely because of strategic considerations. The Europeans, as close neighbors of the Soviet Union, look upon East European trade not only as a source of orders crucial to their capital-goods industries, but also as a way to bridge the political gap between West and East.

A case in point is a recent German chancellery paper prepared by a planning staff before the April 1982 Social Democrats' National Convention.[10] The short discussion paper says that owing to domestic political concerns, "it makes sense and is necessary to place new and controversial foreign policy accents" in the near future. According to the paper, such new accents should steer electoral focus away from the budget deficit, unemployment, and the "campaign financing scandal" that otherwise would be major election topics. Instead, the paper calls for an attack against the monetarist policies of the U.S. and British governments since such policies endanger the attractiveness of the Western system vis-à-vis the communist system, put détente at risk, and threaten the unity of the Western alliance. Germany should anchor its foreign policy in the Atlantic alliance but be more independent in its policies, argues the paper: "a defensive, yielding position won't be successful over the long term against expected criticism from the U.S. . . . Our reaction must be one marked by self-confidence, that one will realize sooner or later that the truest friends are the most critical."

This is but a sample of the world criticism directed at monetarism. Much of it, according to monetarists, is misdirected and self-serving. More useful are recent attempts to gauge the costs of stopping or slowing down inflation, which is a determined monetarist goal in most countries. These attempts focus on the speed of response of inflation to changes in the growth of nominal spending.

Robert J. Gordon considers the reduction in the growth of nominal spending, no matter how it is achieved, as by definition divided between a decline in the rate of inflation and a decline in the growth of real output.[11] An instant and complete response to such policies affects only prices, not output. If response to these policies is slow and incomplete, then output and employment will carry the burden of adjustment. It is these side effects of restrictive policies that make politicians reluctant to sanction their use. Various estimates of the first-year response of inflation to a 1 percent slowdown in nominal spending range from 10 percent in some traditional econometric models to 100 percent in models developed by some proponents of the "new classical macroeconomics."

Gordon considers the speed of response of inflation in 14 historical episodes: the past six decades in the United States and eight foreign countries from the early 1960s through 1979. To judge from the evidence, inflation has responded slowly to changes in U.S. nominal aggregate demand. The one exception to this pattern occurred during and after World War I. Moreover, the pattern of response appears independent of the presidential administration and political party in office. This phenomenon of gradual price adjustment transcends changes in monetary policy procedures and attitudes over the past six decades.

Contrary to expectations, the situation is not much different in other countries. Thus, Gordon reports that only in four of his 14 episodes is a marked slowdown of inflation achieved by restrictive demand policy with only a "minor" loss in output. These are: United States, 1920–22 (where the price level itself was reduced); Japan, 1976–80; France, 1963–66; and Italy, 1963–68.

In Germany in 1965–67 and 1973–76, restrictive policies did in fact slow down inflation, but only at the cost of a substantial slowdown in real output. Switzerland recorded a −0.3 percent annual real GNP trend between 1973 and 1979. Brazil reduced inflation from 90 percent in 1964 to 17 percent in 1971, but output declined about 20 percent below trend during the period of adjustment. Great Britain was much more successful in the period between 1975 and 1978. Gordon, however, does not consider it as a consequence of "pure" restrictive demand policy since it was combined with a "social contract" between the labor government and its labor union supporters. Moreover, the experiences of the past decade of such countries as France, Italy, Brazil, and Israel offer little in the way of guidance to controlling inflation, "since all four countries accommodated the first OPEC oil shock and are still experiencing the permanent acceleration of inflation that resulted from their earlier policy decisions."

Of the four historical episodes he lists, Gordon considers only the experience of France and Italy in the early 1960s as successful. Each of these four, moreover, has limited applicability today. For instance, the U.S. experience during and after World War I predates the advent of three-year staggered union wage contracts, "which has introduced an extra delay into the responsiveness of the U.S. inflation process."[12] In Japan, the success since 1976 can be attributed to "a union bargaining structure in which contracts last only a year and expire simultaneously, and in which unions appear to have entered into an implicit social contract with the monetary authorities." To judge from Gordon's evidence, there is little room for optimism regarding a quick and painless cure for inflation.

On the other hand, Martin J. Bailey, in a more recent study of the experience of 33 nations in the 1970s reports that the battle against inflation is not as costly in terms of employment and output as some economists have thought.[13] For instance, the 1978 annual report of President Carter's Council of Economic Advisers, chaired by Charles L. Schultze, estimated the costs of reducing inflation as very significant indeed. To eliminate 0.5 percent of inflation would require a loss of $100 billion in output. Moreover, it might take six years of such losses, amounting to 7 percent of real GNP, to reduce the rate of inflation by 3 percent. These estimates are based on an earlier study by George Perry of the Brookings Institution.

Bailey's study covers most of the industrial countries, as well as Argentina, Chile, Brazil, India, Pakistan, the Philippines, and South Korea. His estimates suggest that the fight against inflation is five to seven times less damaging than estimated by the council's 1978 report. He finds that, on the average, a 5 percent reduction in the growth of a country's money supply over three years will reduce the inflation rate by about 5 percent. The peak loss of output will average about 2 percent of GNP, with lesser losses extending over about two years.

There is, however, considerable variation among countries and separate business cycles. Bailey estimates the range for the same 5 percent slowdown in money growth from 0 to 5 percent in the peak loss of industrial output and 1 to 3 percent for GNP. These are important losses, amounting to hundreds of billions of dollars.

Still, the losses are nowhere near the magnitude implied by Perry et al. In the United States, for instance, inflation has come down from a peak of 13.3 percent in 1979 to an annual rate of 3.2 percent in the first five months of 1982, or down about 10.3 percent. If we take the earlier estimates seriously, U.S. losses in potential output should be about $2 trillion. They have not been anywhere near that figure.

Moreover, the existence of substantial transitional costs in reducing or eliminating inflation is insufficient reason to reject anti-inflationary policies. The net gains from reducing inflation, as noted elsewhere, may well exceed these transitional costs. It is difficult in our present stage of knowledge to give a precise quantitative value to these benefits and costs.[14] Available estimates differ significantly from each other.

Meyer and Rasche attempt to estimate "*minimum* total costs associated with continued inflation necessary to justify incurring the previously calculated costs of eradicating inflation."[15] Thus, they assume that pursuit of anti-inflation policies incurs transitional costs as unemployment rises above the rate associated with potential output. Inflation costs are likely to involve decreases in potential output owing to disincentives to saving or investment or welfare losses due to anticipated or unanticipated inflation. A gain in eliminating inflation may increase output above the level that would have prevailed had inflation been permitted to continue. Meyer and Rasche note that their "analysis emphasizes the necessity of comparing the transitional cost incurred over the period during which inflation is eradicated with the permanent benefit attributed to the eradication of inflation."[16]

This can be illustrated as follows: take G as the present value of the permanent per period output gain, evaluated from period n to ∞:

$$G = \sum_{t=n} \frac{gt}{(1 + r)^t} \tag{1}$$

If we take to be constant for all $t \geq n$, the illustration is simplified. Meyer and Rasche calculate the value of g, which equates the discounted cost of unemployment, and then the gain from eliminating inflation is calculated. The result gives us the minimum value of the permanent per period gain from eliminating inflation that would justify incurring the transitional costs.

If the gains are expressed more meaningfully as a real sum that grows at the same rate of potential output, then

$$G = \frac{g(1 + \rho)^t}{(1 + r)^t} \qquad (2)$$

where g is the value of the gain in the first period for which it is registered. For $\rho \geq r$, $G \to \infty$. This result by Meyer and Rasche corresponds to a result derived earlier by Feldstein that: "If the cost of inflation grows at a rate equal to or greater than the discount rate, *any positive initial gain (any g > o) is sufficient to justify incurring any finite transitional cost!*"[17]

For instance, Meyer and Rasche calculate the values of g from a Phillips's curve in Perry's (1978) model and Stein's monetarist model, which assess the relation between inflation and unemployment.[18] They assume a 3.3 percent discount rate and apply equation (1). Their calculations yield a minimum value of g from $25 billion per year in the Stein model to $73 billion from Perry's Phillips's curve. Moreover, a gradual policy of lowering inflation will impose a lower cost if the Phillips's curve is nonlinear. At the same time, however, a gradual policy also postpones the benefits from eliminating inflation. Thus, a more aggressive policy to eliminate inflation reduces the size of the permanent per period gain required to justify it.

Indeed, a well-defined, credible anti-inflation policy may induce a more rapid deceleration of inflation expectations than is suggested by such conventional Phillips's curve-based results as those reported by Perry.[19] According to some rational expectations models, they suggest virtually no output loss if monetary deceleration is perfectly anticipated.[20] Others allow for the existence of output loss during transition periods. It takes time for people to become convinced that the central bank intends to decelerate monetary growth and stabilize it at a noninflationary rate.

The learning process on the part of the public is much more complex than simply "watching the central bank." A case in point are businesspeople accustomed in the past ten years to business practices and investment strategies that fit an inflationary environment.[21] A new noninflationary environment changes many of the rules of thumb of business. Many of these businesspeople hold their positions of power and influence because they have done well during the inflationary years. A sudden disinflation means being thrust into situations they do not understand or for which their lack of comparable personal experience makes them ill-equipped to handle important business decisions. As a result, they are in for a powerful relearning process if they wish to continue as decisionmakers.

In an explicit test of Keynesian and monetarist hypotheses, J.L. Stein finds that the monetarist hypothesis is consistent with the data and thus the Keynesian hypothesis is rejected.[22] The monetarist hypothesis sees the significant variable as the change in real balances, while the Keynesian hypothesis sees it as the unemployment rate. In effect, the evidence supports "the monetarist view that inflation is primarily a monetary phenomenon whose driving force is the previous year's growth in real balances."[23] Consistent with the data is the view that "change in real balances also effects the subsequent unemployment rate. There is indeed a social cost involved in reducing the rate of inflation; but it is considerably less than that claimed by the Keynesian and considerably more than that claimed by the NCE [new classical economics]."[24] Policymakers do indeed face transitional costs in winding down inflation.

In the May 1982 issue of *Challenge*, James Tobin argues that it is likely that the U.S. Congress, the Reagan administration, and the Federal Reserve will eventually reach a new "accord for economic recovery." Tobin, along with other Keynesians and antimonetarists, forecasts the "failure" of current policy leading eventually to a significant shift in direction toward greater monetary ease and fiscal restraint (in effect, to go back to business as usual without giving monetarism the benefit of a fair hearing).

According to Tobin, U.S. monetary policy is simply not in tune with the rest of the economy. Monetarists agree that the Federal Reserve is not following monetarist policy. He supports the goal of reducing monetary growth to wind down inflation as do monetarists. The problem, as he sees it, is that the Federal Reserve System's narrow focus on "monetary aggregates of uncertain and shifting meaning and unstable velocity" has resulted in an overly constrictive monetary policy and high interest rates. This is, of course, standard Keynesian fare. Monetarists too are uncertain as to which if any monetary aggregates are targeted by the Federal Reserve.

What will the "new accord" look like? Tobin sees it as the Federal Reserve abandoning M_1 and M_2 and focusing instead on MV (money times velocity) or total spending per year on goods and services. The Fed's new targets will be about 12 percent growth in nominal GNP over the next year and perhaps 10 percent in the succeeding year. Tobin argues that the administration and Congress will agree to a package of spending reductions, suspended income tax cuts, and selective tax increases to shrink the deficits for fiscal 1983 and 1984.

The "accord" advanced by Tobin is similar to James Meade's "national cash target" idea contained in the first volume of *Stagflation: Wage Fixing.*[25] Indeed, there is also a resemblance between Meade's idea and Friedman's rule of a gradual reduction in the growth of the money supply followed by steady growth at a moderate rate. However, Meade doubts (as does Tobin) whether curtailing the stock of money is enough to control the rise of total spending. Meade also emphasizes fiscal policy and wage-fixing. Presumably the second volume of *Stagflation* will spell out the technical details.

A similar approach is also put forth by Samuel Brittan of the London *Financial Times.*[26] Brittan's proposal calls for the British Treasury to choose as its annual target a steady rise in money gross domestic product.

It is, as the *Economist* points out,

a return to original Keynesianism and a logical next step in Britain's past 50 years of running round in macroeconomic circles. . . . In the early 1930s (a) the Treasury thought it should narrow budget deficits even in a slump. Then (b) Keynes recommended pumping extra demand whenever the year ahead looked likely to see a fall in money gdp, undeterred by the fact that nobody could measure it. Then (c) with Keynes coldly in his grave, post war Keynesians said that demand should be stimulated so long as real resources did not look like being fully employed. This was probably sensible in the years up to around 1964 when the stimulation of a 7% rise in money gdp was apt to bring a 4% rise in output and a 3% rise in prices, but by 1974–79 a rise of 20% in money gdp was more usually bringing something like a 1–2% rise in output and a 18–19% rise in prices. So there was a movement (d) towards the supposedly simple aim that the usual rise in money supply should be in some permitted range like 7–11%, because then there would not be the funds to finance a runaway inflation. . . . It proved difficult to control money supply when various measures such as M1, M2, M3, base money grew by very differing amounts, and whichever was chosen by the Bank of England was liable to be the least representative because of the distortions created by the weapons used to control it. So there was an urge to return macroeconomic policy back to (a) where it was proper to narrow budget deficits even in a slump, and now Mr. Brittan suggests moving to (b), even as the main chorus of reflationists urges that (c). . . .[27]

It is quite probable that Tobin, Meade, and others share Brittan's (b). It is also unfortunate that (d) is not given more than lip service by politicians and central bankers. Nevertheless, the problem still remains. Neither (a) nor (b) nor (c) is likely to be effective when many industrial countries remain in the grip of recession and inflation. Moreover, evidence suggests that the various measures of monetary aggregates are highly correlated with one another. Short-run movements in these aggregates are of little concern for the long-run strategy advocated by monetarists.

It is also incorrect to conclude that monetarism has not worked very well in Great Britain. Within a year and a half the British have managed to reduce inflation from 16 percent to about 8 or 9 percent per year by reducing the growth of the monetary base. To be sure, the cost has been significant partly because saving increased while spending in the public sector did not decline. One consequence has been that the increased saving went to finance the public sector deficit and not into economic investment and expansions. Some of the unemployment increase can be attributed to the removal of employment subsidies granted by British governments in the past to major industries.

ARE WE ALL MONETARISTS NOW?

A few years ago Sir Keith Joseph claimed: "We are all monetarists now." What does this mean in terms of policy? Milton Friedman writes that a monetarist policy has five points:

> first, the target should be growth in some monetary aggregate—just which monetary aggregate is a separate question; second, monetary authorities should adopt long-run targets for monetary growth that are consistent with no inflation; third, present rates of growth of monetary aggregates should be modified to achieve the long-run targets in a gradual, systematic, and preannounced fashion; fourth, monetary authorities should avoid fine-tuning; fifth, monetary authorities should avoid trying to manipulate either interest rates or exchange rates.[28]

He goes on to say that

> almost every central banker in the world today agrees verbally to at least the first three of these five points, and most also to the fourth. The fifth is unquestionably the most controversial. However, in most cases the profession of faith, is simply lip service.[29]

Thus, in major industrial countries monetary targets have become the perferred economic lever. Revelation? A truce between Keynesians and monetarists? Fashion? Or desperation? All four, argues the *Economist*.[30]

Rapid growth in money supplies in nearly all countries was followed by inflation in the 1970s. Monetary targetry was the instrument used by countries that appeared the most stable. Such a strategy employed by these countries came to be equated with all that was stable, noninterfering, and free market. Strong countries that believed in money targets were increasingly having to come to the rescue of the weak, who were constrained to pay attention to their rescuers' beliefs. In many countries there was disenchantment with past and current fiscal policy as an instrument for stabilizing the economy. Fine-tuning too had passed into disrepute.

In short, experience in many countries suggests that monetary policy is not an effective instrument for achieving directly full employment or economic growth. It is at its best in promoting price stability over the long run. It is in this sense that "we are all monetarists now."

At the very least, monetarism serves as an early-warning system to governments. Monetary targets, as such, are not very meaningful when they are nice and easy to hit, nor when they are rolled over. They then become little more than a forecasting exercise, as central banks simply adjust their sights after each regrettable monetary lapse. Monetary targets must signify a government's intention not to expand the money supply to accommodate wage and price pressures originating in various sectors of the economy. In effect, the focus of monetary policy must be on control of the absolute level of prices. Again, it is an issue of credibility. On this score there is a significant difference between rhetoric and practice of monetarist policies.

For instance, Friedman's observation regarding the last of his five points as the most controversial of monetarist policy may well serve to undermine the other four. As noted above, there is a movement in Europe and elsewhere to pressure the U.S. administration to reflate its economy in order to stimulate world trade. This is manifested in pushing the U.S. government to intervene in foreign exchange markets to damp down moves in currency values. In effect, Europeans hope that Americans will share with them the burden of currency intervention.

The ultimate objective, of course, is to undermine tight U.S. monetary policy by imposing currency intervention objectives upon the U.S. monetary authority. The dollar has made significant gains against European currencies in recent years. For instance, the German mark fell from 51¢ in late 1980 to a low of 81¢ in 1981. This was a consequence of the narrowing of the gap between U.S. and German inflation rates from 8 percent in 1981 to zero in 1982.

Attempts to keep the dollar down have had undesirable domestic effects in these countries, as we would expect from our earlier discussions. According to data from the St. Louis Federal Reserve Bank, M_1 growth was negative in 1981 in Germany, Belgium, and the Netherlands, while in the United States it was positive and less deflationary. The domestic impact of intervention has been to reduce the money supply in the interventionist countries. The cost to Europeans and others of such intervention has been to intensify recession in their economies. Attempts to substitute an official view of currency values for that of the market are seldom successful and often costly.

Nevertheless, the Europeans are adamant in pushing the case for intervention. The French, for example, are proposing a "tripolar" monetary system based on the dollar, the yen, and the EMS.[31] Under this new system, an exchange rate zone would be established for the currency blocs, and central banks would be obligated to keep rate movements within these zones. As such, the idea represents a partial return to the Bretton Woods System of fixed exchange rates and would require ongoing intervention in foreign exchange markets. If the movements of a currency were too great for intervention to handle, a country would have to alter its domestic economic policies.

Under the French plan, central banks would, presumably, have to stabilize interest rates and exchange rates rather than concentrating primarily on controlling monetary aggregates. For reasons already discussed, this is a sure road to rekindling inflation. It is not surprising that the French plan has been received with something less than enthusiasm. The Americans, British, and Germans seem to agree that the economic fundamentals of inflation rates and trade balances are the primary determinants of exchange rates, and that movements caused by these fundamentals cannot be countered for long by intervention.

Interest rates are the other candidates most likely to provoke disagreement and controversy over monetarist policy. Some evidence suggests that higher and more variable money growth since 1967 in the United States has been primarily responsible for the longer-term rise and increased variability in interest rates.[32] The longer-term evidence does not appear to support such special factors as a significant change in the behavior of velocity or real output growth. This suggests that an extended period of lower and less variable money growth may very well generate lower and more stable interest rates, which is what monetarists advocate.

How are we to get from here to there? Monetarist policy calls for present monetary aggregate growth rates to be gradually reduced to achieve long-run targets consistent with no inflation in a systematic and preannounced fashion. The emphasis on the "gradual, systematic, and preannounced" manner underscored by Friedman will help keep transitional costs politically acceptable. Such evidence as we have on the costs and benefits of inflation control does appear consistent with a gradualist approach.

It is at this point that the credibility of the monetary authority becomes absolutely essential. If the purpose of the monetary targets is their declaratory effect, flexibility, that is, rolling targets, will have the same effect as flexibility in other policy targets. All bend together, undermining the credibility of the monetary authority.

Monetary rules are urged by monetarists to provide the monetary authority with guidelines that will enhance its credibility. This study underscores credibility as the fundamental issue. Unfortunately, even if these rules are adopted, it is likely that the long duration of bureaucratic inertia and behavior in terms of self-interest will simply emasculate the rules. Indeed, Friedman writes:

> Why the enormous resistance of the Fed to moving to monetary aggregates? Fundamentally, I believe, because monetary aggregates permit far more effective monitoring of performance and account-ability for achieving targets than money market conditions. . . . Who of us wants to be held responsible for our mistakes? It's not very nice to have a bottom line, why should we introduce one?[33]

There are alternatives to a strict bottom line for the Federal Reserve System. We have discussed elsewhere institutional arrangements under which central banks in other countries operate. Friedman proposes either to make the Fed a bureau in the Treasury under the Secretary of the Treasury, or to put it under direct congressional control: "Either involves terminating the so-called independence of the system. But either would establish a strong incentive for the Fed to produce a stabler monetary environment than we have had."[34]

Federal Reserve representatives repeatedly argue that there is little the Fed can do to control monetary growth along monetarist lines "under current operating procedures." Monetarists argue that these "procedures" are nothing more than self-imposed restrictions. They are, in fact, what monetarists want changed so as to improve the effectiveness and credibility of the Federal Reserve. Allan Meltzer argues:

> We want to change those rules. Their own research, by Kier and others we have mentioned and by virtually every academic economist who has studied this, supports our view. Our ideas have found their way into the marketplace, into the press, to governments here and in foreign countries. The Swiss are able to control money growth rates

with high variability, but with strong belief that when they announce a target, it is going to be achieved. Their experience could be duplicated here. It is not the variability, it is the credibility of the policy that is important.[35]

This view is shared by Treasury undersecretary Beryl W. Sprinkel:

We believe the Federal Reserve's control mechanism would be improved if the interest rate constraints were removed completely and efforts were concentrated on controlling the adjusted monetary base or adjusted bank reserves. Adoption of contemporaneous reserve accounting and a flexibly oriented discount policy would also help the Federal Reserve match their actions with their policy and thereby restore credibility to anti-inflation efforts. Avoidance of extreme monetary variability is also necessary if policy direction is to be believed. A steady but persistent decline in monetary growth over the next four years will promote stable economic growth, declining inflation, and stable but lower interest rates.[36]

Meltzer favorably quotes Sprinkel, who is one of the most prominent monetarists in the Reagan administration. This is encouraging.

Monetarism incorporates principles that are widely accepted and to which, unfortunately, some central banks pay only lip service. It may well be, as some of its detractors would have it, that the whole world groaned and marvelled to find itself monetarist. Monetarism's adoption and apparent triumph is not necessarily the beginning of its downfall. It is not that the theory was correct until it was put fully into practice. If put into full practice, monetarism will survive the experience.

NOTES

1. For an interesting discussion of methodological and other differences between F. A. Hayek and Milton Friedman, see W. J. Frazer, Jr. and L. A. Boland, "Foundations of Friedman's Methodology," *American Economic Review* (forthcoming, 1983).

2. See for example James Tobin, "The Monetarist Counter-Revolution Today—An Appraisal," *Economic Journal* (March 1981): 29–42; S. Weintraub, *Capitalism's Inflation and Unemployment Crisis* (Reading, Mass.: Addison-Wesley, 1978); Ralph C. Bryant, *Money and Monetary Policy in Interdependent Nations* (Washington, D.C.: Brookings Institution, 1980). For a discussion of related issues, see James H. Gapinski and Charles E. Rockwood, eds., *Essays in Post-Keynesian Inflation* (Cambridge: Harper & Row, Ballinger, 1979) and Abba P. Lerner and David C. Colander, *MAP: A Market Anti-Inflation Plan* (New York: Harcourt Brace Jovanovich 1980). Rockwood argues in favor of price controls but for political reasons. Thus, he doubts that democratic governments will be willing to accept the costs of a transitory increase in unemployment when money growth is reduced. Much the same is true of Lerner's MAP proposal. In any case, both

view controls as a temporary measure to reduce inflationary expectations to levels consistent with lower money growth. Douglas A. Hibbs, Jr., in a paper devoted in part to the political feasibility of disinflationary policies, concludes that the anti-inflation policies favored by the vast majority of economists and the public contrast strongly. Deflationary policies favored by most economists are firmly rejected by the public. Apparently public preferences are for some form of wage and price controls, even if such controls mean a reduction in real wages. If in fact the cost of deflationary policies is high and political pressures favoring an incomes policy are substantial, the public's preferred response to inflation may prevail. It may well be that the combination of an incomes policy and fiscal and monetary restraint would produce more disinflation per unit of foregone real output and employment than standard money macropolicies. See for example Douglas A. Hibbs, Jr., "Public Concern about Inflation and Unemployment in the United States: Trends and Political Implications," *Conference on Inflation*, sponsored by the National Bureau of Economic Research, October 10, 1980, Washington, D.C. It is interesting that public reaction to inflation control is similar in other countries. See George Macesich, *The International Monetary Economy and The Third World*. (New York: Praeger, 1981), pp. 214–15. Thus, in 1966 in Yugoslavia 62 percent of those employed were favorably disposed toward price controls by authorities, 23 percent against such controls, and the remainder of no opinion.

3. *Economist*, May 8, 1982, pp. 12–13.

4. John F. Brothwell, "Monetarism, Wages, and Employment Policy in the United Kingdom," *Journal of Post-Keynesian Economics* 4 (Spring 1982): 386. Quoting from Keynes's "Economic Consequences of Mr. Churchill" (1925), Brothwell leaves to Keynes the final comment: "Credit restriction is an incredibly powerful instrument, and even a little of it goes a long way—especially in circumstances where the opposite is called for. The policy of deliberately intensifying unemployment with a view of forcing wage reduction is already partly in force, and the tragedy of our situation lies in the fact that, from the misguided standpoint which has been officially adopted, this course is theoretically justifiable . . . Deflation does not reduce wages automatically. It reduces them by causing unemployment. The proper object of dear money is to check an incipient boom. Wce to those whose faith leads them to use it to aggravate a depression!"

5. James K. Galbraith, "Monetary Policy in France," *Journal of Post-Keynesian Economics* 4 (Spring 1982): 402. See also articles by Nicholas Kaldor, "Fallacies of Monetarism," S. Weintraub, "Monetarisms' Muddles," M. Bronfenbrenner, "Price Changes and Output Change: A Short-Run Three-Equation Analysis," *Kredit und Kapital*, 1981, Heft 4.

6. Art Pine, "Europeans Pessimistic as Recession Appears Deep, Hard to Reverse," *Wall Street Journal*, May 10, 1982, pp. 3, 20.

7. John Urquhart, "Canada Ties Relief from Unemployment, a Postwar High in April, to U.S. Policy," *Wall Street Journal* May 10, 1982, p. 14.

8. Ibid.

9. See G. Macesich, *The International Monetary Economy and the Third World*. (New York: Praeger, 1981).

10. John M. Geddes, "German Squabbling over Foreign Policy Could Put Damper on Visit by Reagan," *Wall Street Journal* May 20, 1982, p. 30.

11. Robert J. Gordon, "Why Stopping Inflation May Be Costly: Evidence from Fourteen Historical Episodes," *Conference on Inflation*, February 27, 1981, National Bureau of Economic Research, Washington, D.C.

12. Ibid. See also a related study by Robert J. Gordon, "Wages and Prices Are Not Always Sticky: A Century of Evidence for the United States, United Kingdom, and Japan," Working Paper No. 847, January 1982, National Bureau of Economic Research.

John B. Taylor, "Staggered Wage in a Macro Model," *American Economic Review, Papers and Proceedings*, (May 1979): 108–13. Anna J. Schwartz, "Empirical Findings of the Study of Monetary Trends in the United States and the United Kingdom," and Richard T. Selden, "Money and Inflation in the United States, Canada and Europe," *Proceedings and Reports*, Center for Yugoslav-American Studies, Research and Exchanges, Florida State University, Tallahassee, Florida, Volume 15, 1981.

13. Martin J. Bailey's paper reporting his results was presented before the National Bureau of Economic Research Conference in Cambridge, Mass., in April 1982.

14. See Martin S. Feldstein, "The Welfare Cost of Permanent Inflation and Optimal Short-run Economic Policy," *Journal of Political Economy* (August 1979): 749–67; Lawrence H. Meyer and Robert H. Rasche, "On the Costs and Benefits of Anti-Inflation Policies," *Review*, Federal Reserve Bank of St. Louis (February 1980): 3–14; Stanley Fisher and Frances Modigliani, "Towards an Understanding of the Real Effects and Costs of Inflation," *Weltwirtschaftliches Archiv* 4 (1978): 810–33; John A. Tatom, "The Welfare Cost of Inflation," *Review*, Federal Reserve Bank of St. Louis (November 1976): 9–22.

15. Meyer and Rasche, "Costs and Benefits," p. 13.

16. Ibid.

17. Ibid., p. 14.

18. George L. Perry, "Slowing the Wage Price Spiral: The Macro-economic View," *Brookings Papers on Economic Activity* 2 (1978): 259–91; Jerome L. Stein, "Inflation, Employment and Stagflation," *Journal of Monetary Economics* (April 1978): 193–228.

19. See for instance William Fellner, "The Credibility Effect and Rational Expectations: Implications of the Gramlich Study," *Brookings Papers on Economic Activity* 1 (1979): 167–78.

20. Paul A. Anderson, "Rational Expectations Forecasts from Monetarist Models," *Journal of Monetary Economics* (January 1979): 67–80; Robert J. Barro, "Unanticipated Money Growth and Unemployment in the United States," *American Economic Review* (March 1977): 101–15.

21. John Rutledge, "Decision-Makers Now Confront Disinflation," *Wall Street Journal*, May 24, 1982, p. 20.

22. Jerome L. Stein, "Monetarist, Keynesian and New Classical Economics," *American Economic Review Papers and Proceedings* (May 1981): 139–44.

23. Ibid., p. 144.

24. Ibid. Monetarists, according to Stein, include Milton Friedman, Karl Brunner, Alan Meltzer; Keynesians are James Tobin, Franco Modigliani, Sydney Weintraub; new classical economists are Thomas Sargent, Robert Lacos, and Robert Barro.

25. James Meade, *Stagflation: Wage Fixing*, Vol. 1 (London: Allen and Unwin, 1982).

26. Samuel Brittan, *How to End the 'Monetarist' Controversy* (London: Institute of Economic Affairs, 1980).

27. *The Economist*, (August 22, 1981): 71.

28. Milton Friedman, "Monetary Policy: Theory and Practice," *Journal of Money, Credit and Banking* (February 1982): 101.

29. Ibid.

30. *Economist*, July 2, 1977.

31. This is similar to early postwar proposals for monetary reform based on key currency concepts. See Macesich, *The International Monetary Economy and the Third World*.

32. See for example G. J. Santoni and C. C. Stone, "What Really Happened to Interest Rates?: A Longer-Run Analysis," *Review*, Federal Reserve Bank of St. Louis

(November 1981): 3–14. See also, "Is the Federal Reserves' Monetary Control Policy Misdirected?" A Debate: for the affirmative, R. A. Rasche and A. Meltzer; for the negative, P. D. Sternlight and S. H. Alilrod; Moderator Cong. C. P. Wylie (Ohio), *Journal of Money, Credit and Banking* (February 1982): 119–47.

33. Friedman, "Monetary Policy," p. 115. Friedman's paper contains a good historical documentation of the Federal Reserve System's attempts to steer clear of any course set for it by Congress.

34. Ibid., p. 118. He proposes a simple version of congressional control in an eight-point program that would involve a congressional directive to the Fed to adopt and implement it.

35. Meltzer in "Is the Federal Reserve's Monetary Control Policy Misdirected?" p. 146. The reference to Kier is Peter Kier, "Impact of Discount Policy Procedures on the Effectiveness of Reserve Targeting," in *New Monetary Control Procedures*, Federal Reserve Staff Study (Washington, D.C.: Board of Governors of the Federal Reserve System, February 1981).

36. Beryl W. Sprinkel, statement before the Monetary and Fiscal Subcommittee of the Joint Economic Committee, April 8, 1981, p. 12. Also quoted by Meltzer, "Is the Federal Reserve's Monetary Control Misdirected?" pp. 146–47.

BIBLIOGRAPHY

CHAPTER 1

Anderson, L. "The State of the Monetarist Debate." *Federal Reserve Bank of St. Louis Review*, December 1978.

Birnbaum, E. A. and P. Braverman. "Monetarism—Broken Rudder of Reaganomics." *Wall Street Journal*, July 23, 1981.

Brunner, Karl. "The 1976 Nobel Prize in Economics." *Science*, November 5, 1976.

Cobham, David. In *Lloyds Bank Review*, April 1978, and reprinted in T. M. Havrilesky and J. T. Boorman, eds., *Current Issues in Monetary Theory and Policy*. Arlington Heights, Ill.: AHM Publishing, 2d ed., 1980.

Fischer, S., ed. *Rational Expectations and Economic Policy*. Chicago: University of Chicago Press, 1980.

Frankel, S. Herbert. *Money and Liberty*. Washington, D.C.: American Enterprise Institute for Public Policy Research, 1980.

_____. *Two Philosophies of Money: The Conflict of Trust and Authority*. New York: St. Martin's Press, 1977.

Friedman, Benjamin. "The Theoretical Nondebate about Monetarism" Discussion Paper No. 472, April 1976, Harvard Institute of Economic Research, Harvard University, Cambridge, Mass.

Friedman, Milton. "Monetary Policy: Theory and Practice." *Journal of Money, Credit and Banking*. February 1982.

_____. *The Optimum Quantity of Money*. Chicago: Aldine, 1969.

_____. "The Role of Monetary Policy." In *The Optimum Quantity of Money and Other Essays*. Chicago: Aldine, 1969.

_____ and Anna J. Schwartz. *A Monetary History of the United States, 1867–1960*. Princeton: Princeton University Press, 1963.

_____ and _____. *Monetary Trends in the United States and the United Kingdom; Their Relation to Income, Prices and Interest Rates, 1867–1975.* Chicago: University of Chicago Press, 1982.

Galbraith, John K. "Up from Monetarism and Other Wishful Thinking." *New York Review of Books,* August 13, 1981.

Hahn, F. H. "Monetarism and Economic Theory." *Economica,* February 1980.

Havrilesky, T. M. and Boorman, T. T., eds. *Current Issues in Monetary Theory and Policy.* Arlington, IL; AHM, 2d ed., 1980.

Johnson, Harry. "The Ideology of Economic Policy in the New States." In *Chicago Essays on Economic Development,* D. Wall, ed. Chicago: University of Chicago Press, 1972.

_____. "The Nobel Milton." *Economist,* October 23, 1976.

Kantor, B. "Rational Expectations and Economic Thought." *Journal of Economic Literature,* December 1979.

Laidler, David. "A Review of Frankel's Study." *Journal of Economic Literature,* June 1979.

_____ and Nicholas Rowe. "Georg Simmel's *Philosophy of Money:* A Review Article for Economists." *Journal of Economic Literature,* March 1980.

Lucas, R. E., Jr. "Tobin and Monetarism: A Review Article." *Journal of Economic Literature,* June 1981.

Macesich, George. *The International Monetary Economy and the Third World.* New York: Praeger, 1981.

_____ and H. Tsai. *Money in Economic Systems.* New York: Praeger, 1982.

Mayer, T. "The Structure of Monetarism." *Kredit und Kapital* 8, Nos. 2 and 3, 1975.

Mayer, Thomas. *The Structure of Monetarism.* New York: Norton, 1978.

Meiselman, David, ed. *Varieties of Monetary Experience.* Chicago: University of Chicago Press, 1970.

Modigliani, Franco. "The Monetarist Controversy or Should We Forsake Stabilization Policies?" *American Economic Review,* March 1977.

Poole, W. *Money and the Economy: A Monetarist View.* Reading, Mass.: Addison-Wesley, 1978.

Purvis, O. D. "Monetarism: A Review." *Canadian Journal of Economics,* February 1980.

Schwartz, Anna J. "Why Money Matters." *Lloyds Bank Review,* October 1969.

Selden, R. T. "Monetarism." In *Modern Economic Thought,* Sidney Weintraub, ed. Philadelphia: University of Pennsylvania Press, 1976.

Simmel, Georg. *The Philosophy of Money.* Trans. T. Bottomore and D. Frisby. London and Boston: Routledge and Kegan Paul, 1977, 1978.

Wilson, Thomas. "Robertson, Money and Monetarism." *Journal of Economic Literature,* December 1980.

CHAPTER 2

Bailey, Martin J. *National Income and the Price Level.* New York: McGraw-Hill, 1962.

Clower, R. W. "Productivity, Thrift, and the Rate of Interest." *Economic Journal,* March 1954.

Fisher, Irving. *Purchasing Power of Money.* New York: Macmillan, 1911.

Friedman, Milton. "Money: Quantity Theory II." In *International Encyclopedia of the Social Sciences,* Vol. 10, 1968.

_____. "The Optimum Quantity of Money." In *The Optimum Quantity of Money and Other Essays.* Chicago: Aldine, 1969.

_____. *Price Theory.* Chicago: Aldine, 1962.

Hansen, Alvin H. *A Guide to Keynes.* New York: McGraw-Hill, 1953.

Hart, A. G. "Money: General I." In *International Encyclopedia of the Social Sciences,* Vol. 10, 1968.

Hayek, F. A. *The Constitution of Liberty.* Chicago: University of Chicago Press, 1960.

Hetzel, Robert L. "The Quantity Theory Tradition and the Role of Monetary Policy." *Economic Review*, Federal Reserve Bank of Richmond, May/June 1981.

Hicks, J. R. "Mr. Keynes and the 'Classics': A Suggested Interpretation." *Econometrica*, April 1937.

Keynes, John M. *The General Theory of Employment, Interest and Money.* London: Macmillan, 1936.

Klein, Lawrence R. *The Keynesian Revolution.* New York: Macmillan, 1947.

Kurihara, Kenneth K., ed. *Post-Keynesian Economics.* New Brunswick: Rutgers University Press, 1954.

Lerner, Abba P. "On the Marginal Product of Capital and the Marginal Efficiency of Investment." *Journal of Political Economy*, February 1953.

Macesich, George and H. Tsai. *Money in Economic Systems.* New York: Praeger, 1982.

Modigliani, Franco. "Liquidity Preference and the Theory of Interest and Money." *Econometrica*, January 1944.

Patinkin, Don. *Money, Interest and Prices.* Evanston: Row, Peterson, 1965.

Robertson, D. H. *Money.* London: Nisbet, 1948.

Robinson, Joan. *Introduction to the Theory of Employment.* London: Macmillan, 1937.

Scott, Ira O., Jr. "An Exposition of the Keynesian System." *Review of Economic Studies* 19, 1951.

Selden, R. T. "Velocity of Circulation, III." In *International Encyclopedia of the Social Sciences*, Vol. 10, 1968.

Vickers, D. *Studies in the Theory of Money, 1690–1776.* Philadelphia: Chilton, 1959.

CHAPTER 3

Burger, Albert E. *The Money Supply Process.* Belmont, Calif.: Wadsworth, 1971.

Evans, Michael K. *Macroeconomic Activity*. New York: Harper & Row, 1969.

Fand, David I. "Some Issues in Monetary Economics." *Review*, Federal Reserve Bank of St. Louis, January 1970.

Frankel, Jacob A. and Harry G. Johnson, eds. *The Monetary Approach to the Balance of Payments*. London: George Allen and Unwin, 1978.

_____ and _____. "The Monetary Approach to the Balance of Payments: Essential Concepts and Historical Origins." In *The Monetary Approach to the Balance of Payments*. London: George Allen and Unwin, 1978.

Friedman, Milton. "The Demand for Money—Some Theoretical and Empirical Results." *Journal of Political Economy* 67, June 1959.

_____. "A Monetary Theory of National Income." *Journal of Political Economy* 79, April/May, 1971.

_____, ed. *Studies in the Quantity Theory of Money*. Chicago: University of Chicago Press, 1956.

_____. "A Theoretical Framework for Monetary Analysis." *Journal of Political Economy* 78, April/May 1970.

Goldfeld, S. *Commercial Banking Behavior and Economic Activity: A Structural Study of Monetary Policy in the United States*. Amsterdam: North-Holland, 1966.

Hein, Scott E. "Dynamic Forecasting and the Demand for Money." *Review*, Federal Reserve Bank of St. Louis, June/July 1980.

Hendershoot, P. H. and F. De Leeuw. "Free Reserves, Interest Rates and Deposits: A Synthesis." *Journal of Finance* 25, June 1970.

Horwich, George. "Elements of Timing and Response in the Balance Sheet of Banking, 1953–55." *Journal of Finance* 12, May 1957.

Johnson, Harry G. *Macroeconomics and Monetary Theory*. London: Gray-Mills, 1971.

_____. "Monetary Approach to the Balance of Payments: A Nontechnical Guide." In *The Contemporary International Economy: A Reader*, John Adams, ed. New York: St. Martin's Press, 1979.

Keynes, John Maynard. *The General Theory of Employment, Interest and Money*. New York: Harcourt, Brace, 1936.

_____. "Theory of the Rate of Interest." In *Readings in the Theory of Income Distribution*, ed. W. Feller and B. F. Healey. Philadelphia, Pa. 1946.

Laidler, David. *The Demand for Money: Theories and Evidence*. Scranton, Pa.: International Textbook, 1969.

Macesich, George. *The International Monetary Economy and the Third World*. New York: Praeger, 1981.

_____ and H. Tsai. *Money in Economic Systems*. New York: Praeger, 1982.

McDonald, Stephen L. "The Internal Drain and Bank Credit Expansion." *Journal of Finance* 7, December 1953.

Meigs, A. J. *Free Reserves and the Money Supply*. Chicago: University of Chicago Press, 1962.

Meltzer, Allan H. "The Behavior of the French Money Supply, 1938–54." *Journal of Political Economy* 67, June 1959.

Minsky, H. P. "Central Banking and Money Market Changes." *Quarterly Journal of Economics* 71, May 1957.

Parkin, N., I. Richards, and G. Zis. "The Determination and Control of the World Money Supply under Fixed Exchange Rates, 1961–71." *Manchester School* 43, September 1975.

Patinkin, Don. *Keynes' Monetary Thought*. Durham: Duke University Press, 1976.

_____. *Money, Interest, and Prices*, 2d ed. New York: Harper & Row, 1965.

_____ and J. Clark Leita, eds. *Keynes, Cambridge, and the General Theory*. Toronto: University of Toronto Press, 1978.

Putman, Bluford H. and D. Sykes Wilford, eds. *The Monetary Approach to International Adjustment*. New York: Praeger, 1978.

Smith, Lawrence B. and John W. L. Winder. "Price and Interest Rate Expectations and the Demand for Money in Canada." *Journal of Finance*, June 1971.

Zecher, J. Richard. Preface to *Monetary Approach to International Adjustment*, Putman and Wilford, eds. New York: Praeger, 1978.

CHAPTER 4

Ando, Albert and Franco Modigliani. "The Relative Stability of Monetary Velocity and the Investment Multiplier." *American Economic Review*, September 1965.

Ball, R. J. "Some Econometric Analyses of the Long-Term Rate of Interest in the United Kingdom, 1921–1961." Manchester School of Economic and Social Studies, January 1965.

Barber, C. L. "The Quantity Theory and the Income Expenditure Theory in an Open Economy, 1926–1958: A Comment." *Canadian Journal of Economics and Political Science*, August, 1966.

Baumol, W. J. "The Transactions Demand for Cash: An Inventory Theoretical Approach." *Quarterly Journal of Economics*, November 1952.

Bronfenbrenner, M. and T. Mayer. "Liquidity Functions in the American Economy." *Econometrica*, October 1960.

Brunner, K. and A. H. Meltzer. "Predicting Velocity: Implications for Theory and Policy." *Journal of Finance*, May 1963.

Cagan, Phillip. "The Monetary Dynamics of Hyperinflation." In *Studies in the Quantity Theory of Money*. Milton Friedman, ed. Chicago: University of Chicago Press, 1956.

Chow, G. C. *Demand for Automobiles in the United States: A Study in Consumer Behavior*. Amsterdam: North Holland, 1964.

_____. "On the Long-Run and Short-Run Demand for Money." *Journal of Political Economy*, April 1966.

Christ, C. F. "Interest Rates and 'Portfolio Selection' among Liquid Assets in the United States." In C. F. Christ et al., *Measurement in Economics: Studies, in Memory of Yehuda Grunfeld*. Palo Alto, n.p., 1963.

Close, F. A. "A Study of the Comparative Stability of the Investment Multiplier and Monetary Velocity for Twenty-Two Countries." Ph.D. diss., Florida State University, June 1968.

Courchene, T. and H. Shapiro. "The Demand for Money: A Note from the Time Series." *Journal of Political Economy* 72, October 1964.

DePrano, Michael and Thomas Mayer. "Tests of the Relative Importance of Autonomous Expenditures and Money." *American Economic Review*, September 1965.

Eisner, Robert. "Another Look at Liquidity Preference." *Econometrica* 31, July 1963.

Friedman, Milton. "The Demand for Money—Some Theoretical and Empirical Results." *Journal of Political Economy* 67, June 1959.

_____. "The Quantity Theory of Money—A Restatement." In *Studies in the Quantity Theory of Money*. Chicago: University of Chicago Press, 1956.

_____ and David Meiselman. "The Relative Stability of Monetary Velocity and the Investment Multiplier in the United States, 1897–1958." In *Stabilization Policies*. Englewood Cliffs, N.J.: Prentice Hall for the Commission on Money and Credit, 1963.

_____ and _____. "Reply to Ando and Modigliani and to DePrano and Mayer," and rejoinders by Ando and Modigliani and DePrano and Mayer. *American Economic Review*, September 1965.

Goldsmith, R. W. *A Study of Savings in the United States*. Princeton, N.J.: Princeton University Press, 1956.

Gurley, J. *Liquidity and Financial Institutions in the Post-War Economy*. Study Paper 14, Joint Economic Committee, 86th Congress, 2d Session, Washington, D.C., 1960.

Hamburger, N. J. "The Demand for Money by Households, Money Substitutes, and Monetary Policy." *Journal of Political Economy* 74, December 1966.

Harberger, Arnold G. "The Dynamics of Inflation in Chile." In Christ et al., *Measurement in Economics, Studies in Mathematical Economics and Econometrics*. Stanford, Calif., n.p., 1963.

Hein, Scott E. "Dynamic Forecasting and the Demand for Money." Federal Reserve Bank of St. Louis *Review*, June/July 1980.

Heller, H. R. "The Demand for Money: The Evidence from the Short Run Data." *Quarterly Journal of Economics* 79, May 1965.

Hester, D. H. "Keynes and the Quantity Theory: A Comment on the Friedman-Meiselman CMC Paper, 'Reply to Donald Hester' and Hester's 'Rejoinder'. *Review of Economics and Statistics*, November 1964.

Johnson, Harry G. *Macroeconomics and Monetary Theory.* Chicago: Aldine 1967.

_____. "Monetary Theory and Policy." *American Economic Review,* June 1962.

Khusro, A. M. "Investigation of Liquidity Preference." *Yorkshire Bulletin of Economic and Social Research,* January 1952.

Kisselgoff, A. "Liquidity Preference of Large Manufacturing Corporations." *Econometrica,* October 1945.

Laidler, David E. *The Demand for Money: Theories and Evidence.* Scranton, Pa.: International Textbook, 1969.

_____. "The Rate of Interest and the Demand for Money—Some Empirical Evidence." *Journal of Political Economy* 74, December 1966.

_____. "Some Evidence on the Demand for Money." *Journal of Political Economy* 74, February 1966.

Latane, H. A. "Cash Balances and the Interest Rate—A Pragmatic Approach." *Review of Economics and Statistics,* November 1954.

Lee, T. H. "Alternative Interest Rates and the Demand for Money: The Empirical Evidence." *American Economic Review* 57, December 1967.

Lerner, Eugene. "Inflation in the Confederacy 1861–65." In *Studies in the Quantity Theory of Money,* Milton Friedman, ed. Chicago: University of Chicago Press, 1956.

Macesich, George. *Economic Stability: A Comparative Analysis.* Belgrade: BGZ, 1973.

_____. "Empirical Testing and the Income Expenditure Theory." *Canadian Journal of Economics and Political Science,* August 1966.

_____. *The International Monetary Economy and the Third World.* New York: Praeger, 1981.

_____. *Money and the Canadian Economy.* Belgrade: National Bank of Yugoslavia, 1967.

_____. "The Quantity Theory and the Income Expenditure Theory in an Open Economy Revisited." *Canadian Journal of Economics,* August 1969.

_____. "The Quantity Theory and the Income Expenditure Theory in an Open Economy: Canada 1926–1958." *Canadian Journal of Economics and Political Science,* August 1964.

_____ and F. A. Close. "Comparative Stability of Monetary Velocity and Investment Multiplier for Austria and Yugoslavia." *F.S.U. Slavic Papers,* Vol. 3, 1969.

_____ and _____. "Monetary Velocity and Investment Multiplier Stability Relativity for Norway and Sweden." *Statsokonomisk Tidskrift,* 1969.

_____ and Frank Falero, Jr. "Permanent Income Hypothesis, Interest Rates, and Demand for Money." *Weltwirtshaftliches Archiv,* September 1969.

_____ and H. Tsai. *Money in Economic Systems.* New York: Praeger, 1982.

Meiselman, David, ed. *Varieties of Monetary Experience.* Chicago: University of Chicago Press, 1970.

Meltzer, Allan. "The Demand for Money: The Evidence from the Time Series." *The Journal of Political Economy* 71, June 1963.

_____. "Yet Another Look At the Low Level Liquidity Trap." *Econometrica* 31, July 1963.

Selden, Richard. "Monetary Velocity in the United States." In *Studies in the Quantity Theory of Money,* Milton Friedman, ed. Chicago: University of Chicago Press, 1956.

Teigen, R. L. "The Demand for and Supply of Money." In W. L. Smith and R. L. Teigen, *Readings in Money, National Income, and Stabilization Policy.* Homewood, Ill.: Irwin, 1965.

Tobin, James. "Liquidity-Preference as Behavior Toward Risk." *Review of Economic Studies,* February 1958.

_____. "Liquidity Preference and Monetary Policy." *Review of Economics and Statistics,* February 1947.

Turvey, R. *Interest Rates and Assets Prices.* London, George Allen and Unwin, 1960.

CHAPTER 5

Auerbach, Robert D. *Money, Banking, and Financial Markets.* New York: Macmillan, 1982.

Brunner, Karl, ed. *Targets and Indicators of Monetary Policy.* San Francisco: Chandler, 1969.

Burger, Albert E. *The Money Supply Process.* Belmont, Calif.: Wadsworth, 1971.

_____, Lionel Kalish, III, and Christopher T. Babb. "Money Stock Control and Its Implications for Monetary Policy." *Review,* Federal Reserve Bank of St. Louis, October 1971.

Carlson, Keith and Scott E. Hein. "Monetary Aggregates as Monetary Indicators." *Review,* Federal Reserve Bank of St. Louis, November 1980.

Clark, Lindley H., Jr. "Looking for Ways to Overcome Uncertainty." *Wall Street Journal,* March 23, 1982.

Dewald, William G. and Harry Johnson. "An Objective Analysis of American Monetary Policy, 1952–1961." In *Monetary Studies,* Deanne Carson, ed. Homewood, Ill.: Irwin, 1963.

Dimitrijević, D. and George Macesich. *Money and Finance in Contemporary Yugoslavia.* New York: Praeger, 1973.

Friedman, Benjamin. "The Inefficiency of Short-run Monetary Targets for Monetary Policy." In *Brookings Papers on Economic Activity,* Vol. 2, A. Okun and G. L. Perry, eds. Washington, D.C.: Brookings Institution, 1975.

_____. "Targets, Instruments, and Indicators of Monetary Policy." *Journal of Monetary Economics,* October 1975.

Friedman, Milton. "Churning at the Fed." *Newsweek,* August 31, 1981.

_____. "The Federal Reserve and Monetary Instability." *Wall Street Journal,* February 1, 1982.

_____. "A Memorandum to the Fed." *Wall Street Journal,* January 30, 1981.

_____. "Monetary Policy: Theory and Practice." *Journal of Money, Credit and Banking,* February 1982.

_____. "The Role of Monetary Policy." *American Economic Review,* March 1968.

_____. "The Yo-Yo Economy." *Newsweek,* February 15, 1982.

Granger, C. W. J. "Investigating Causal Relations by Econometric Models and Cross Spectral Methods." *Econometrica*, July 1969.

Hafer, R. W. "The New Monetary Aggregates." Federal Reserve Bank of St. Louis *Bulletin*, February 1980.

_____. "Selecting a Monetary Indicator: A Test of the New Monetary Aggregates." *Review*, Federal Reserve Bank of St. Louis, February 1981.

Hamburger, M. J. "Indicators of Monetary Policy: The Arguments and Evidence." *American Economic Review, Papers and Proceedings*, May 1970.

Holbrook, K. and H. Shapiro. "The Choice of Optimal Intermediate Economic Targets." *American Economic Review, Papers and Proceedings*, May 1970.

Keran, M. W. "Selecting a Monetary Indicator—Evidence from the United States and Other Developed Countries." *Review*, Federal Reserve Bank of St. Louis, September 1970.

Levin, F. J. "The Selection of a Monetary Indicator: Some Further Empirical Evidence." *Money Aggregates and Monetary Policy*, Federal Reserve Bank of New York, 1974.

Macesich, George and H. Tsai. *Money in Economic Systems.* New York: Praeger, 1982.

Poole, William. "Optimal Choice of Monetary Policy Instruments in a Stochastic Macro Model." *Quarterly Journal of Economics*, May 1970.

_____. "Rules of Thumb for Guiding Monetary Policy." *Open Market Policies and Operating Procedures—Staff Studies*, Board of Governors of the Federal Reserve System, 1971.

Rasche, Robert H. "A Review of Empirical Studies of the Money Supply Mechanism." *Review*, Federal Reserve Bank of St. Louis, July 1976.

Roos, Lawrence K. "The Attack on Monetary Targets." *Wall Street Journal*, February 3, 1982.

Schdrack, F. C. "Our Empirical Approach to the Definition of Money." *Money Aggregates and Monetary Policy*, Federal Reserve Bank of New York, 1974.

Schwartz, Anna J. "Short-Term Targets of Three Foreign Central Banks." In *Targets and Indicators of Monetary Policy*, Karl Brunner, ed. San Francisco: Chandler, 1969.

Sims, C. A. "Money, Income and Causality." *American Economic Review*, September 1972.

Tanner, J. Ernest. "Indicators of Monetary Policy: An Evolution of Five." *Banca Nazionale del Lavoro Quarterly Review*, December 1972.

Vane, Howard R. and John L. Thompson. *Monetarism: Theory, Evidence and Policy*. New York: Wiley, (A Halstead Press Book), 1979.

Zecher, Richard. "Implications of Four Econometric Models for the Indicator Issue." *The American Economic Review, Papers and Proceedings*, May 1970.

CHAPTER 6

Ahearn, Daniel S. *Federal Reserve Policy Reappraised, 1951–1959*. New York and London: Columbia University Press, 1963.

Angell, James W. "Appropriate Monetary Policies and Operations in the United States Today." *Review of Economics and Statistics* 42, August 1960.

Attiyeh, Richard. "Rules versus Discretion: A Comment." *Journal of Political Economy* 73, April 1965.

Bronfenbrenner, Martin. "Monetary Rules: A New Look." *Journal of Law and Economics* 8, October 1965.

_____. "Statistical Tests of Rival Monetary Rules." *Journal of Political Economy* 69, February 1961.

_____. "Statistical Tests of Rival Monetary Rules: Quarterly Data Supplement." *Journal of Political Economy* 69, December 1961.

Felner, William. *Towards a Reconstruction of Macroeconomics: Problems of Theory and Policy*. Washington, D.C.: American Enterprise Institute, 1976.

Fisher, Irving. *Stabilizing the Dollar*. New York: Macmillan, 1920.

Friedman, Milton. "Commodity Reserve Currency." *Journal of Political Economy* 59, June 1951.

_____. "The Lag in Effect of Monetary Policy." *Journal of Political Economy* 69, October 1961.

_____. "A Monetary and Fiscal Framework for Economic Stability." *American Economic Review* 38, June 1948.

_____ and Anna J. Schwartz. *A Monetary History of the United States.* National Bureau of Economic Research, Studies in Business Cycles, No. 12. Princeton, N.J.: Princeton University Press, 1963.

_____. *The Optimum Quantity of Money and Other Essays.* Chicago: Aldine, 1969.

_____. "Price, Income, and Monetary Changes in Three Wartime Periods." *American Economic Review, Papers and Proceedings,* May 1952.

_____. *A Program for Monetary Stability,* the Millar Lectures, No. 3. New York: Fordham University Press, 1960.

_____. "The Role of Monetary Policy." *American Economic Review* 58, March 1968.

_____. "Should There Be an Independent Monetary Authority?" In *In Search of a Monetary Constitution,* ed. L. B. Yeager. Cambridge, Mass.: Harvard University Press, 1962.

Gramley, Lyle E. "Guidelines for Monetary Policy—The Case against Simple Rules." In *Readings in Money, National Income, and Stabilization Policy,* ed. W. L. Smith and R. L. Teigen, rev. ed. Homewood, Ill.: Irwin, 1970.

Gurley, John G. and Edward S. Shaw. "Financial Aspects of Economic Development." *American Economic Review* 45, September 1955.

Hamovitch, William, ed. *The Argument from Keynes' Treatise to Friedman.* Boston, Mass.: D. C. Heath, 1966.

Hart, Albert G. "The 'Chicago Plan' for Banking Reform." *Review of Economic Studies* 2, 1935.

Lerner, Abba P. "Milton Friedman's 'A Program for Monetary Stability': A Review." *Journal of the American Statistical Association* 58, March 1962.

Macesich, George. *Geldpolitik in einem gemeinsamen europaischen Market.* (Money in a European Common Market). Baden-Baden: Nomos Verlagsgesellschaft, 1972.

_____. "Monetary Policy in the Common Market Countries: Rules versus Discretion." *Weltwirtschaftliches Archiv* 198, 1972.

_____ and H. Tsai. *Money in Economic Systems*. New York: Praeger, 1982.

Mayer, Thomas. "The Lag in Effect of Monetary Policy: Some Criticisms." *Western Economic Journal* 5, September 1967.

Melitz, Jacques. Compendium, U. S. Congress Joint Economic Committee, *Standards for Guiding Monetary Action*, Report of the Joint Economic Committee. Washington, D.C.: Government Printing Office, 1968.

Mints, Lloyd W. "Monetary Policy and Stabilization." *American Economic Review, Papers and Proceedings* 41, May 1951.

_____. *Monetary Policy for a Competitive Society*. New York: McGraw-Hill, 1950.

Modigliani, Franco. "Some Empirical Tests of Monetary Management and of Rules versus Discretion." *Journal of Political Economy* 72, June 1964.

Okun, Arthur M. *The Political Economy of Prosperity*. Washington, D.C.: Brookings Institution, 1970.

Samuelson, Paul A. "Reflections on Central Banking." *National Banking Review* 1, September 1963.

Schneider, Erich. "Automatism or Discretion in Monetary Policy." *Banca Nazionale del Lavoro Quarterly Review* 23, June 1970.

Schotta, Charles, Jr. "The Performance of Alternative Monetary Rules in Canada, 1927–1961." *National Banking Review* 1, December 1963.

Shaw, Edward S. "Monetary Stability in a Growing Economy." In *The Allocation of Economic Resources: Essays in Honor of B. F. Haley*. Stanford, Calif.: Stanford University Press, 1959.

Simons, Henry C. "A Positive Program for Laissez Faire: Some Proposals for a Liberal Economic Policy." In *Public Policy Pamphlet*, No. 15, ed. H. D. Gideonse. Chicago: University of Chicago Press, 1934.

_____. *Economic Policy for a Free Society*. Chicago: University of Chicago Press, 1948.

_____. "Introduction: A Political Credo." In *Economic Policy for a Free Society*. Chicago: University of Chicago Press, 1948.

_____. "The Requisites of Free Competition." *American Economic Review* Supplement, 26, March 1936.

_____. "Rules versus Authorities in Monetary Policy." *Journal of Political Economy* 44, February 1936.

Snyder, Carl. *Capitalism the Creator: The Economic Foundations of Modern Industrial Society.* New York: Macmillan, 1940.

_____. "The Problem of Monetary and Economic Stability." *Quarterly Journal of Economics* 49, February 1935.

Stuper, Rainer, "An Empirical Analysis of the Debate over Rules versus Discretion with Special Reference to the Monetary Management of the German Bundesbank from 1958 to 1970." Ph.D. dissertation, Florida State University, March, 1973.

Tucker, Donald P. "Bronfenbrenner on Monetary Rules: A Comment." *Journal of Political Economy* 71, April 1963.

Viner, Jacob. "The Necessary and the Desirable Range of Discretion to Be Allowed to a Monetary Authority." In *In Search of A Monetary Constitution*, ed. L. B. Yeager. Cambridge, Mass.: Harvard University Press, 1962.

Walker, Charles E. "Fact and Fiction in Central Banking." In *Essays in Monetary Policy in Honor of Elmer Wood*, ed. P. C. Walker. Columbia, Miss.: University of Missouri Press, 1965.

Warburton, Clark. "How Much Variation in the Quantity of Money Is Needed?" *Southern Economic Journal* 18, April 1952.

_____. "The Misplaced Emphasis in Contemporary Business Fluctuation Theory." *Journal of Business* 19, October 1946.

_____. "Rules and Implements of Monetary Policy." *Journal of Finance* 8, March 1953.

_____. "The Secular Trend in Monetary Velocity." *Review of Economics and Statistics* 30, March 1948.

_____. "The Volume of Money and the Price Level between the World Wars." *Journal of Political Economy* 53, June 1945.

Whittlesey, Charles R. "Rules, Discretion, and Central Bankers." In *Essays in Money and Banking in Honour of Richard S. Sayers*, ed. C. R. Whittlesey and J. S. Wilson. London: Oxford University Press, 1968.

Yohe, William. "The Intellectual Milieu at the Federal Reserve Board in the 1920s." Presented at the Annual Meeting History of Economic Society, Duke University, May 25, 1982.

CHAPTER 7

Attiyeh, Yossef A. "Wage-Price Spiral versus Demand Inflation: United States, 1949–1955" Ph.D. diss., University of Chicago, December 1959.

Auerbach, Robert D. and Ronald Moses. "The Phillips Curve and All That: A Comment." *Scottish Journal of Political Economy*, November 1974.

Barth, J. R. and J. T. Bennett. "Cost-Push versus Demand-Pull Inflation: Some Empirical Evidence." *Journal of Money, Credit and Banking*, August 1975.

Batten, D. S. "Inflation: The Cost-Push Myth." *Review*, Federal Reserve Bank of St. Louis, June/July 1981.

Bowen, William G. "Cost Inflation versus Demand Inflation: A Useful Distinction?" *Southern Economic Journal* 26, January 1960.

Fisher, Irving. "A Statistical Relation between Unemployment and Price Changes." *International Labour Review*, June 1926.

_____. *The Theory of Interest*. New York: Kelley, 1961.

Foster, J. "Tests of the Simple Fisher Hypothesis Utilizing Observed Inflationary Expectations: Some Further Evidence." *Scottish Journal of Political Economy*, November 1977.

Friedman, Milton. "Current Critical Issues in Wage Theory and Price." Industrial Relations Research Association, *Proceedings of the Eleventh Annual Meeting*, Chicago, 1959.

_____. "Government Revenue from Inflation." *Journal of Political Economy*, July/August 1971.

_____., ed. "The Monetary Dynamics of Hyper Inflation." In *Studies in the Quarterly Theory of Money*. Chicago: University of Chicago Press, 1956.

_____. Nobel Lecture: "Inflation and Unemployment." *Journal of Political Economy*, June 1977.

_____. "The Role of Monetary Policy." *American Economic Review*, March 1968.

_____. *Unemployment versus Inflation? An Evolution of the Phillips Curve*. London: Institute of Economic Affairs, 1975.

Gibson, N. "Price Expectations Effects on Interest Rates." *Journal of Finance*, March 1970.

Johnson, Harry G. *Macroeconomics and Monetary Theory*. Chicago: Aldine, 1967.

Lipsey, R. G. "The Relation between Unemployment and the Rate of Change of Money Wage Rates in the United Kingdom, 1861–1957: A Further Analysis." *Economica*, February 1960.

Lucas, Robert E., Jr. "Rational Expectations and the Theory of Economic Policy." *Journal of Monetary Economics*, January 1976.

_____. "Rational Expectations." *Journal of Money, Credit and Banking*, November 1980.

_____. "Tobin and Monetarism: A Review Article." *Journal of Economic Literature*, June 1981.

Lustgarten, S. *Industrial Concentration and Inflation*. Washington, D.C.: AEI, 1975.

Macesich, George. *Comparative Economic Stability*. Belgrade: Beogradski Graficki Zavod, 1973.

Meiselman, David. *The Term Structure of Interest*. Englewood Cliffs, N.J.: Prentice-Hall, 1962.

Modigliani, Franco. "The Monetarist Controversy or Should We Forsake Stabilization Policies?" *American Economic Review*, March 1977.

Morton, Walter. "Trade Unionism, Full Employment and Inflation." *American Economic Review*, March 1950.

Muth, John F. "Rational Expectations and the Theory of Price Movements." *Econometrica*, July 1961.

Phelps, Edmond S. "Phillips Curves, Expectations of Inflation and Optimum Unemployment Over There." *Economica*, August 1967.

Phillips, A. W. "The Relationship between Unemployment and the Rate of Change of Money Wage Rates in the United Kingdom, 1861–1957." *Economica*, November 1958.

Rees, Albert. "Do Unions Cause Inflation?" *Journal of Law and Economics*, October 1959.

_____ and Mary T. Hamilton. "The Wage-Price Productivity Perplex." *Journal of Political Economy*, February 1967.

Samuelson, Paul A. and Robert M. Solow. "Analytical Aspects of Anti-Inflation Policy." *American Economic Review*, May 1960.

Sargent, Thomas. "A Note on the 'Accelerationist' Controversy." *Journal of Money Credit and Banking*, August 1971.

_____ and Neil Wallace. "Rational Expectations and the Theory of Economic Policy." *Studies in Monetary Policy* 2, Federal Reserve Bank of Minneapolis, 1975.

Schlesinger, James R., "Market Structure, Union Power, and Inflation," Southern Economic Journal, January, 1959.

Tobin, James. "Inflation and Unemployment." *American Economic Review*, March 1972.

Vance, H. R. and J. L. Thompson. *Monetarism: Theory, Evidence, and Policy.* New York: Wiley, 1979.

Weiss, L. "The Role of Active Monetary Policy in a Rational Expectations Model." *Journal of Political Economy*, April 1980.

Wolozin, Harold. "Inflation and the Price Mechanism." *Journal of Political Economy* 67, October 1959.

CHAPTER 8

Anderson, L. C. and J. L. Jordan. "Monetary and Fiscal Action: A Test of Their Relative Importance in Economic Stabilization." *Review*, Federal Reserve Bank of St. Louis, November 1968.

Andro, A. "Some Aspects of Stabilization Policies, the Monetarist Controversy, and the MPS Model." *International Economic Review*, October 1974.

Arnowitz, Victor. "On the Accuracy and Properties of Recent Macroeconomic Forecasts." *American Economic Review*, May 1978.

Blinder, A. S. and R. M. Solow. "Does Fiscal Policy Matter?" *Journal of Public Economics*, November 1973.

_____ and _____. "Does Fiscal Policy Still Matter?" *Journal of Monetary Economics*, November 1976.

Brunner, K. and A. H. Meltzer. "Money, Debt and Economic Activity." *Journal of Political Economy*, September/October 1972.

Carlson, K. M. "Monetary and Fiscal Actions in Macroeconomic Models." *Review*, Federal Reserve Bank of St. Louis, January 1974.

_____ and Roger W. Spencer. "Crowding Out and Its Critics." In *Review*, Federal Reserve Bank of St. Louis, December 1975.

David, P. A. and J. L. Scadding. "Private Savings: Ultrarationality, Aggregation,, and 'Denison's Law.'" *Journal of Political Economy*, March/April 1974.

Evans, Michael. "Bankruptcy of Keynesian Econometric Models." *Challenge*, January/February 1980.

Friedman, B. M. "Even the St. Louis Model Now Believes in Fiscal Policy." *Journal of Money, Credit and Banking*, May 1977.

Friedman, Milton. "Comments on the Critics." *Journal of Political Economy*, September/October 1972.

_____, ed. *Essays in Positive Economics*. Chicago: University of Chicago Press, 1953.

Fromm, Gary and Lawrence R. Klein. "A Comparison of Eleven Econometric Models of the United States." *American Economic Review*, May 1973.

Hafer, R. W. "The Role of Fiscal Policy in the St. Louis Equation." In *Review*, Federal Reserve Bank of St. Louis, January 1982.

Infante, E. F. and J. L. Stein. "Does Fiscal Policy Matter?" *Journal of Monetary Economics*, November 1976.

Keran, M. W. "Monetary and Fiscal Influences on Economic Activity—The Historical Evidence." *Review*, Federal Reserve Bank of St. Louis, November 1969.

_____. "Monetary and Fiscal Influences on Economic Activity: The Foreign Experience," *Review*, Federal Reserve Bank of St. Louis, February, 1970.

Keynes, J. M. *The General Theory of Employment, Interest, and Money*. New York: Harcourt, Brace, 1936.

Klein, Lawrence R. "Commentary on the State of the Monetarist Debate." *Review*, Federal Reserve Bank of St. Louis, September 1973.

Knight, F. H. "Capital and Interest." In *Readings in the Theory of Income Distribution*. Philadelphia: Blakiston, 1949.

Larosiere, J. de. "Coexistence of Fiscal Deficits, High Tax Burdens Is Consequence of Pressures for Public Spending." *IMF Survey* March 22, 1982.

Sliger, Bernard, Ansel M. Sharp, and Robert L. Sandmeyer. "Local Government Revenues: An Overview." In *Management Policies in Local Government, Finance*, J. R. Aronson and Eli Schwartz, eds. Washington: International City Management Association, 1975.

Spencer, R. W. and W. P. Yohe. "Crowding Out of Private Expenditures by Fiscal Policy Actions." *Review*, Federal Reserve Bank of St. Louis, October 1970.

Stein, Herbert. *Fiscal Revolution in America*. Chicago: University of Chicago Press, 1969.

Tobin, J. "Friedman's Theoretical Framework." *Journal of Political Economy*, September/October 1972.

CHAPTER 9

Anderson, L. C. and T. M. Carlson. "A Monetary Model for Economic Stabilization." *Monthly Review*, Federal Reserve Bank of St. Louis, April 1970.

DeLeeuw, Frank and Edward Gramlich. "The Channels of Monetary Policy." *Federal Reserve Bulletin*, June 1969.

_____ and _____. "The Federal Reserve-MIT Econometric Model." *Federal Reserve Bulletin*, January 1968.

Dusenberry, James et al., eds. *The Brookings Quarterly Model of the United States*. Chicago: Rand-McNally, 1965.

Fox, Carl A. *Intermediate Economic Statistics*. New York: Wiley, 1968.

Klein, L. R. and Gary Fromm. "The Brookings-SSRC Quarterly Econometric Model of the United States: Model Properties." *American Economic Review*, May 1965.

Klein, R. L. and A. S. Goldberger. *An Econometric Model of the United States, 1929–1952*. Amsterdam: North-Holland, 1955.

Macesich, George. "Money, Monetary Policy and Econometric Models." *Jugoslovensko Bankarstvo*, December 1973.

Modigliani, F. and R. Sutch. "Innovations in Interest Rate Policy." *American Economic Review*, May 1966.

Nerlove, Mark. "A Tabular Survey of Macro-Economic Models." *International Economic Review*, May 1966.

Rasche, Robert H. and Harold T. Shapiro. "The FRB-MIT Econometric Model: Its Special Features." *American Economic Review*, May 1968.

Spivey, W. Allen and William J. Wrobleski. *Econometric Model Performance in Forecasting and Policy Assessment*. Washington, D.C.: AEI for Public Policy, 1979.

Theil, H. *Principles of Econometrics*. New York: Wiley, 1971.

CHAPTER 10

Bilson, John F. O. "The Current Experience with Floating Exchange Rates: An Appraisal of the Monetary Approach." *American Economic Review*, May 1978.

_____. "Profitability and Stability in International Currency Markets." Working Paper No. 664, National Bureau of Economic Research, April 1981.

Cagan, Phillip. "The First Fifty Years of the National Banking System: An Historical Appraisal." In *Banking and Monetary Studies*, Deanne Carson, ed. Homewood, Ill.: Irwin, 1963.

Dornbusch, Rudiger. "Exchange Rate Economics: Where Do We Stand?" *Banking Papers on Economic Activity* 1, 1980.

_____, Jacob A. Frenkel, and Marc C. Miles. Discussion in *America's Economic Review*, May 1978.

_____. "Monetary Policy under Exchange-Rate Flexibility: The Recent Experience" In *Managed Exchange Rate Flexibility: The Recent Experience*, J. R. Artus et al. Boston: Federal Reserve Bank of Boston, 1978.

Frenkel, Jacob A. "Exchange Rates, Prices and Money: Lessons from the 1920's." *American Economic Review*, May 1980.

_____. "A Monetary Approach to the Exchange Rate: Doctrinal Aspects and Empirical Evidence." In *The Economics of Exchange Rates*, Jacob A.

Frenkel and Harry G. Johnson, eds. Reading, Mass.: Addison-Wesley, 1978.

_____. "The Forward Exchange Rate, Expectations and the Demand for Money: The German Hyperinflation." *American Economic Review*, September 1977.

_____. "Purchasing Power Parity: Doctrinal Perspective and Evidence From the 1920s." *Journal of International Economics*, May 1978.

Friedman, Milton "The Case for Flexible Exchange Rates." In *Essays in Positive Economics*. Chicago: University of Chicago Press, 1953.

_____. "Monetary Policy: Theory and Practice." *Journal of Money, Credit and Banking.* February 1982.

_____ and Anna J. Schwartz. *A Monetary History of the United States, 1867–1960.* Princeton: Princeton University Press, 1963.

Girton, Lance and Don Roper. "A Monetary Model and Exchange Market Pressure Applied to the Postwar Canadian Experience." *American Economic Review*, September 1977.

Halm, George. "The Case for Greater Exchange Rate Flexibility in an Interdependent World." In *Issues in Banking and Monetary Analysis*, G. Pontecarvo et al., eds. New York: Holt, Rinehart and Winston, 1967.

Humphrey, Thomas H. *Essays on Inflation*. Richmond: Federal Reserve Bank of Richmond, 1980.

_____ and Thomas A. Lawler. "Factors Determining Exchange Rates: A Simple Model and Empirical Tests." In *The Monetary Approach to International Adjustment, Bluford H. Putnam and D. Sykes Wilford, eds. New York: Praeger, 1978.*

Johnson, Harry G. "The Case for Flexible Exchange Rates, 1969." *Review*, Federal Reserve Bank of St. Louis, June 1969.

Kemp, Donald S. "A Monetary View of the Balance of Payments." *Review*, Federal Reserve Bank of St. Louis, April 1975.

Kenan, Peter B. "New Views of Exchange Rates and Old Views of Policy." *American Economic Review*, May 1978.

Kreiner, M.E. and L.H. Officer. *The Monetary Approach to the Balance of Payments: A Survey.* Princeton: Princeton Studies in International Finance No. 43, 1978.

Krueger, Anne O. "Balance of Payments Theory." *Journal of Economic Literature*, March 1969.

Leger, John M. "U.S. Is Urged to Watch Dollar Exchange Rates: Group of Monetary Experts Advocate Readiness to Intervene in Markets." *Wall Street Journal*, May 10, 1982.

Macesich, George. "International Trade and United States Economic Development Revisited." *Journal of Economic History*, September 1961.

_____ and H. Tsai. "A North American Common Market: The Issue of Independent Monetary Policy." A paper presented at the NAESA in Washington, D.C., December 1981.

_____. "Source of Monetary Disturbances in the United States, 1834–45." *Journal of Economic History*, September 1960.

Magee, Stephen P. "The Empirical Evidence on the Monetary Approach to the Balance of Payments and Exchange Rates." *American Economic Review*, May 1976.

Meade, James E. *The Balance of Payments.* London: Oxford University Press, 1951.

Miller, Norman C. "Monetary vs. Traditional Approaches of Balance of Payments Analysis". *American Economic Review*, May 1978.

Mills, Terry C. and Geoffrey E. Wood. "Money-Income Relationships and the Exchange Rate Regime." In *Review*, Federal Reserve Bank of St. Louis, August 1978.

Officer, L.H. "The Purchasing Power Point Theory Exchange Rates." *IMF Staff Papers*, March 1976.

Putnam, Bluford H. and D. Sykes Wilford. "International Reserve Flows: Seemingly Unrelated Regression." In *The Monetary Approach to International Adjustment*, Bluford H. Putnam and D. Sykes Wilford, eds. New York: Praeger 1978.

_____ and _____. "Money, Income and Causality in the United States and the United Kingdom: A Theoretical Explanation of Different Findings" *American Economic Review*, June 1978.

Tanner, J. Earnest and Vittorio Bonemo. "Gold, Capital Flows, and Long Swings in American Business Activity." *Journal of Political Economy*, January/February 1968.

Willet, Thomas D. *International Liquidity Issues*. Washington: American Enterprise Institute for Public Policy Research, 1980.

Willett, T.W. "International Specie Flows and American Monetary Stability." *Journal of Economic History*, March 1968.

CHAPTER 11

Anderson, Paul A. "Rational Expectations Forecasts from Monetarist Models." *Journal of Monetary Economics*, January 1979.

Barro, Robert J. "Unanticipated Money Growth and Unemployment in the United States." *American Economic Review*, March 1977.

Bronfenbrenner, Martin. "Price Changes and Output Change: A Short-Run Three-Equation Analysis." *Kredit und Kapital*, 1981, Heft 4.

Brothwell, John F. "Monetarism, Wages, and Employment Policy in the United Kingdom." *Journal of Post Keynesian Economics* 4, Spring 1982.

Bryant, Ralph C. *Money and Monetary Policy in Interdependent Nations*. Washington, D.C.: Brookings Institution, 1980.

Feldstein, Martin S. "The Welfare Cost of Permanent Inflation and Optimal Short-Run Economic Policy." *Journal of Political Economy*, August 1979.

Fellner, William. "The Credibility Effect and Rational Expectations: Implications of the Gramlich Study." *Brookings Papers on Economic Activity* 1, 1979.

Fisher, Stanley and Frances Modigliani. "Toward an Understanding of the Real Effects and Costs of Inflation." *Weltwirtschaftliches Archiv* 4, 1978.

Friedman, Milton. "Monetary Policy: Theory and Practice." *Journal of Money, Credit and Banking*, February 1982.

Galbraith, James K. "Monetary Policy in France." *Journal of Post Keynesian Economics* 4, No. 3, Spring 1982.

Gapinski, James H. and Charles E. Rockwood, eds. *Essays in Post-Keynesian Inflation*. Cambridge: Harper & Row, 1979.

Geddes, John M. "German Squabbling over Foreign Policy Could Put Damper on Visit by Reagan." *Wall Street Journal*, May 20, 1982.

Gordon, Robert J. "Wages and Prices Are Not Always Sticky: A Century of Evidence for the United States, United Kingdom and Japan." Working Paper No. 847, January 1982, National Bureau of Economic Research.

_____. "Why Stopping Inflation May Be Costly: Evidence from Fourteen Historical Episodes." In *Conference on Inflation*, February 27, 1981. National Bureau of Economic Research, Washington, D.C.

Hibbs, Douglas A., Jr. "Public Concern about Inflation and Unemployment in the United States: Trends and Political Implications." In *Conference on Inflation*, sponsored by the National Bureau of Economic Research, October 10, 1980, Washington, D.C.

Kaldor, Nicholas. "Fallacies of Monetarism." *Kredit und Kapital*, 1981, Heft 4.

Kier, Peter. "Impact of Discount Policy Procedures in the Effectiveness of Reserve Targeting." In *New Monetary Control Procedures*. Federal Reserve Staff Study. Washington, D.C.: Board of Governors of the Federal Reserve System, February 1981.

Lerner, Abba P. and David C. Colander. *MAP: A Market Anti-Inflation Plan.* New York: Harcourt Brace Jovanovich, 1980.

Macesich, George. *The International Monetary Economy and the Third World.* New York: Praeger, 1981.

Meyer, Lawrence H. and Robert H. Rasche. "On the Costs and Benefits of Anti-Inflation Policies." In *Review*, Federal Reserve Bank of St. Louis, February 1980.

Perry, George L. "Slowing the Wage Price Spiral: The Macro-Economic View." *Brookings Papers on Economic Activity 2*, 1978.

Pine, Art. "Europeans Pessimistic as Recession Appears Deep, Hard to Reverse." *Wall Street Journal*, May 10, 1982.

Rutledge, John. "Decision-Makers Now Confront Disinflation." *Wall Street Journal*, May 24, 1982.

Santoni, G.J. and C.C. Stone. "What Really Happened to Interest Rates?: A Longer-Run Analysis." In *Review*, Federal Reserve Bank of St. Louis, November 1981.

Schwartz, Anna J. "Empirical Findings in the Study of Monetary Trends in the United States and the United Kingdom." In *Proceedings and Reports,*

Center for Yugoslav-American Studies, Research, and Exchanges, Florida State University, Tallahassee, Florida, Vol. 15, 1981.

Selden, Richard T. "Money and Inflation in the United States, Canada and Europe." In *Proceedings and Reports*, Center for Yugoslav-American Studies, Research, and Exchanges, Florida State University, Tallahassee, Florida, Vol. 15, 1981.

Stein, Jerome L. "Inflation, Employment and Stagflation." *Journal of Monetary Economics*, April 1978.

_____. "Monetarist, Keynesian and New Classical Economics." *American Economic Review Papers and Proceedings*, May 1981.

Tatom, John A. "The Welfare Cost of Inflation." *Review*, Federal Reserve Bank of St. Louis, November 1976.

Taylor, John B. "Staggered Wage in a Macro Model." *American Economic Review, Papers and Proceedings*, May 1979.

Tobin, James. "The Monetarist Counter-Revolution Today—An Appraisal." *Economic Journal*, March 1981.

Urquhart, John. "Canada Ties Relief from Unemployment, a Postwar High in April, to U.S. Policy." *Wall Street Journal*, May 10, 1982.

Weintraub, S. *Capitalism's Inflation and Unemployment Crisis*. Reading, Mass.: Addison-Wesley, 1978.

_____. "Monetarism's 'Muddles.'" *Kredit und Kapital*, 1981, Heft 4.

INDEX

Larosiere, J. de 181
Latane, H. A. 66, 67, 70, 79
Law, John 9, 19
Lawler, Thomas A. 207
Lee, T. H. 84
Lerner, Abba P. 163
liquidity effect 25
Lerner, Eugene 85
liquidity preference theory 32, 49–50, 66
Locke, John 9, 119
Lothian, James R. 211–12, 213
Lucas, Robert E. 158
Luxembourg 181

Macesich, George 62, 86, 87, 95, 131, 194, 206, 209
macroeconomic models 72
marginal efficiency of capital 33
marginal efficiency of investment 34–35
Marshall, Alfred 49
Marxian Theory 110
Mayer, Thomas 66, 68, 69–70, 71–72, 73, 125, 130
MacEachen, Allan 220
Meade, James 57, 227
Meiselman, David 62, 64, 194
Melitz, Jacques 125
Meltzer, Allan 51, 71, 72, 74–80, 83, 177–78, 231, 232
Menger, Carl 9
Mexico 206, 207, 209
Michigan model 194
Mill, John Stuart 20, 201
Mints, Lloyd W. 121, 122
Modigliani, Franco 52, 64, 129–30, 193
monetarists 3, 13–14, 22, 43, 101, 117, 118, 139, 144–58, 163, 164, 168, 184, 203, 217, 218, 219, 228–29, 232
monetary analysis 27, 43
monetary base 51, 52, 54, 100
monetary disturbances 20
monetary influences on nominal income 93
monetary dynamics 19

monetary stability 21, 61
money, quantity 72
money, role of 19
money, demand for 36, 47, 48, 49–50, 67, 72, 73, 76, 77, 79, 82, 86
money market 40
money supply 22, 51, 52, 56, 65
Mundell, Robert 57
Muth, John F. 157

Napoleonic Wars 20
National Bureau of Economic Research 122, 209
national wealth 68
Nerlove, Mark 184
net money receipts 32
Netherlands 86, 99, 100, 118, 131, 181, 230
New International Economic Order 11
Nixon administration 134
nominal income theory 47
nominal money 24, 48
nominalist 14
Norway 181

Okun, Arthur M. 127, 130
OPEC 140, 167

Pakistan 223
Parkin, M. 58
permanent income models 82, 83, 84
Perry, George L. 223, 225
Phelps, Edmund S. 157
Phillipines 223
Phillips Curve 7, 44, 94, 150, 152, 153, 155–58, 225
Pigou, A. C. 49
Portugal 181
post World War I 20
post World War II 99
precautionary motive 48, 49
price anticipation effect 25, 27, 50, 145, 146, 147
price level 44, 50–51, 82, 139–41, 177, 211, 213
Purchasing Power Parity theory 203–04

Putman, Bluford H. 57, 206, 207

quantity theory equations (velocity and
  cash balances) 23, 26–27, 139
quantity theory of money 3, 4, 5, 19,
  22, 23–26, 27, 28, 44, 51, 58, 61–
  62 63, 65, 110, 139, 203

Rasche, R. H. 52, 224
Reagan, President Ronald 7, 8, 165,
  214, 218, 221, 232
real cash balances 7, 24
recession 217
reform liberalism 7, 23
Rees, Albert 146, 147, 153
Ricardo, David 20, 201
Richards, I. 58
Roosevelt, President F. D. 8, 162
Rowe, Nicholas 12
Russia 151

Samuelson, Paul 152
Schotta, Charles 129
Schultze, Charles L. 223
Schwartz, Anna 6, 102, 122
Selden, Richard 86, 123, 128
Shapiro, H. T. 84
Shaw, Edward S. 124–25
Simmel, Georg 9, 11, 13, 15–16
Simons, Henry C. 119, 120–21
Sims, C. A. 103
Smith, P. E. 52
Snyder, Carl 121
Social Economic Council of the Neth-
  erlands 99
Solomon, Anthony 214
Solow, Robert 152, 156, 171, 177, 178
Soviet Union 11, 221
Spain 100, 181
specie standard 26, 199
speculative motive 50
Spencer, R. W. 171–76, 178
Sprinkel, Beryl W. 232
stagflation 227
Stein, J. L. 226

supply-side economics 7, 8, 9, 22
Sutch, R. 193
Sweden 86, 96, 118, 131, 181, 220
Switzerland 101, 109, 231–32

Tanner, Ernest J. 102
Teigen, Ronald L. 52, 56–57, 84
Thatcher, Margaret 219
third world 10, 11, 221
Thornton, Henry 20
Tobin, James 13, 68, 155, 170, 177, 226,
  227
traditionalist monetary policy 45, 62,
  93, 94, 95–98, 99, 102, 110, 118,
  121, 122–23, 164–65, 168, 176,
  191, 194, 195, 197, 214, 220, 229
transaction motive 36, 48–49
Tsai, H. 86, 87, 95, 131, 206, 209
Tucker, Donald P. 129
Turnovsky, S. J. 156

unemployment 21, 24, 152, 154, 155,
  156–58, 217
unions 143, 145, 146, 150
United Kingdom 86, 87, 96, 97, 101,
  102, 108, 131, 134, 141, 152, 156,
  162, 181, 213, 217, 219, 227, 228
United States 86, 87, 96, 98, 99, 100,
  102, 103, 109, 111, 118, 122, 128,
  131, 132, 155, 163–64, 166–67,
  180, 200, 206, 207, 209, 211, 212,
  213, 214, 217–18, 220, 222
University of Chicago 163 (and the
  preface)
utility maximization 50

Volcker, Paul 218
Von Mises, Ludwig 9

Wallich, Henry 214
Walrasian equations 44
Warburton, Clark 121, 122, 123,
  124–25
wealth models 74, 78, 80, 83

ABOUT THE AUTHOR

GEORGE MACESICH is Professor of Economics and Director of the Center for Yugoslav-American Studies, Research, and Exchanges at Florida State University in Tallahassee. He received his Ph.D. in economics from the University of Chicago. His books, among others, include *The International Monetary Economy and the Third World* and, with Hui-Liang Tsai, *Money in Economic Systems*.